THE SCOTTISH HIGHLANDERS

The Scottish Highlanders

a personal view

Charles MacKinnon
of Dunakin

ROBERT HALE · LONDON

ISBN 0 7090 1292 6

Robert Hale Limited
Clerkenwell House
Clerkenwell Green
London EC1R 0HT

Photoset in Ehrhardt by
Kelly Typesetting Limited
Bradford-on-Avon, Wiltshire
Printed in Great Britain by
St Edmundsbury Press
Bury St Edmunds, Suffolk
Bound by Hunter & Foulis Limited

Contents

This book is affectionately
dedicated to
DR CLAUDE BILLOT
cher toubib

List of Illustrations

ACKNOWLEDGEMENTS

Alexander Ramsay: 1, 3, 9, 10, 13, 14, 17, 18, 22, 23, 24, 27; The National Trust for Scotland: 2; Derek G. Widdicombe, 4; National Galleries of Scotland: 5, 6; G. Douglas Bolton: 8, 12, 16; Royal Collection: 19; John Dewar & Sons Ltd: 20; Noel Habgood/Derek G. Widdicombe: 26, 33, 34; Frieda Stanbury/Derek G. Whitticombe: 32; Royal Library: 28; National Army Museum: 30, 31.

Clan Crest Badges reproduced by kind permission of Art Pewter Silver Ltd, East Kilbride, Scotland.

Author's Foreword

Sir Steven Runciman, in his preface to his three-volume *History of the Crusades*, makes the important observation:

> History writing today has passed into an Alexandrian age, where criticism has overpowered creation. Faced by the mountainous heap of the minutiae of knowledge and awed by the watchful severity of his colleagues, the modern historian too often takes refuge in learned articles or narrowly specialized dissertations, small fortresses that are easy to defend from attack. His work can be of the highest value; but it is not an end in itself. I believe that the supreme duty of the historian is to write history, that is to say, to attempt to record in one sweeping sequence the greater events and movements that have swayed the destinies of man.

He goes on to add, 'The writer rash enough to make the attempt should not be criticized for his ambition, however much he may deserve censure for the inadequacy of his equipment or the inanity of his results.'

I begin this book by quoting Sir Steven Runciman because nobody could put the problem better. Every historian is faced with the necessity for over-simplification and of selection from far too much detailed material. The result can, in the worst instances, lead not merely to glib half-truths but to even glibber downright untruths. The very act of being selective is in itself a form both of censorship and of propaganda.

If the professional historian fighting his battles on ever-increasingly narrow fronts is daunted by the amount of material at his disposal (to say nothing of the mountain of unlisted and uncatalogued material waiting to be studied, which may overturn many current ideas), how much more frightening is it for an amateur historian trying to depict the history of a race over a period of more than fifteen hundred years in a single, small volume?

Longer books than this have been written on single clans; scores of volumes have been written about some of the more important single clans. One could, if one were adequately equipped for the task, write an enormous multi-volume encyclo- paedia on the Highlands; and that, let it be noted, would omit the history of the Lowlands and the Borders, whose role in the history of Scotland was considerably more important and is far better documented.

I began my passionate love-affair with the Highland clans as a boy of twelve, and this enthusiasm has never abated. Some twenty years ago I wrote a little book entitled *The Highlands In History*, which was mainly aimed at correcting what I considered to be serious misconceptions. I realized afterwards that I had left unsaid most of what I really wanted to say and that I had been far too partisan, too slanted in my opinions.

People have been pouring out books about the Scottish High- landers ever since Sir Walter Scott (who really knew very little about them or what terrible things were happening to them in his lifetime) started the fashion. He also master-minded the State Visit of King George IV to Edinburgh where that Hanoverian monarch appeared in full Highland dress and where he was greeted and attended by 'his' chiefs similarly dressed up in fanciful Highland garb, in a great ceremonious burying of an old enmity.

The Highlands became a craze, and the misconceptions, the fallacious picture of the noble savage in tartan and silver finery, proud, pure, loyal to the death to his 'rightful' kings, began to assume formidable proportions.

Queen Victoria set her seal on the whole movement by falling in love with Balmoral, the Highlands (around Balmoral—her trip to the western Highlands was a dismal failure), tartan and, since her family ruled in Britain because they were descended from Protestant *Stuarts*, and not at all by virtue of their Hanoverian ancestry, she became quite openly Jacobite in her sympathies!

Highland and clan histories began to proliferate, and the whole thing got thoroughly out of hand and has stayed that way, becom- ing firmly set in a mould of flowery misconception and vague untruth.

Why in that case does any man in his right mind want to add to the mountain of myth? I have already admitted that a work of this sort, which is at best no more than a sketchy personal view of centuries of history, must be highly selective. There can be no escape from this; it is a hard fact of the job of writing history.

I have found all my life that my favourite books on clans and tartans rarely provide an outline of the broad sweep of general history into which I can fit the clan histories. And the historians of Scotland rarely have very much to say about the clans, which they evidently regard as politically unimportant. What I am attempting here, and it is only an attempt, is to provide an outline history that puts the Highland story into some sort of orderly perspective and sets it against the 'greater events and movements' that have swayed the destiny of the Highland clansman. In Part Two the clan histories have been made to fit, so far as this is possible, into the broad outline of major events of Part One.

Of course I am as slanted in my outlook as any other impartial writer of history. On the other hand I do not mind revealing in which direction this slant lies. Above all I want to disperse the myth which obscures the real nature of my ancestors and which, despite its cloying romanticism and the attractive tartan package in which it is presented, does my people less than justice.

They were real people, just like any others. They were of their time and of their place. Their story, and it is a bitter one, illustrates the basic lesson of history that when men are put into certain geographical and climatological locations and into certain political situations and are subjected to strong pressures of certain sorts, they will tend to behave exactly as other men will in the same circumstances.

History does not like absolutes but rather seems to revel in curious contradictions and anomalies and in rules which can perhaps be best inferred from their many exceptions. What is most surprising about it, to me at any rate, is the way it takes hold of the imagination.

I began this book with a very clear idea of what I wanted to say and how I intended to say it, but as it progressed I found it had the power to speak for itself, sometimes despite me. I came to *know* the race about which I was writing in an extremely personal way, as if I had lived among them during all the long centuries and shared their experiences. What was wonderful about this was that they were so recognizable and understandable, not in the least remote from the present.

And I am quite certain that if I attempted a similar study of *any* other people, exactly the same thing would occur. This, I think, is one of the great gifts that history has to offer to us.

Another is that history frequently displays a charm and a niceness of its own entirely out of keeping with the amount of cruelty and suffering which men have always inflicted on one another; so that frequently one comes to the sort of happy ending in the most unlikely circumstances, which no novelist would dare to devise for fear of being accused of faking.

If any of the joy and the sheer charm of history comes across in this book, I shall have achieved far more than I ever set out to do—but it is not something that can easily be conveyed. It seems to like to take one by surprise, in its own way.

I hope that, when the curtains of romantic balderdash have been slightly parted, the clansman of today will find something of real and lasting interest to him about his Highland ancestors.

Acknowledgements

The author wishes to thank William Collins, Sons & Co. Ltd, for permission to draw on material used in his earlier book *The Highlands In History* published by them in 1961.

The author also wishes to acknowledge that it would have been almost impossible to write Chapter 9 on the Highland Clearances without making extensive use of the facts revealed in John Prebble's masterly definitive history published under that title by Penguin Books Ltd.

The Museum of Scottish Tartans

The repressive measures expressly forbidding 'Tartan, Plaid or Kilt' subsequent to the Rising of 1745 drew strong public resistance. The opposition was reinforced by the undoubted courage of the Highland Regiments in foreign fields and this inspired the formation of many Highland, Caledonian, etc., Societies which led, almost entirely, to the Repeal of the Act in 1782.

It was not until 1963 that the fervour of the original movements was to crystallize in the inauguration of the Scottish Tartans Society by the Lord Lyon King of Arms. Thirteen years later and almost 230 years to the day from the signing of the Act of Proscription the Society opened the Scottish Tartans Museum in Comrie. The first Museum dealing solely with this part of Scotland's heritage in its first year won the coveted Museum of the Year Award.

Today, world famous for its exciting interpretation of the story of Clans and Tartan it houses the most comprehensive collection on the subject while its Museum shop sells those symbols of Clan and Family in which the Scots take pride. The Society research service traces connections between surnames, Clans and Tartans, and the subsequent right to wear the Crest Badge of one's Clan in designs approved by the Standing Council of Scottish Chiefs.

The Museum is open all year and is equidistant from both Edinburgh and Glasgow. Enquiries are welcome but enquirers are asked to enclose stamps to the value of a reply since the

Museum is not funded from Public funds but by private sub-scription.

> The Scottish Tartans Museum,
> COMRIE,
> Perthshire,
> Scotland, PH6 2DW.
>
> Telephone: (0764) 70779

PART ONE

The Background

1

The Land and the People

All Scotland is, as all Gaul once was, divided into three parts. There are three distinct and easily distinguishable geographical regions, and they have provided three distinct types of Scotsman. It is important to bear this in mind, because there is still a tendency among some people to imagine Scotland as being divided across the centre into Highlands in the north and Lowlands in the south.

The land areas of the constituent parts of Great Britain are, in round figures, England 50,000 square miles, the whole of Ireland 32,000, Scotland 30,000 and Wales 8,000. England, then, occupies about 40 per cent of the total land area. What is interesting about these figures is the fact that to this day eminent English historians dismiss Scotland, Ireland and Wales as the 'Celtic fringe'. Which is to say, in other words, that the British Isles are and were 60 per cent fringe and 40 per cent whole fabric!

From the English point of view, there were 8,000 square miles of mountainous country to the west, occupied by a strange mountain race; and another 30,000 square miles to the north separated from them by a long line of hills running east–west, which formed a natural frontier.

It is no wonder that the English kings never felt easy about this, for, in the politics of the pre-medieval and medieval period, any neighbour over whom you did not hold sway was not only a permanent *potential* enemy but usually an actual enemy.

The southern part of Scotland, where it borders with England, is the easiest part to describe, because it consists of wild moorland country with hills rising to substantial heights. The border, which is marked principally by the Cheviot Hills, has been a remarkably

stable one over a considerable period of history. This is not to say
that it was not constantly disputed. The Scottish kings tried to
push it further south, and King David I, who died in 1153,
succeeded in acquiring the English northern counties of
Northumberland, Cumberland and Westmorland; but his son
lost these territories. Likewise the English at various times tried
to thrust up by the east coast into the Lothians, which at an earlier
time were in any case English, and so to push the Scottish border
further north towards the old Antonine Wall from Clyde to Forth.

But the border remained more or less where it is today.

This hilly border region has produced the borderers, a hardy
fighting people who guarded Scotland's frontier with England
and, when they were not feuding and fighting with the English
across the border, feuded and fought among themselves. They
provide some of the best-known Scottish surnames—the
Armstrongs, Elliots, Kerrs, Scotts, Douglases, Hepburns, Bruces
and Johnstons among them. Their role in Scottish history was
crucial, but they do not concern us directly in this particular
account.

Beyond the borders lie the Scottish Lowlands. The Lowland
region not merely runs east–west across the centre of Scotland,
usually described as the central Lowlands, but sweeps northwards up the east coast. The Lowland border with the Highlands
begins in the west at Dumbarton, on the north bank of the River
Clyde, and progresses northwards and eastwards to embrace an
eastern plain which stretches from Fife, through the rich Carse of
Gowrie, up past Aberdeen and then sweeps round the north-east
shoulder of Scotland and along the edge of the Moray Firth, past
Nairn right up to Inverness itself, which is and always has been a
'frontier' town, where Highlanders were not specially welcome.

This triangular Lowland area was the heartland of Scotland
and contained the national capital from the days of Kenneth
MacAlpin onwards, who moved his seat of power from the
western Highlands to Scone in Perthshire; later it was moved to
Dunfermline and finally to Edinburgh, which lies at some
distance from the Highlands.

The Highlanders always resented this absence of *their* king
from *their* midst.

The third geographical region was the great mountainous mass
commonly called simply the Highlands. This is dominated by two

main mountain ranges. One is the long range running north–south along the axis of Scotland from Loch Lomond up to the Pentland Firth, the great backbone of Scotland. The other is a range curving off north-eastwards to form the Grampians.

The Grampians were never a formidable barrier, because not only are there a number of passes over them but they open onto a plain at their east end, so that it is merely necessary to go round them.

But the central Highlands were much more formidable, and the only practicable way to penetrate them was through the Great Glen, which runs from Inverness in the north-east to Fort William, further south on the west coast. However, while it was comparatively simple to penetrate up into the north of Scotland along its low-lying east coast, it was a different matter to venture into the Great Glen, which led the intrepid explorer further and further away from civilization and safety, into an unknown world which remained to a remarkable extent cut off from the rest of Scotland till the aftermath of the Jacobite rising of 1745–6.

The Great Glen, in fact, was much more useful to the Highlanders, to *get out* in order to raid the rich agricultural plains of north-east Scotland, than it was for other people to *get in* at the Highlanders.

The Highlanders disliked roads except for their own drove-roads by which they themselves could easily traverse a region which has always been bewildering to outsiders. It was only when General Wade built proper roads in the Highlands in 1725 that they became comparatively easy of access, despite which there are still places on the west coast where it is easier and far shorter to travel by boat than directly overland.

The Scottish people are an amalgam of races, as indeed are most people apart from the extremely primitive who have had no contact with the rest of the world. When the Romans arrived in Britain in 55 BC to begin their conquest of a country which had not yet been identified as an island, they began by subduing the people they found in the south and midlands of modern England, whom they called Britons. Many of the Britons preferred not to subject themselves to the Roman yoke and retreated into the western mountains to form the Welsh people who really represent the ancient Britons as opposed to the Romano-Britons who accepted the benefits of Roman civilization.

Inevitably in their push northwards the Romans came to what is very roughly speaking the present national boundary from Tweed to Solway, along the southern face of the Cheviots; and here they found another race, extremely warlike and fierce. They were formidable enough to halt the Roman advance for a time, and the Romans called them Caledonians, but from the start they seem to have been nicknamed Picts.

Agricola was the first to make a serious attempt to conquer the Picts, and he pushed up into Fife, from there made a foray further northwards against the Picts and in AD 83 inflicted a crushing defeat on them at Mons Graupius.

At this time the entire northern end of Britain, roughly corresponding to modern Scotland, seems to have been occupied by this one people. No doubt they were themselves an amalgam of more than one earlier settlement, but in fact almost nothing at all is known about them other than the reports that went to Rome and the later and very dubious accounts of monks like the Venerable Bede who never saw Scotland and believed that you turned right at the Scottish border and went off into the North Sea. His map of Britain shows Scotland lying at right-angles to England, and the central mountain range which has always divided east and west is shown as a barrier between north and south.

Curiously enough, few historians seems to have taken note of this when evaluating the theory that the Picts were divided into northern and southern Picts, separated by the Grampians, which, as we have seen, were not an effective barrier at all. It is much more probable that Bede's 'northern' Picts were the ones who lived inside the modern Highland Line, particularly in the western Highlands, and that they were not northern Picts at all but *western* Picts.

The Romans did not exploit their victory at Mons Graupius. It is debatable whether in any case the Romans could have penetrated and held down the Highlands proper. We know that in those times the mountains were dark areas of dense forest where the light did not penetrate easily, far less soldiers far removed from their lines of supply. This is, of course, speculative, but it is necessary to counter the wild remark of the historian Tacitus that, in recalling Agricola after Mons Graupius, Rome had entirely thrown away a 'completely conquered' Britain. It is a far cry from the edge of the Grampians to the western Highland seaboard or the extreme north.

What Agricola did do, however, was to send the fleet which had accompanied his army on its march northwards along the eastern coastline, on a voyage of expedition and discovery. They rounded the north of Scotland, sailed back down along the western seaboard and finally returned home to England with the astonishing news that Britain was an island.

If anybody else knew that Britain was an island prior to this time, the fact has not been recorded anywhere that we know of yet.

The Romans attempted two settlements. One was along Hadrian's Wall, somewhat south of the present border; and then they pushed the Picts back a considerable distance and built a wall from the Forth to the Clyde, called the Antonine Wall. They occupied all of southern Scotland between the walls for more than two centuries, but finally they were forced to withdraw their armies because of the situation in Rome and to leave Britain altogether.

They left behind a new Romanized nation in southern Scotland, in what became known as the kingdom of Strathclyde, which originally stretched across to the east coast, but it was difficult to hold the flatter eastern seaboard, and soon Angles began to push north from Northumbria to establish an English kingdom in the Lothians. Edinburgh is named after one of the English leaders, Edwin.

While this was going on in the south, other things were happening in the north. There were repeated attacks on the eastern and western coasts by Danes and Norsemen, but in the west there was a more serious invasion by the Scots of Northern Ireland. These were a Gaelic-speaking Celtic people, and they settled first in some of the Hebridean islands such as Skye and Mull, and finally, in 501, Fergus Mor the son of Erc established the mainland kingdom of Dalriada, principally in the modern county of Argyll. The Scots had finally arrived in Scotland.

The purpose of this account is merely to establish a broad perspective of what happened, and not to become involved in detail, which does not change the basic outline of events and can, in the telling, sometimes obscure them. So far we have met five races—the Picts, probably themselves an amalgam of races from more distant times; the Romano-Britons of Strathclyde; the Angles of the Lothians; the Irish (who, to confuse matters, are called Scots) who settled in the Inner Hebrides and founded the mainland kingdom of Dalriada; and finally the Norse invaders.

The first race to disappear were the Picts, and 'disappear' they did. The vexed question 'Who were the Picts?' used to turn otherwise mild antiquaries into furious enemies as they propounded their various theories. According to the latest information today, however, nobody yet knows who they were or even what happened to them. Nor do we know what language they spoke, except that it was not the Gaelic of the Scoto-Irish invaders from Antrim who brought Irish civilization to Scotland.

Columba is supposed to have converted the northern Picts to Christianity, but, as has been pointed out, the 'northern' Picts were probably the western Picts among whom he had his original mission. Columba was not an innovator, for Christianity had reached western Scotland from Ireland when the Scots first settled. Ireland was a cradle of Christianity and of learning. Even earlier, St Ninian had established himself in Galloway, and there he founded a missionary enterprise which followed the eastern lowland route to the far north, to Inverness and beyond. Archaeologists are still uncovering much information about both how far the Romans penetrated northwards in expeditions from their southern bases, and how far Ninian and the other early pre-Columban saints penetrated.

If, as is stated, Columba went up the Great Glen into eastern Pictdom and converted King Brude in Inverness, Brude was probably a lapsed Christian, for Ninian and his followers had been there long before Columba. It was Ninian, incidentally, who converted Patrick and sent him back to Ireland to spread Christianity there.

It is probable that a common religious background made it easy for the Dalriadic Scots to establish relations with the Picts, but little is known of the relationship between the two kingdoms with their separate kings until in 843 Kenneth, the son of Alpin of Dalriada, succeeded to the Pictish throne and united the two peoples under one ruler.

The mystery lies in the fact that thereafter the Picts disappear entirely. There are theories about great battles and about treachery during which Kenneth killed all the Pictish royal family and their nobles, but nobody knows exactly why the language, oral traditions about their origin, their customs and even their real name (for Picts was a Latin nickname) vanished. They did vanish, however, and the smaller kingdom of Dalriada gave Scotland its name, its language (Gaelic), its customs and its rulers. Kenneth was known after 843 as King of the Scots, and Scotland had finally been born.

There was, of course, still *another* 'Scotland' in Northern Ireland, in Antrim, but that is merely one of history's irritating complications. Until about the twelfth century the use of the word 'Scots' on any document has to be looked at closely to see whether it refers to the Scots in Ireland or the Scots in Scotland.

The Scots, with whom we now include the vanishing Picts who nevertheless exist genetically in the Scots since the two nations fused into one, finally extended their rule southwards over their two southern neighbours, Strathclyde and Lothian. King Malcolm II managed to annex the Lothians to his Scottish kingdom in 1016 or 1018. His grandson Duncan, who succeeded him as king, had already become King of Strathclyde, and so, when he succeeded to Scotland in 1034, he ruled over a country which corresponded approximately to modern Scotland, all of which was now called Scotland.

The Norsemen took rather longer to disappear from the scene, but in the islands which they shared with the intruding Scots, the Norse became absorbed into the local life. The inhabitants of Skye and Mull and other Hebridean islands are of original Pictish stock but strongly overlaid with Scottish-Norwegian elements. It is this three-cornered racial mixture which is the heritage of almost all the Highlanders.

This is a greatly over-simplified account of how a country of three distinct geographical regions became settled by several races and finally in 1034 theoretically united under one crown; but it is substantially what happened.

The union remained for the moment, however, a theoretical one. The Highlanders, with whom we are concerned in this history, belonged to a different race from the rest of Scotland. They were predominantly Celto-Irish in their culture, traditions and language. The rest of Scotland outside the Highlands was either predominantly Romano-British or English.

The Highlanders, who regarded themselves with some

justification as the 'real' Scots, regarded their richer southern neighbours as strangers and foreign interlopers, not belonging to the kingdom at all. This attitude underlies much of the antagonism which grew up, for, to the southerner, the Highlander was a wild man of the mountains, hated and feared, and his proprietorial airs were ridiculous.

The Lowlanders, from the outset, did not like the Highlanders any more than the Highlanders liked them. Inevitably a series of powerful magnates succeeded in establishing territories along the Highland Line, as it became called, and became frontiersmen or wardens of the marches similar to those in England who occupied territories adjacent to Wales.

In Scotland some of these 'frontier nobility' possessed lands in both Highlands and Lowlands. The Murrays, Drummonds, Grahams and Ogilvies are examples of Highland clans who possessed this dualistic aspect.

Indeed, in discussing the Highlanders it is important to be specific not only as to the period under discussion but also as to the geographical location. The inhabitants of the western Highlands and the islands were remote, occupying less fertile lands, and were cut off from the rest, whom they heartily despised. The nearer the various clan territories were to the plains, the less pronounced was the difference between Highlander and Lowlander.

A chief living near the mouths of the glens where they opened out onto the plains was obviously interested in the material advantages of acquiring lands there if possible; and, if not, at least of trading and acquiring some of the benefits of civilization. And, of course, they established marriage alliances with Lowland families in the course of time and tried to expand into the fertile Lowlands that way, which is how the great frontier clans came into existence—by intermarriage. The Murrays, Lowland noblemen of foreign extraction, commanded three thousand Highlanders in time of war, which made them Highland chiefs to be reckoned with.

Of the three peoples of Scotland, the Highlanders probably had to be and to remain more self-sufficient and independent, because of their remoteness from the trade routes and the fact that normally they did not have much money. Their wealth lay in their clan and its fighting force, and its cattle.

Although there is ample evidence that in the Moray Firth area, for instance, and in Wester Ross the climate was surprisingly mild and agreeable, and although the whole Highland area was well wooded and full of game, the Highlanders were the poorest of the three divisions of Scotland.

Nevertheless, the people were not poor in everything. They were a hardy, active and warlike people—of this there is no possible doubt. Everybody who has left early evidence testifies to it, and not generally in flattering terms. Such people need to be well nourished, and the Highlanders were always great meat-eaters. They bred cattle in their glens, and their woods were full of game which they loved to hunt. At a time when the Lowlander of central Scotland was little better than a serf, tyrannized by greedy bonnet lairds, and lived mainly off brose and oatmeal, the Highlander was well fed.

His clothing was of necessity more primitive the further removed he was from contact with the outside world, but it was warm, comfortable and well adapted to his needs. We know that he wore the saffron shirt of the Irish, a warm garment reaching to the knee and belted at the waist. He went bare-legged and often bare-footed, which has given rise to the curious description of the Highlanders as 'red-shanked'.

This does not mean that they were red-haired. They were no more red-haired than any other British race. The native Gael is predominantly dark, and the Norse infusion produced many fair-haired islanders. The simple explanation is that the High-landers had tanned legs at a time when most men kept their legs covered, and this gave an impression of redness which was nothing more than the effect of weather.

All Highlanders tend to be clannish, whether in Wales, in the Ozark Mountains of America or in Scotland. They tend to feud a good deal, because their holdings are, by the very geographical nature of things, comparatively small; and instead of one broad stretch of land supporting one people (with whatever social distinctions), there were numerous little enclaves supporting small groups, all seeking means of expansion and looking very warily at all neighbours stronger than themselves.

2

The Clans: Who and What they were

The question of who the clans were is surprisingly difficult to solve, and impossible to be dogmatic about. Part of the reason for this, curiously enough, lies in the beauty of Scottish tartan. All over the world people love to display it—tartan umbrellas in Japan, tartan ties in France, tartan shopping-bags in militant black Africa, tartan skirts for women and girls literally anywhere where there are women and girls.

When the great tartan revival began, in 1822, all the chiefs of the clans hurried to discover their clan's tartan. Very few of the present tartans are what was really being worn prior to 1746, when the wearing of Highland dress became proscribed. Indeed, it is doubtful if there were as many as twenty 'clan' tartans then—that is to say, uniform tartans worn by all clansmen in time of war.

This, however, is scarcely relevant, for many of the present tartans are now almost two centuries old, even if they do not correspond to the older patterns. For forty years after Culloden the wearing of tartan and Highland dress was an offence heavily penalized, so it is hardly surprising that original patterns were lost. In 1822, during George IV's visit to Edinburgh, the chiefs were asked to appear in their tartans, and so tartans were provided for the occasion; and the clansmen, now free to wear what they liked, hurried to buy 'their' clan tartan.

The thing was such a success that the tailors obviously wished there were many more tartans, because everybody wanted to be 'entitled' to a clan tartan. This resulted in two things. One was the largely bogus genealogy called 'sept names', a long list of which every seller of tartan will happily provide on request. These prove

that, for instance, if your name is White, you are miraculously a member of either Clan Lamont or Clan MacGregor, or presumably of both if you wish. One only has to consider the number of Lowland and English Whites to see the nonsense in this proposition.

Secondly, Lowland and Border 'houses' miraculously became 'clans' and were provided with tartans. Anyone who imagines that the Border Bruces prior to 1746 regarded themselves as a 'clan' (which is a Gaelic word) or that they sported Bruce or any other tartan, fails to understand the general contempt in which the Highlands and Highlanders were held at that time.

When clan life under the chiefs ended in 1746, how many clans were there? Records are unsatisfactory and do not go back beyond the end of the sixteenth century, but in the accounts which do exist the total figure given is usually under forty, which often includes listing the MacDonalds as five separate clans, so that the ceiling is more like thirty-six.

Nevertheless, there are curious omissions in these lists, for whereas some clans with their own chiefs attached themselves to greater clans such as the MacKenzies or the Gordons, there were independent clans who do not figure on the lists. The inference is that these lists, including the famous list of Lord President Forbes of Culloden (see Appendix II) submitted to London in 1747, were concerned with practical politics and were lists of chiefs and captains in the Highlands who were able to bring men into the field on one side or the other on their own account and not in the tail of a greater chief. This would explain the fact that the MacDonalds of Glencoe and the MacKinnons, both small clans, are almost always listed, while some of the larger clans are not. But there are still omissions—Forbes omits, for instance, MacNeil and Macnab, who were both out in 1715 and who were both out again in 1745, as clans in their own right under their own clan leaders.

The fifty-six clans discussed in detail in Part Two (which includes the MacDonalds as one, not five, and which omits the MacAlpins who are discussed in Appendix I) seem to be a probable picture of the clans under chiefs who existed between the fifteenth and the eighteenth centuries. But a study of the clan histories reveals the existence of earlier clans, and it is plain that the number and identity of clans varied from time to time. The powerful Bisset Lords of Lovat disappeared from the Highlands, providing a ready-made clan for the Fraser chiefs and for one or two others.

However, there is no such thing as a fully definitive list of clans, and if the number of clans today has proliferated greatly since 1746, it is a considerable compliment to the Highlanders and their way of life.

The fighting strength of the clans in 1745 was around 22,000, of which about 10,000 were reckoned to be loyal to the Government and 12,000 of Jacobite sympathy. This military strength must not be mistaken for the full fighting strength of the clans. Evidently no sane chief would denude his lands of men capable of bearing arms. If he did, he would find when he came home from war that one of his enemies had taken over his clan and his lands. When the chief went off to war with his best fighting men—and there was really little or no point in taking anybody else—he left behind a 'Home Guard' who could protect the clan lands during his absence.

The fighting strength of 22,000 given by General Wade and Forbes of Culloden cannot represent more than 15 per cent of the total Highland clan population, which gives us a clan population of at least 135,000.

Before leaving the question of the various clans, it is worth taking a closer look at the sept-names which sell so much tartan. The Highland clansmen did not have surnames at all. The chiefs had Gaelic patronymics which sometimes became surnames; and it was the chiefs and greater chieftains, who had dealings with the central government in the Lowlands, who first had a need of surnames.

The chief of the MacDonalds of Glencoe was known as MacIan. Just that. The clan, part of the great Clan Donald, had been founded by an Ian, and the chief was MacIan for ever afterwards and the clan became known in the Highlands as the MacIans. They lived in Glencoe. Outside the Highlands, however, the chief became known as MacDonald of Glencoe, which was infinitely more useful since it conformed with Lowland usage in describing landed proprietors, and it indicated where his loyalties lay (to the high chief of Clan Donald) and where his lands were.

The clansmen, however, would be known by a combination of

genealogical-descriptive Christian names, and not surnames. Thus somebody might be Ian the Red, son of Hugh the Smith, son of Farquhar; or Little Mary, the daughter of James the Red, son of Lachlan the Dumb. Should a clansman find himself far from home and forced to reveal his identity to other High-landers, he would name his chief, i.e. he would say he was Black Hugh the Brewer, who followed MacIan, and everybody would be satisfied.

Surnames were forced on the Highlanders when they them-selves were forced south in search of work after the chiefs were scattered, or else when census-takers and others invaded the Highlands to compile the inevitable statistics. One branch of the MacDonalds were the MacDonalds of Sleat, whose Highland patronymic was Huisdean because their progenitor or name-father was Hugh. Clan Huisdean were the Sleat MacDonalds, and when many of them were compelled to give a surname, they did not think to say they were MacDonalds but that they belonged to Clan Huisdean, and so the perfectly genuine sept-name of Houston was born and is widespread today. Anybody called Houston can be pretty sure that he is both a Highlander and a Skye MacDonald, as opposed to the Browns, Smiths, Whites or Brewsters (MacGrowthers in Gaelic) who might belong in any clan, or in many cases might not be either Scottish or Highland at all.

This leads naturally to the obvious question of the difference between a Scottish Highland clan and the other Scottish 'clans'? What in fact was a Highland clan?

First of all it was geographically Highland—that goes without saying. But what distinguished the Highland clansmen from the followers of Lowland lords and border chiefs was their relation-ship to the chief. The word '*clann*' in Gaelic means 'children', and the Highland clan was above all things a family, a family in which everybody believed that they were all, from chief to blacksmith, descendants of one founder or progenitor. They regarded them-selves as kinsmen in a very definite sense. Evidently this was not entirely true, yet it was true enough to put its hallmark on the social organization of the Highlanders.

Lack of mobility was part of it too. It has already been pointed out that the mountainous and tortuous nature of the country, consisting as it did of hundreds of glens and of lochs and fjords, lent itself to a great many little, distinct groups of people, rather than to large, cohesive groups.

Some of the first chiefs, such as the Siol Alpin chiefs who were grandsons and great-grandsons of King Alpin I, were given grants of land because they were of royal stock, close enough to the King to merit a patrimony. Other chiefs acquired land by being the first to settle on it. Yet others chased out earlier occupants.

Throughout Highland history, land was acquired by force, although a surprisingly large number of clans managed to retain their ancient lands, or substantial parts of them. The simplest way of 'colonizing' was to settle with your brothers and have a large number of children. By this method in a very few generations three or four brothers settling in a glen would have descendants running into hundreds, as well as absorbing into their community weaker families already in the glens.

There is no record of precisely what went on inside the Highlands during the first several centuries after the Picts and Scots fused into one Scottish people. In some areas several 'settlers' might have risen and fallen before one stock finally took root and dominated the area and formed the clan.

Evidently the extent of the blood relationship was variable. Small groups finding large and powerful neighbours springing up around them, and fearing the loss of their own patrimony, would be quick to attach themselves to a strong chief. Such strangers were not descended from the founder of the clan, but, as they would intermarry with clansmen who were, in a generation or two probably all their descendants would have genuine blood lines with the chief's family.

The basis of the Highland clan was the patriarchal chief and his authoritative form of government. The chief provided protection and handed out justice. He was the father, the clan the children, and they were loyal to him because only in that way would he have the *means* of providing the security they all needed.

It is easy to paint a falsely idyllic picture of the clan as a happy congregation of a thousand or more relatives, all loyal to their loving 'father'. It is equally easy to fall into the currently fashionable mistake of regarding the chiefs as unscrupulous tyrants terrorizing their serfs into obedience.

No Highland clan could have survived on this basis.

Interdependence was the hallmark of the clan, and its strength lay in its solidarity. Loyalty was not a high-minded philosophy but a simple defence-mechanism, and so they were on the whole remarkably loyal. Any chief who tried to tyrannize or oppress his clansmen beyond an acceptable level would be deserted by them and jumped upon by his sharp-eyed neighbours, always on the look-out for a means to expand their own frontiers. It was not in the chief's interest to dissipate his inheritance of men, and this may explain why women and children were apparently so honoured by the clan, for they were the key to its future. The Highland economy can be described as a cattle-economy, but it was even more a people-economy.

In the clan histories in Part Two, many instances can be found of chiefs who were killed or deposed and replaced by one of the chiefly family more acceptable to the clan. Instances will be found in abundance of clans acting independently of their chiefs. Clan-power was a very real thing even into the eighteenth century, but obviously the further west one goes into the lochs and glens and the islands, the greater the clan cohesion; and the nearer the Lowlands, the more it might become weakened. The great 'frontier' chiefs were as much proprietors and noblemen as they were chiefs. More so in many cases. Their attitude towards their clansmen could be and often was much more high-handed.

Nevertheless, at times when the issues at stake were not religious or otherwise powerfully emotive, the clan tended to function as an efficient unit. The current fashion of making out that during the Jacobite rebellions the chiefs forced their clansmen into battle at sword point, without the poor ignorant wretches knowing what they were fighting for, is grossly exaggerated and presented out of sensible context. It is, of course, an inevitable reaction to the sickly-sweet pictures of the Highlander as a natural-born aristocrat, full of flowery noble sentiments, uttering ridiculous statements and ready to die for his rightful king no matter what.

Certainly the chief, with his particular clan council if he had one, decided clan policy. It is more than likely that during the Jacobite rising of 1745 many clansmen did not understand their chiefs' reasons for backing the Stuart cause, although there were quite valid reasons, which had little to do with loyalty in the abstract. Such clansmen certainly did not know what they were fighting about.

In 1939 the 'chiefs' in Westminster decided to go to war against Germany (it was Britain who declared war on Germany in both world wars). Their reasons were very imperfectly understood by many young men of 18 who were called upon to go and die—they could go at 17½ if they wanted to fly in aeroplanes. Conscription was introduced to make sure that the young men *would* 'want' to go.

Some did not, either because they were afraid, or else because they were opposed to the war on real grounds of conscience. Tribunals had a difficult job trying to sort out their motives. Those who were regarded as genuine were offered non-combatant jobs and might find themselves medical orderlies or ambulance drivers in the front line, under fire, where they were just as much in danger of their lives as any of the combatants but with the disadvantage that they couldn't fight back. Others were thrown into prison; in 1939 a prison sentence for a respectable member of the community was a terrible punishment to his wife and children, and not very much of a pleasure for the prisoner.

This comparison is an important one. No Highland chief could force young boys to go and be slaughtered in battle unless the clan as a whole felt that he was right in doing so.

Some chiefs, we know, did resort to threats. Some clansmen may afterwards have felt very bitter about the whole of the second Jacobite rising. Most, like the young men of 1939, just did what they were told and hoped for the best. As for the chiefly power, perhaps the most amusing example of it is that of the MacIntosh chief who was an officer in one of the Hanoverian Highland regiments but whose wife, Lady Anne MacIntosh, raised the clan during his absence to fight against the Government.

Barbara Tuchman in the Foreword to *A Distant Mirror* states the position very well. Writing about the Middle Ages, she says: 'Any statement of fact . . . may (and probably will) be met by a statement of the opposite or a different version. Women out-numbered men because men were killed off in wars; men out-numbered women because women died in childbirth. Common people were familiar with the Bible; common people were un-familiar with the Bible. Nobles were tax exempt; no, they were not tax exempt. French peasants were filthy and foul-smelling and lived on bread and onions; French peasants ate pork, fowl and game and enjoyed frequent baths in the village bathhouses.'

She adds, 'I would ask the reader to expect contradictions, not uniformity. No aspect of society, no habit, custom, movement, development, is without cross-currents. Starving peasants in hovels live alongside prosperous peasants in featherbeds. Children are neglected and children are loved. Knights talk of honour and turn brigand. . . . No age is tidy or made of whole cloth.'

What Barbara Tuchman writes about fourteenth-century France is true of Highland Scotland in any century, including the present. There are no absolutes in history. A study of the exceptions merely established basic trends.

The basic rule of the clan was that it was organized round the chief and his family, with whom at any given moment most of the clan—no matter what their origin—had a blood relationship because of constant intermarriage between younger sons of the chiefs and clan members. The chiefly strain ultimately ran in all of them, however much distilled.

The Highlanders themselves called themselves 'families'. They were the children of the chief, which is what 'clan' means. They accepted a patriarchal rule because it was the best system there could be for governing the clan, surrounded as it was by greedy-eyed neighbours ready to jump at the first chance of ousting them from their possessions. It was a simple question of finding a workable system which fitted the needs of time and place and prevailing conditions. That such patriarchal and authoritarian government is no longer acceptable in the western world today is totally irrelevant.

All our circumstances are different, and our judgement of what went on in distant times must never allow itself to be clouded by our current problems and our ways of dealing with them. The clan was organized as a family and liked to consider that it *was* a family. It is no part of the job of the modern historian to decide that a thousand years of clansmen were all wrong and did not know what they were talking about. It is our job to see and understand them for what they actually were and believed themselves to be, the second being as important as the first.

In the case of the Anglo-Norman clans who have provided some of Scotland's proudest Highland names—Chisholm,

Fraser and Stewart among others—the clans were there from the beginning, and it was the chiefs who were the incomers, not the clansmen. Brought to Scotland by David I and given extensive grants of land in Highlands and Lowlands and in the Borders, some of these Anglo-Norman chiefs became more Highland than the Highlanders. It is important to remember that younger sons descended in the social scale, marrying into humbler clan families, so that the chiefly blood was carried downwards into the clan and in a very short space of time the incoming chiefs (and we are talking of six and seven centuries ago, and longer) had established blood-ties with the whole of their new clan.

From the purely practical point of view, there were some fifty or sixty Highland clans at the height of the clan system. There could not have been many more, and there might not have been as many. Many Highlanders bear names which do not fit neatly into the clan names. Their ancestors were probably attached to or belonged to one clan or another. Due to the haphazard system of recording non-existent surnames, it is now impossible to tell to which clan they may have belonged.

The clans were patriarchal and familial, bound tightly together by geographical location and the need for physical security. The clansmen needed the chief, and he certainly needed his clansmen, who could and did depose him if necessary.

3

The Securing of the Kingdom

Scotland, as we have seen, became united in 1034—more or less.
It was not till 1266 that the Western Isles were finally ceded by
Norway, and not till 1472 that the Orkneys and Shetlands were
annexed.

The England across the border was not the England that we
know now, because the Norman invasion was still thirty-two years
distant. During these first ten and a half centuries of existence,
following the birth of Christ, recorded history is not plentiful in
the way it is in respect of the later medieval period.

It is when Robert Bruce steps onto the stage of history that the
Highlanders do the same. For eight centuries, from the advent of
Fergus Mor MacErc and the founding of Dalriada, which was to
have such a profound effect on Scotland's future, until Bruce had
himself crowned king, the Highlanders were evolving behind the
barrier of their mountains in a way which today can only be
imperfectly glimpsed.

Certainly they had evolved, for the painted primitive Picts of
the Romans had given way to a comparatively cultured race.
There are many reasons, conjectural and otherwise, for this. The
Scots were Irish at a time when Ireland was a great centre of
learning, when scholars travelled from Europe to Ireland and
when there was a constant exchange of ideas between the island,
on the one hand, and Continental Europe and the Mediterranean
basin on the other. In addition the Romans had left two centuries
of civilizing legacy in Strathclyde.

There must have been constant contact between Ireland and
the Highlands, and probably also between the Highlands and the
Lowlands.

Nevertheless, the Highlanders do not figure largely in national affairs before Robert Bruce. In order to understand the background to what follows, it is necessary to outline the interplay of relationships between Scotland and England.

Kenneth MacAlpin had been the first Scottish king to push his boundary southwards into the Lothians, and he would have liked to go further south, to the River Tees. This ambition seems to have been remembered by his successors, for Malcolm III, known as Malcolm Canmore, who was born around 1030 and who reigned 1058–93, saw the Norman invasion of England as an opportunity. The confusion which followed the conquest of the south was too good a chance to miss. His goal was to annex the northern counties of England to Scotland. Although the general impression given by some historians is that it was England which was the aggressor in the constant attempt to conquer Scotland, the original expansionist enterprise was a *Scottish* one— southwards.

Malcolm Canmore's repeated attempts to annex northern England—there were five and he was killed at Alnwick during the course of the fifth—were a failure; but they set an unhappy pattern. In 1072 the Conqueror marched towards Scotland in strength and forced Malcolm to take an oath of homage and to send his eldest son Duncan to the English court as a hostage.

Following Malcolm's death, William II of England (Rufus) supported the cause of his son Duncan against Malcolm's brother Donald Ban who had seized the throne. Duncan was able to march north with an English army and unseat Donald Ban, but he did not live long to enjoy his victory.

Another of Malcolm Canmore's sons, Edmund, now made common cause with his uncle Donald Ban. They killed Duncan, and there was then a short, curious spell during which Scotland was divided into two kingdoms, with Donald Ban ruling north of the Forth–Clyde line (the old Antonine Wall of the Romans) and his nephew Edmund south of it.

William Rufus now supported yet another of Canmore's sons, Edgar, against these joint rulers. Edgar finally succeeded in becoming King of Scotland in 1097, but at the cost of acknowledging the English king as his feudal superior. This dangerous business of homage, first entered into by Canmore, had now been repeated.

Homage played an important part in the feudal system, for without it the system would have collapsed and anarchy resulted. To break one's oath of homage was a serious crime. To what extent kings took it seriously between *themselves* is hard to say. It normally happened when one king had his back to the wall and had to do homage to get rid of a powerful enemy. Homage and hostages were thus often the price of freedom; but whether Canmore or Edgar had any real intention of submitting his kingdom to the English is very doubtful.

Edgar was succeeded by his brother Alexander, and when Alexander died, he was succeeded at last by the youngest of Canmore's sons, King David I. David was the vassal of the English king for his earldom of Huntingdon. His English possessions were considerable, and he brought north to his kingdom many of his Anglo-Norman friends, among them such famous names as Balliol, Bruce and Stewart.

David did not regard himself as an English vassal except in respect of his English possessions. On the contrary, renewed in him was the burning desire to extend Scotland southwards. This he succeeded in doing, and at the time of his death he ruled over a Scotland which included the northern English counties of Cumberland, Westmorland and Northumberland. He ruled in his own right as a fully independent ruler and to the end did homage only for his English lands.

The gain was only temporary. Malcolm IV of Scotland was compelled by Henry II of England to restore the northern counties. Malcolm died young and was followed by his brother William the Lion. He tried to regain the lost English counties but was captured and taken prisoner. He was sent to Normandy, and there he had to recognize Henry II as the overlord of Scotland in order to regain his own freedom. He took the oath and came home.

His submission was of short duration. Following the death of Henry II of England, Richard the Lionheart began to raise funds for the third Crusade and sold back the sovereign rights of Scotland to Scotland's king. He did more. He agreed that they had originally been surrendered under duress, and in an agreement called the Quitclaim of Canterbury he set forth the English acknowledgement of Scotland's independence.

This was the state of affairs before the reign of King Edward I of England. Scottish kings had done homage for Scotland to three English kings—William the Conqueror, William Rufus and Henry II. But they had also repeatedly invaded northern England in attempts to annex it to Scotland. Finally Richard the Lionheart had agreed in writing that England had no valid claim to the kingdom of Scotland.

Alexander III was Scotland's king when Edward I succeeded to the English throne. The two men were brothers-in-law and to some extent friends. It was at this point in history that the Scottish king ran out of male heirs. Alexander's sons died without having children of their own, and his daughter, Margaret, who had married King Erik II of Norway, had also died, so that the heir to the Scottish throne was Alexander's granddaughter Margaret, known as the Maid of Norway.

Alexander III was killed as the result of an accident in 1286, and Margaret was at once recognized as the Scottish queen.

Edward I here saw an opportunity to unite the two kingdoms peaceably, something which might have had a considerable effect on European history if it had succeeded. It was agreed that Margaret of Scotland would marry Edward's heir, Prince Edward. Alas for high hopes. In 1290, during the voyage from Norway to Scotland, the young Queen died. She had been queen for four years, and she was only seven years old when she died.

Scotland was without a ruler.

Onto the stage now stepped a number of claimants. The three most serious were the descendants of David, Earl of Huntingdon, who was a brother to both Malcolm IV and William the Lion.

David of Huntingdon had had three daughters, and their descendants now claimed the Scottish throne. The descendant of the eldest daughter, Margaret, was John Balliol. According to the rules of primogeniture, generally acknowledged, he had the best claim to the throne.

However, the descendant of the second daughter, Isabella, Robert Bruce of Annandale, was one generation nearer the throne. He was a great-great-grandson of King David I; Balliol was a great-great-great-grandson. But Bruce's claim was based not on primogeniture but on the fact that Alexander II had recognized Robert Bruce as his heir, before the birth of his son Alexander III. This invoked the law of tanistry, the naming of the heir by the incumbent ruler, which was and in some instances still is Scottish law. The descendant of the third daughter had an even more tenuous claim, so that the principal contenders became Balliol and Bruce.

The question now arose of who was competent to judge between the claimants, and whose judgement they would accept. There were thirteen of them altogether, and every claim had to be meticulously examined. It was sensibly argued that only a king could judge in the cause of a vacant kingship, and the obvious and convenient candidate was Edward I, brother-in-law of Alexander III and almost but not quite father-in-law of the seven-year-old Queen who had just died.

Up to this point relations between Scotland and Edward had been friendly.

Once more Edward seized his chance. He agreed to arbitrate, but in order to do so, he said, it would be necessary for each of the competitors to acknowledge him as his feudal superior. It was a neat trick and a logical one, for who could judge *but* a superior? They had invited him, but he was not going to waste his time if they would not listen to him. It did not take long for the claimants to realize that any who refused to do homage stood no chance of being elected. They all complied.

Edward quite correctly decided in favour of John Balliol, who became Scotland's one and only King John in 1292. One may note in passing the curious parallel that in England, Scotland and France the name John was not a lucky one for a king.

Edward had finally solved the problem of boundaries, the problem of having a powerful neighbour who was independent of him sitting on his northern doorstep and from time to time invading England. He immediately forced Balliol to do homage to him for the kingdom of Scotland. This made a fourth time, and a dangerous precedent was established.

Edward now set about humiliating Balliol shamelessly, with the express purpose of trying to push him into revolt. If Balliol, having done homage, were to rebel, Edward could declare him a forfeit rebel and seize his possessions—his possessions in this case being the kingdom of Scotland. He would then legally obtain physical possession of the northern kingdom.

Balliol finally repudiated his allegiance to Edward and entered into an alliance with France in 1295, an alliance which endured until 1603 when Scotland and England became united under the

Scottish crown—a fact which is not always very obvious in the relationship which followed, and which today is generally overlooked.

Edward invaded Scotland in force and occupied it, in much the same way that Nazi Germany occupied France and various other European countries during World War II. Balliol was forced to surrender and was sent to the Tower of London. Scotland was seemingly conquered.

For ten years Scotland lay under England's yoke, and resentment smouldered. Finally a knight from Renfrewshire, William Wallace of Elderslie, rallied the Scottish resistance. He slew an English governor and fought a battle at Stirling Bridge in which he inflicted a humiliating defeat on the English, but a year and a half later he himself was defeated at Falkirk and had to go into hiding. After seven years he was betrayed, captured and executed. But in all he had done he had made it clear that he was acting for King John Balliol, Scotland's rightful king.

So far the Highlanders had not been greatly involved in what was happening. Wallace does not seem to have sought their help. He lived close to the Highlands but was separated from them by the estuary of the River Clyde. Although he spoke Gaelic and French far better than he spoke English, he made no attempt to muster the clans. This was left to Bruce to do.

It is interesting to consider speculatively how at this point the Highlanders regarded events in the south. Probably not very seriously, for what went on outside the Highlands did not concern them a great deal. They certainly did not share the feelings of burning rage that filled the hearts of the Scots in the Lowlands and Borders. The English did not occupy the Highlands. It was far simpler to 'contain' the clansmen. It is doubtful if they took the clans very seriously, and there is no reason why they should have done.

So far nobody had sought clan support. The Bruce who did so was the *grandson* of the Robert Bruce of Annandale who had been Balliol's closest competitor for the crown.

This, then, is the background to the Highland Arrival. One notes dispassionately that, if the English kings made repeated attempts to bring Scotland under their direct rule, Scottish kings made equally repeated attempts to annex northern England. Unfortunately for Scotland, they had waited till the Anglo-

Saxons had been invaded by the Normans, and it was the might of Norman feudal power with which Scotland had to contend.

Robert Bruce did not seek Highland support as a matter of calculated policy. Although he had had himself crowned in March 1306, he had aroused the anger of many of the powerful Scottish barons, including the family of Comyns, who were, like his ancestors, Anglo-Normans who had come to Scotland with David I.

Apart from his feud with the Comyns and their supporters, he had aroused suspicion among some of the barons by submitting to Edward of England in 1302. In 1306, before his coronation, he had murdered John, Lord of Badenoch, known as 'the Red Comyn', and had been excommunicated for this. The murder took place in the Church of the Minorites in Dumfries. It seems to have been partly in retaliation for an affair in Selkirk Forest in 1299 in which Bruce himself had nearly been killed.

The Comyns were part-Highland, part-Borderers. They owned lands in England and estates in Roxburghshire, and they had acquired their northern possessions by marriage. The Red Comyn had himself a substantial claim to the crown. Indeed, in the Bruce–Comyn feud, patriotism is well concealed behind a very obvious struggle to obtain the crown.

Three months after his coronation, Bruce was defeated near Perth by the Earl of Pembroke and forced to seek refuge in the Highlands There he sought the support of all who would give it—and not all did. Apart from the Comyns, who were at the time Earls of Buchan and Atholl, as well as Lords of Badenoch, the MacDougalls and the Macnabs were against him. The MacDougalls almost caught and killed him at Dalry near Tyndrum.

He eventually reached shelter on the Scottish island of Arran, where it is said he was befriended by the MacKinnons, who as a reward were later given considerable estates in Skye, where up to that time they had only a foothold at Dunakin, their principal clan lands being in Mull.

In 1307 Bruce managed to defeat Pembroke, and soon afterwards Edward I of England died. Bruce's strength now grew. He defeated the Comyn Earl of Buchan at Inverurie and harried Buchan. 'Harried' is a very polite word indeed and cloaks a great many atrocities that are better left cloaked, but there has never been a time when atrocities were unfashionable, and Bruce was merely doing what any other sensible ruler of his day would have done.

The following year he took Dunstaffnage from the MacDougalls. He began to consolidate his kingdom, raided into England, fought-off English counter-attacks and seized the Isle of Man.

His most famous partisan was 'the Good' Sir James Douglas, but he had found many supporters in the Highlands. By 1314 his army contained numerous clans, including Camerons, Campbells, Drummonds, Frasers, Grants, MacDonalds, MacFarlanes, MacGregors, MacKays, MacKenzies, MacIntoshes, MacLeans, Macphersons, Munros, Robertsons, Rosses, Sinclairs and Sutherlands—and Stewarts.

When Bruce had been on the run, as a crowned king, he had done as anyone else would have done. He had promised considerable rewards for all those who would help him establish and consolidate his kingdom. There was nothing disinterested or 'noble' about the Highland support. Men followed where their interests seemed to lead. If they were lucky, they backed the winning side, and if not they could always claim to have supported the 'rightful' side. It is an oddity of history that losers are usually 'rightful'. This is not a cynical appraisal of the chiefs. It means simply that they were sensible, responsible men who took calculated risks.

Those who supported Bruce did not regret it. Many clan fortunes took a considerable turn for the better after the victory over the English at Bannockburn in 1314. Some, of course, such as those of the Comyns, suffered a reversal from which they never recovered. The MacDougalls were clever and married Bruce's granddaughter and so recovered much of their lands—but not Dunstaffnage Castle, which became a Campbell stronghold and still is. Sir Neil Campbell of Lochow and Alexander MacDonald, brother of the MacDonald chief, were two of his most devoted Highland supporters and were rewarded handsomely.

The appearance of the Highlanders on the national scene may therefore be regarded as to a considerable extent accidental. If Bruce had had the support of his nobility, he would never have been forced into hiding in the mountains. The Highlanders had not acquired miraculously and from nowhere a sudden sense of

'Scottish' identity, in the wider meaning of the expression. They quite probably did not regard the English as essentially much worse than any other 'Sassenach' or Lowlander. But in the non-Highland Bruce ran the blood of the ancient Dalriadic kings, and evidently if they helped him he could do much to help them in return.

In a later chapter, mention will be made of the eternal Highland dream of a restoration of their Gaelic kingdom. They hated the absence of the kings from the Highlands, among the Sassenachs or Lowlanders. This was a strong motivation in everything the chiefs did, but the kingdom of the Gael remained a dream to the bitter end.

There was no miraculous unity of Scotland after the wars of independence. That took centuries to arrive—one could argue that it has still not arrived. Certainly Scotland itself was not very united in 1603 when the crowns of Scotland and England were united, and it is perhaps the fate of some countries to remain eternally divided among themselves.

The Highlanders had given Scotland her name and her kings, her *Scottish* kings. But the House of Alpin had moved its political centre right away from the Highlands into the eastern lowland plain, and the subsequent House of Dunkeld had remained estranged. Indeed, as will be seen in the next chapter, Bruce himself had unwittingly sown the seeds of what became a very serious attempt to wrest the kingship away from the House of Stewart and return it to the Highlands.

The Highlanders were no different from anyone else. The Comyns had their supporters, and Bruce had his. There was no treason or dishonour involved in the choosing of sides.

Nevertheless, the Highlanders, although undoubtedly unaware of the fact, had helped to set the stage for the Arbroath Declaration of 1320 in which the Scottish nobility in a stirring declaration of independence declared that, so long as one hundred remained alive, the Scots would never submit to the English, 'for it is not for glory we fight, for riches or for honours, but for freedom alone, which no good man loses but with his life'. They went on to add that any king who tried to submit Scotland to England would be driven out by the Scots, and Bruce himself is said to have been responsible for that clause.

Gropingly and for mixed motives, the Scottish leaders,

Lowland, Border and Highland, had enunciated the principle of the contract which must exist between a king and his people if a monarchy is to survive.

At this point the national picture has begun to unfold, and at last the Highlanders are present. They deserve as much credit as the Good Sir James Douglas or anyone else who picked the winning side in a time of much confusion.

Much more important, a precept had been established by which in future Scottish kings would remember that Highland support had been helpful to Bruce, perhaps even essential to him, and so might be worth cultivating again. If the clans retreated back into their glens after Bannockburn, they were not forgotten.

Feared, despised and often persecuted when they could be with impunity—they were never again forgotten.

4

The Lordship of the Isles

Some names and titles have acquired a romantic flavour all of their own. 'Lord of the Isles' is such a title, but the reality was a good deal less romantic than the sound of the name.

This is where the MacDonalds and Campbells enter into the history, and this is where it becomes necessary to put an end to one of those emotive myths with which popular history abounds. It runs something like this:

The MacDonalds were *real* Highlanders. They were the victims of crafty, conniving newcomers called Campbell. With the help of distant kings who knew nothing of events in the Highlands, the Campbells deprived the MacDonalds of much of their lands by dirty tricks.

The great MacDonald–Campbell feud permeates the history of the Highlands from the time of Bruce onwards, and, like the struggle between Bruce and the Comyns, it was a struggle for power.

The MacDonalds trace their origins to one Somerled, who in the twelfth century made himself master of Morven and Lochaber by heading a rising which expelled Norwegian raiders who had settled there. Later King David I gave him Arran, Bute and the Isle of Man, and he was also Lord of Argyll. His sons were known as Kings of the Isles.

Somerled then decided to make war against the King of Scotland, Malcolm IV (The Maiden). He was defeated in 1164, but the Crown's troubles with the MacDonalds had only just begun.

Of Somerled's descendants, one became the progenitor of the Clan MacDougall; another, Donald of Islay, became the

MacDonald progenitor; the third was the founder of the MacRuari (MacRory) clan in Bute, which did not survive as a distinct clan.

In the time of Bruce, Alexander (or Alisdair, the names are interchangeable) the chief of the MacDonalds and Alexander the chief of the MacDougalls made common cause against Bruce in support of the Comyns. Alexander MacDonald was imprisoned, but his brother Angus Og rallied the clan in support of Bruce. When it was all over, Angus Og was confirmed in all his brother's possessions.

After the death of Bruce, the MacDonalds changed sides again in a second revolt against the House of Bruce and lost their lands; but in 1344 John, the MacDonald chief, was reinstated. His possessions included Islay, Jura, Mull, Colonsay, Tiree and Lewis, plus great landholdings on the mainland. In 1346 he took to himself the title of '*Lord of the Isles*'.

There were only four Lords of the Isles, although after the forfeiture of the lordship there were claimants who made a nuisance of themselves for a number of years. It has already been said that John, the 1st Lord, rebelled and was pardoned by King David II in 1344.

Donald, the 2nd Lord, considered that he was the rightful Earl of Ross and accepted English aid in establishing his claim. He was beaten at the Battle of Harlaw in 1411 and never did become Earl of Ross.

Alexander, the 3rd Lord, following what was by now a family tradition, took arms against the Scottish king and in 1427 was thrown into prison as a result. Two years later he succeeded quite legally to the earldom of Ross and was liberated. He was not at all grateful for this royal clemency—indeed, royal favour. Furious about having been imprisoned, he promptly raised his clans of the Isles and of Ross, ravaged the Crown lands in Inverness-shire and burned the town of Inverness itself. James I of Scotland defeated him, forced him to submit and imprisoned him again. He died finally in 1449 after a turbulent life and was succeeded by his son John.

John, the 4th Lord, was no more peaceful than his predecessors. In 1462 or 1463 he entered into an intrigue with King Edward IV of England. The plan was that John, and the Earl of Douglas would overthrow the ruling Scottish dynasty. Thereafter

John would rule over the entire north of Scotland, north of the old Antonine Wall, and the Earl of Douglas would rule over the southern part of the country. In return for his support, they would, of course, do homage to the English king for their separate kingdoms.

The scheme came to nothing, but in 1493 the Lordship was declared forfeit to the Crown. John lived for a further ten years, becoming a monk at Paisley.

The MacDonald intrigues with the English were not over, for, jumping a little in history, we find in 1545 Donald Dubh MacDonald, the last pretender to the forfeit Lordship, entering into an alliance with King Henry VIII of England against the Scottish king. They were not exactly patriots these Lords of the Isles and their descendants.

It is hardly surprising that the Scottish kings did not regard the MacDonalds very kindly for some time after all this. The MacDonalds had remained in power as a result of Angus Og having helped Bruce. If he had not, the MacDonalds would have been severely penalized, like the Comyns and the rest of their friends. Angus Og was amply rewarded, but his successors were rebellious to the point of weariness, and they constituted a perpetual danger and threat to the peace of Scotland. It is difficult to describe them in milder terms.

There is no doubt that the MacDonalds saw things from the purely Celtic point of view, of course. Scotland's kings had become detested Sassenachs, dwelling away from the land of their Dalriadic ancestors. There is undoubtedly something rather magnificent about the MacDonald attempts to turn the Highlands into a separate kingdom, and it certainly had some sort of historical precedent, for King Kenneth MacAlpin had been king of a kingdom which stretched roughly northwards from the Forth–Clyde line. The Lothians and Strathclyde were only added later.

The MacDonalds were the first great power-group in the Highlands. What about the Campbells? Who and what were they?

The progenitor from whom they take their Gaelic patronymic was Sir Colin Mor Campbell of Lochow, who was killed in 1294. This does not mean that Campbells appeared from nowhere in 1294. They had an ancestry going back to distant Irish-Celtic origins, and they had been settled in Argyll long before their famous ancestor Sir Colin, who died roughly a century after Somerled.

Sir Colin's son Neil, like Angus Og MacDonald, supported Bruce. Neil was the first to bear the name MacCailein Mor, son of Colin Mor, which the Dukes of Argyll carry to this day. All the Campbell chiefs are the descendants of Sir Colin of Lochow.

Neil too was rewarded by Bruce for his support. Unlike the MacDonalds, who had been great magnates before the arrival of Bruce, the Campbells were quick to see how their rewards had been earned and where their interests could best be served. They became devoted supporters of the Scottish kings and of the central government.

By about 1425 Sir Duncan Campbell of Lochow had become Lord Campbell, and soon afterwards, in 1457, the second Lord Campbell, Colin, was created the 1st Earl of Argyll and became Lord High Chancellor of Scotland.

The Scottish kings, having discovered that rewarding and flattering MacDonald chiefs were distinctly unprofitable things to do, had to find some way of keeping them in check in order to secure peace in the Highlands. The Campbells were ready to hand, grateful for their rewards and anxious to earn more. Their chiefs were as Celtic and Highland as any clan chiefs in Scotland and were, viewed through royal eyes, model citizens.

It was James IV of Scotland, popular with the Highlanders not only because he visited the Highlands but because he took the trouble to learn to speak Gaelic which had pretty well died out in the Lowlands, who resolved the MacDonald question. He used the Campbells to hold the MacDonalds in check. Whenever there was trouble in the western Highlands, the Campbells were given a royal commission to quell it. Where lands became forfeit to the Crown, they were given to the Campbells. Their possessions grew, as did their prestige, and they formed powerful connections by marriage. Everything they did and everything they acquired was buttressed by royal warrants and charters and the approval of the Privy Council.

Loyalty, of course, is not an absolute, and only the individual can possibly separate his loyalty from self-interest or necessity. The Campbells and the MacDonalds were both playing the same game in the west, trying to establish an effective power-base from which they could protect their own interests and those of their descendants, and from which they could climb ever upwards. The main difference between the two clans is that they had different ideas on the rules of the game. If the Campbells ever had any idea of grasping the ultimate power, the crown, for themselves, the fact is well concealed. The MacDonalds, however, made no bones about it. They did not want *any* overlord in the Lowlands. They wanted the kingdom of the Gael with the MacDonald lords as its princes or kings.

One can sympathize easily with the MacDonalds—and Highland historians usually have, at the expense of the Campbells. Somerled had established the MacDonald power in the west and had made himself supreme so that his sons were known as kings. His descendants felt that they virtually owned the Highlands and islands. Other clans on the western seaboard had become vassal clans to the MacDonald power. The MacDonalds were in a very good position to form a 'breakaway' kingdom of the Gael, independent from the rest of Scotland. It is the sort of temptation that is very difficult to resist.

In 1509 James IV, the most brilliant of the Stewart kings, made the Earl of Huntly his sheriff in the north, and the Earl of Argyll his sheriff in the west. He turned two powerful but loyal clans into an effective police force to control the Highlands. Whether the loyalty of the Gordons and Campbells was fed by self-interest is quite beside the point.

As the MacDonalds saw their power being stripped from them by Scottish kings, and watched the rise of the Campbells, whom they understandably came to hate at an early date, their bitterness grew. Out of this bitterness came the myth that the MacDonalds were 'real' Highlanders who had 'always' been there and that the Campbells were despicable newcomers who held their lands by new-fangled charters and other underhand methods.

The MacDonalds, of course, had 'won' their land at swordpoint.

The Campbell rise to power took place admittedly some two centuries after Somerled's early rise, but the MacDonalds were not the 'original' Highlanders. Like all west Highland clans, they were an amalgam of Irish-Scot and 'original' Pict—whoever and whatever he was—and Norse settler and invader. So were the Campbells, as can be seen by consulting their short history in Part Two.

The MacDonalds and Campbells were both very much of their time, and the principal difference between them was the Campbell use of royal authority and the MacDonald contempt for it.

It is highly unlikely that at the time of the failure of the Lordship of the Isles the other clans felt particularly partisan. Indeed, many of them who had been vassal clans were now able to pursue independent policies of their own. The MacLeans were able to increase their own power and standing as a result of MacDonald misfortunes; and after the end of the Lordship we find the MacLeans and the MacKinnons, who under the MacDonald rule had been enemies, becoming friends and acting together along with the MacQuarries. This was completely normal, for shifting power-bases and changing circumstances always result in new alignments.

It is only in the time of Archibald, the 7th Earl of Argyle (it was spelt that way for a long time, although the modern spelling is Argyll), that the general unpopularity of the Campbells with the other clans begins to assume any real dimension. The 7th earl's persecution of the MacGregors and others, and especially his betrayal under trust of MacGregor of Glenstrae and seven of his clan in 1604, earned the Campbell clan many enemies in the Highlands. His son the 8th earl and 1st marquis was the one who fought against that romantic figure Montrose and was labelled 'master-fiend' despite the fact that he personally put the crown on Charles II in Scone and supported him until he was sent back into exile after the Battle of Worcester (see Chapter 5).

From that time on we discover emotive and romantic nonsense clogging the pages of Highland history, but by that time the issues at stake had ceased to be mere power-struggles and become issues of religion and conscience. When that happens, propaganda, which has been a potent political weapon ever since the early Church began to write history (and had a monopoly of it for centuries), challenges popular sentiment with a mixture of truth, half-truth and judicious bare-faced lying.

Who, after all, cannot envisage the scene with the little fair-haired boy in blue silk suit, with white lace collar and cuffs, standing up like a little man before his beetle-browed, scowling, menacing, rather brutal questioners? On the left of the painting we see the father, a Cavalier, sword in hand, hiding behind the panelling listening. The caption reads simply: 'When did you last see your father?'

It is the most powerful piece of partisan propaganda imaginable, and it made it impossible for anybody to like the Roundheads. The Cavaliers were dashing, noble, loyal and true. It is a totally false picture, created by a seven-word sentence which in *itself* makes no statement—which must be the acme of propaganda-writing. Many of the gentry supported Cromwell, many of the poor and simple country people supported the King. Families were divided among themselves.

So, when the Campbells supported the Solemn League and Covenant (see page 65), after persecuting (which is to say killing) MacGregors and other small clans, and many of the clans came out in support of Montrose and the King, it became easy to add all the early MacDonald grievances as fuel to the flame.

Later, after the Glencoe affair (discussed on pages 78–80), the whole Campbell–MacDonald feud entered into the field of pure fiction.

The fact is that the Lords of the Isles had had their chance, and they had failed to make good use of it. They had royal favour, royal leniency, vast possessions, tremendous standing among the other clans. They could easily have made themselves the masters of a sub-kingdom. It was the 'sub' they despised, and for that they paid the penalty.

The MacDonalds were neither right nor wrong. History does not work that way. Each important figure on the historical stage has to make his own policy and his own decisions, is the inheritor of his own past and is a prey to all his own prejudices, inherited and otherwise. And, of course, each figure nurses his own secret ambitions. None of us ever has the hindsight of history about ourselves—that is something we can enjoy only in relation to other people, long after events have taken place.

It was a great pity that the MacDonalds took the line that they did. There is little doubt that Scotland as a whole and the Highlands in particular would have been spared centuries of grief and bloodshed if the MacDonalds had not chosen to confront the royal House in a trial of strength. The Campbells would probably have ended up being no more than important vassals and followers of the MacDonalds, as was the case with other clans.

Historical imponderables are always tempting and enjoyable, but they are full of uncertainty. Perhaps it would not have turned out so well at all. We shall never know.

5

Montrose and Argyle—a Study in Contrasts

After Bannockburn some of the Highland clans took the part of
the Scottish kings from time to time. They were present at the
Battle of Halidon Hill in 1333 when David II of Scotland was
engaged in a second war of independence against Edward III of
England, and they were probably represented at Duplin Moor
and Neville's Cross in the same era.

They formed a part of James III's army against his rebels at
Sauchieburn in 1488, in the aftermath of which the King was
murdered; and they were certainly out in strength in support of
James IV at Flodden in 1513.

It was during the Wars of the Covenants, the Bishops' Wars,
that religion fully entered into the picture, and it was at this time
that the Highlanders captured the imagination with their lightning campaigns under the King's Lieutenant-General, James
Graham, Marquis of Montrose. From this time on, the Highlanders played a more and more central role in what happened in
Scotland's history.

Montrose and Argyle, his chief opponent, have often been
represented as opposites, but this is an over-simplification. They
had a great deal in common, more than is usually admitted, and
for a brief spell they were allies.

James Graham, 5th Earl and 1st Marquis of Montrose, was
only thirty-eight when he was executed in 1650. He is essentially
a likeable character in history. He won golden opinions in his
student days at St Andrews University, he was possessed of great
personal magnetism and charm, and there is a hint of gay
insouciance about him, a sort of careless gallantry which came so

naturally to him that his detractors have not hesitated to equate it with a lack of responsibility.

The troubles which brought Montrose and Argyle to the forefront of Scotland's historical stage reached a peak in 1638 when Charles I tried to force his new prayer book on the Scots, who did not want it. The Reformation had followed a different path in Scotland from that which it followed in England. The original Reformation Church was the Catholic Church minus the Pope and very little else. In the time of Henry VIII of England, a Catholic attending a service, after Henry had made himself Head of the Church *in* England (it was not yet thought of as being *of* England), would have noticed virtually no difference from a Catholic service anywhere else in the world.

The work of reforming went on under Elizabeth, and eventually 'popery' became a dirty word, which to some extent it has always remained in the United Kingdom; but the structure of the Church remained what it was under Henry, the king aided by his bishops responsible for all forms of worship in England.

In Scotland the doctrines of Calvin had taken root, and at the time of the Union of the Crowns the Scots regarded the hierarchy of English Church as an encroachment on people's liberty of worship. They required neither bishops nor kings to advise them in matters of the spirit, and they did not intend to allow them to do so.

If Charles I had allowed his Scottish subjects the freedom in religious matters which they were already enjoying before his time, the conflict between king and people would have been avoided, or at least postponed. He chose not to do so. The Scots were to have his bishops and his prayer book.

As a result, the National Covenant was drawn up and read in Greyfriars Churchyard in Edinburgh and was immensely popular. The National Covenant (often referred to as the first Covenant) protests the loyalty of the people to the king, but it also states Scotland's undoubted right to its own Church and its own Parliament. It was a natural response to a piece of ill-advised interference on the part of a Government in London which knew little and cared less about the wishes of the Scottish people.

Neither Montrose nor the others who subscribed to this 1638 National Covenant considered themselves rebellious subjects. Montrose, indeed, belonged to a family which had won an enviable reputation for loyalty to the Crown. They had come to Scotland in the wake of King David I, it was the Scottish Crown which had established their fortunes and given them their titles, and they considered themselves devoted and trustworthy servants of their kings. Nevertheless, the Grahams were not giddy monarchists. The old saying 'Right, wrong, follow the king, else wherefore born?' was never a Graham sentiment, nor a Scottish sentiment.

It has already been noted that three centuries earlier the Arbroath Declaration of Independence of 1320 had made it clear that there existed a contract between the king and his people, a contract which both sides had to honour. Any king, therefore, who tried to interfere with the freedom of worship of the Scots was bound to be resisted—on that specific point. The young Montrose, therefore, enthusiastically jumped on top of a barrel at the first protest against the new prayer book. There was nothing inconsistent between this fact and the fact that he was a lover of legality, of law and order, a firm believer in a strong central authority.

Charles's reaction to this piece of Scottish impudence was to raise an army, and the Covenanters promptly followed suit. Montrose steps forth as the first Covenanting general, and he won his first battle against the Royalists at Bridge of Dee in 1639. It was not much more than a skirmish, but in it he displayed some of the qualities which made him so formidable in what followed.

The Royalist defeat was followed by a truce and negotiations. The more extreme of the Covenanters now saw a chance to assert a number of conditions which cut across the royal prerogatives. Beating the King's forces in battle proved to be a heady wine.

Argyle now suffered what seems from all the evidence to have been a genuine religious conversion. He became head of the extreme faction. He was the most powerful noble in Scotland. Only the Marquis of Huntly could match his power, but Huntly did not enjoy nearly as much prestige outside the Highlands as the Campbell chief did.

When the Solemn League and Covenant (the second Covenant) of 1643 was drafted, Montrose took the difficult decision to abandon the Covenanting army. There is no question but that it was a bitter and difficult decision. He was a Presbyterian and remained one all his life, and he had been one of the most devoted adherents to the first Covenant. It was no betrayal of his family tradition to oppose any king who came in arms against the Scots people in order to force religion on them. But in the second Covenant he felt strongly that Argyle and the others were determined, under the cloak of religion, to establish a theocracy in Scotland with themselves at its apex—a theocracy under which the King would be a puppet figure. They were anxious to impose government by the Church instead of government by the King.

Montrose went south to see the King and to offer his services to him. Charles had never been friendly towards him. As a young man Montrose had been snubbed by his monarch, something which he must have remembered all his life. He had great difficulty in persuading Charles to accept his services, but in the end he was given a commission as the royal Lieutenant-General in Scotland. He was despatched to try to win Scotland to the King's cause, but he was despatched empty-handed, without arms, troops or money.

Whatever he was going to achieve in Scotland he was going to have to achieve it on his own.

He managed to avoid the Covenanting troops, who were everywhere, and to reach momentary safety at Tullibelton, the home of Patrick Graham of Inchbrakie. With two followers and horses but no baggage, he is ready to undertake his life's work. Everywhere he is surrounded by enemies.

Eventually he learned that Alexander MacDonald, known as 'Colkitto', had arrived in Atholl with a great army of Irish levies, eager to fight for the King. He had raised some Highlanders, mostly his own clansmen from Islay and Kintyre. Montrose set out to meet him. He found Colkitto drawn up facing watchful levies at Blair, Highlanders of the east who distrusted the men of the west and feared the wild Irish.

Suddenly, without any warning, between the two sides with their hackles raised and ready for the onset walked two men—Montrose and Patrick Graham of Inchbrakie, known as 'Black Pate' Graham. Montrose wore trews and a plaid and carried a Highland broadsword and a targe.

The Atholl men and the Irish and the clans from the west forgot that they had been on the point of a pitched battle, and Montrose had acquired his army. It happened very much as it has been related here, and there is no doubt that it was a romantic beginning to a year of miracles.

Against the Covenanting forces Montrose managed to raise a force of Highland clans to fight beside the Macdonells from Antrim, and for one year, in 1644 and 1645, he made a war with his Highlanders, a war of remarkable forced marches, of lightning attacks, of brilliant generalship.

Among the clans who supported him and the King's cause were the Macnabs, MacGregors, Gordons, the various branches of the great MacDonald confederation, Appin Stewarts, Farquharsons, Macphersons, MacLeans, MacKinnons and Camerons. Together they won startling victories, beginning at Tippermuir, where his small army was virtually weaponless. He pointed at the well-armed and superior force facing them and told his weaponless men blithely that *there* there were arms in plenty for the taking. Many of the Highlanders fought with stones, and they carried the day. Tippermuir was followed by Inverlochy, where Montrose and his army carried out an incredible forced march over snowbound, mountainous, inhospitable country lacking roads of any sort, in order to fall on Argyle's army, when nobody could have believed that he was anywhere within miles of them. Further victories followed at Auldearn and Kilsyth, and after Kilsyth he was able to say truthfully to his king that he was the master of Scotland.

Had Charles been able to exploit the situation, matters would have been very different. But Charles was in difficulties of his own in England, where he was far less well served against his puritanical subjects. Montrose was left waiting, and the Highlanders became impatient and began to drift off home to their glens.

From the purely Highland point of view, they had served Montrose far better than he had any right to expect. They had succumbed to his charisma, and they thought the world of him. He had held them always on a very tight rein. They must have felt, with justice, that they had little booty to show for all the risks they had taken, all the great deeds achieved. Certainly nobody *paid* them as soldiers; so no booty meant work for nothing while the clan lands were neglected. At the first slackening of the pace, the first period of inactivity, they slipped off home with what goods they had acquired, to make sure that all was well with their families, from whom they had been separated for a long time.

Colkitto, having been knighted by a grateful Montrose, went off on his own with his wild Irishers to harry Argyle's country in pursuance of the long-standing MacDonald loathing and hatred for all things Campbell.

Montrose was taken by surprise at Philiphaugh at the end of 1645, with only the nucleus of an army, and only just managed to save his life in the rout which followed. He retired to the Highlands to lie up for the winter.

At this point everything was by no means lost. What he had shown could be done once, could certainly be done a second time and perhaps better. He planned to mount a new offensive after the spring of 1646 and busied himself arousing support from the clans whom he knew would follow him.

Out of the blue, word reached him that Charles had surrendered himself to a Covenanting army at Newark on Trent in England. Charles commanded that Montrose instantly disperse what forces he had and personally go abroad. Charles had pledged his kingly word that Montrose would obey him.

Montrose had no option but to do so. He went to France and kicked his heels at the futile and gossip-ridden court of the Queen in exile. Three years after his surrender, King Charles I was taken out one morning and beheaded.

The next year, 1650, Charles II sent Montrose back to Scotland—once again with nothing substantial in the way of troops and with no money. It was up to him to repeat his performance and to raise an army in Scotland, retake the country and then go on to defeat Cromwell and re-establish Charles II on his proper throne in London.

Charles II was no more sensible, no more dependable than his father had been. He could not resist the temptation to back both ends against the middle. Having promised to do nothing, he immediately entered into negotiations with Argyle, who by this time was Montrose's bitter enemy. Charles was determined that if he could not win back his throne with Montrose's help, then he would try to win it with Argyle's help. All that mattered was to get back the throne. In opening negotiations with Argyle, he sent Montrose to certain death.

Montrose arrived in the far north, was defeated in what seems to have been only a skirmish at Carbisdale and took to the heather. He was betrayed to his Covenanting enemies by MacLeod of

Assynt before he had any opportunity to make contact with his loyal chiefs. They took him to Edinburgh to execute him, and in his pocket he carried Charles's commission as the royal viceroy and Captain-General of Scotland. The Covenanters took him prisoner in the King's name and executed him in Edinburgh in the King's name. They were *all* acting for the King—which is the measure of Charles II's duplicity.

During the dozen years which separate the signing of the first Covenant by Montrose and others, and Montrose's execution, his counterpart on the Covenanting side was Archibald Campbell, 8th Earl and 1st Marquis of Argyle. He was eight years older than Montrose, and there has been a suggestion of a rivalry between the two men going back to student days at St Andrews, but this does not seem very likely.

Argyle was in many ways the opposite of Montrose. He had reddish hair, he was far from handsome in appearance, having a cast in one eye, and above all he was a cold, calculating, unattractive character. This may have been due to an intensely unhappy childhood. His mother, who belonged to the great Douglas House of Morton, died in his infancy, and he was ignored and neglected by his eccentric, unlovable father. His boyhood must have been intensely unhappy, and yet he was heir to the most powerful Highland chiefship in Scotland.

Of all the clans the Campbells were the most secure and the most powerful and enjoyed most prestige outside the Highlands. Following the death of his father, the young Earl was fully occupied with financial and other affairs. He was not at all involved in the great religious question of his time. He did not sign the first Covenant—and nobody knew with any certainty which side he would choose in the coming conflict.

Like the Grahams, the Earls of Argyle belonged to a family which had founded its fortunes on loyalty to the Crown. They had consistently supported the central government. It was their policy to do so. If Argyle lacked Montrose's charisma, he could match him and outreach him in all things concerning loyalty to the crown of Scotland.

Argyle was not a religious man, but he had a keen brain and he was by nature cut out to be a statesman, a career to which his great rank would have paved the way in ordinary times of peace. He was of Celtic stock, and his clan were completely Highland, whereas

Brice Mackinnon's tomb at Iona. The galley on the shield is common to many west Highland clans

ROBERT
THE
BRUCE
KING
OF
SCOTS
1306-1329

The Bruce Monument at Bannockburn where, in 1314, Robert the Bruce defeated the English and secured Scottish independence

Mingarry Castle, stronghold of MacIain of Ardnamurchan, occupies a strategic
position on the Sound of Mull at the northernmost reach of the South Isles

Dusk over Loch Leven, Highland Region

Leading Covenanter Archibald Campbell, 8th Earl and 1st Marquis of Argyle, crowned Charles II at Scone in 1649, but was executed at the Restoration for his collaboration with Cromwell

James, Duke of York, later James VII and II – the Jacobites named themselves after him

Montrose rallied the Highland clans to Charles I in 1644, but was sacrificed to Charles II's policy of reconciliation with the Covenanters and executed in 1650

Soldier's Leap, Pass of Killiecrankie, where the Battle of Killiecrankie took place in 1689

Glencoe: scene of the massacre of the MacDonalds of Glencoe in 1692

Following the 1715 rising, Eilean Donan, seat of the Mackenzies of Kintail, was garrisoned in 1719 by Spanish Jacobite groups, and blown up by an English man-of-war

James Stuart, the Old Pretender

Castle Stalker in Appin, occupied during the Jacobite risings by the Government against the Stewarts of Appin

Duntulm Castle on Skye, seat of the MacDonalds of Sleat. At nearby Floddigarry, Flora MacDonald lived after her marriage in 1750

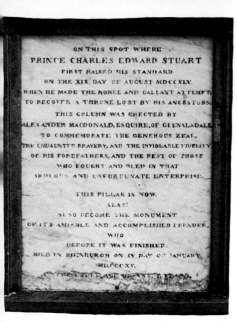

Inscription on the Jacobite Monument
in Glenfinnan

Flora MacDonald helped Bonnie Prince
Charlie escape after the failure of the '45 Risin

A deserted croft at Shieling near Second Coast, Ross

Glenfinnan Monument. In 1745 the Duke of Atholl and Rannoch raised Prince Charles Edward's standard here and the Rising began

The MacGillivray cairn at Culloden, 1746

Montrose was descended from a certain William de Graham who followed David I into Scotland in the same way as the Bruces, Balliols and Stewarts, as well as some Highland chiefs such as the Frasers, Chisholms and Colquhouns. The Graham clan was half Highland, half Lowland, a frontier clan.

It is Argyle's lack of charisma which has made him so unattractive to historians and has resulted in his being accorded rather less than his due.

Both men were Presbyterians (that is to say they believed in a Church ruled over by a presbytery elected from within, and not by bishops appointed by the king). Both men were loyal supporters of the Crown. Both men remained so, and it is important to remember that, in all which follows.

It was when the Glasgow Assembly met at the end of 1638, the best part of a year after the first Covenant had been signed, that Argyle went through a profound spiritual experience. He was thirty-four at the time, prince of an independent west Highland kingdom, the most important Protestant nobleman in the country.

When he decided to join forces with the Covenant, he did so whole-heartedly. At no time did he ever flinch from the consequences or waver in his religious zeal, which, as so often happens in the case of sudden conversions, bordered on fanaticism. Of course, in his fanaticism he was not alone. Other Covenanting leaders outdid him in it, and indeed he may well have picked up his extremist views from his new friends.

Argyle was undeniably the driving force behind the new Solemn League and Covenant to which Montrose could not subscribe. The difference between the two men is simply stated. Montrose wanted the King to leave the Scots in peace in matters affecting their religious faith and in the proper exercise of their parliamentary rights. The adherents of the second Covenant not only wanted no bishops in Scotland—they wanted none in England either. They profoundly distrusted the combination of king and bishop.

That many of the Covenanters saw in the second Covenant a chance to establish a theocracy in Scotland, with all its attendant benefits to those at the top, is plain. What is less plain is the amount of self-interest which motivated Argyle, for he at least enjoyed an almost unique position in Scotland under its kings. It is not easy to see what Argyle stood to gain that he did not already possess, and one is forced to attribute his part in history to his religious faith. Certainly Argyle at no time ever sought to overthrow the monarch or the monarchy. His family had a remarkable record of public service and high office. If the MacDonalds and their friends loathed him, the reigning dynasty had no reason to.

Like all the Scots, Argyle was scandalized when the English beheaded Charles I. The Scots have been roundly accused of having sold Charles to the English. It was certainly to a Scottish Covenanting leader that he surrendered himself, and the Scots handed him over to the English; as part of the bargain they demanded arrears of pay for the army which they had maintained in England in support of the English Puritans. But the Scots army could not remain in England much longer, and if they had tried to carry off the King, the English would not have permitted it. In handing Charles over, they submitted to *force majeure*, and if they took the opportunity to haggle over back pay, one cannot blame them, however suspicious the combination of events may look in the eyes of later generations.

The fact is that, if Charles had allowed the Scots their presbytery, the Scots people might well have supported him against those of his English subjects who were in rebellion. The Highlanders, with whom we are concerned, were neither for nor against the king. They disliked Argyle and the Campbells, and if the second Covenant was going to increase Argyle's power, they were ready to dislike the Covenant. But the theological question did not touch the Highlanders very closely at that time, and if Montrose, Argyle and the King had been united in a common cause, the Highlanders would have risen for the King along with much of the rest of Scotland.

Argyle had no sense of having 'sold' his king merely in exchange for some arrears of pay for soldiers. So far as Argyle was concerned, at the time Charles was handed over to the English (among whom Charles, his father and his grandfather had chosen to make their home), the ultimate question of how Crown and religion were going to become reconciled was still unanswered. He could not have foreseen the execution of the King three years later. John Buchan, in his *Montrose*, says that there exists a declaration of a Commission of the General Assembly of the Scottish Church that the Scots did not hand over Charles until they had received assurances that the safety of his royal person would be respected by the English Parliament.

Immediately Charles was executed, it was Argyle who had Charles II proclaimed King of the Scots, while Cromwell was busy demolishing the monarchy in England.

The antagonism between Montrose and Argyle was professional. Montrose had cut the Covenanters to ribbons for an entire year and almost defeated their religious aspirations. Montrose was therefore plainly the sworn enemy of the second Covenant to which Argyle ardently subscribed. Montrose was a religious moderate in an age when almost nobody was moderate about anything.

An Episcopal Church in England and a Presbyterian one in Scotland, united under one Crown, was not only undesirable to the Covenanters but must have been regarded as pure moonshine. It is the kind of idiotic compromise that only the British people can make feasible. The curious position of Queen Elizabeth today, with two different 'established' Churches in her 'United' Kingdom, is the sort of situation that outsiders will never be able to understand.

When Argyle was presented with the chance to destroy Montrose, he did not hesitate to take it. While Montrose lived, the Covenanters would never sleep peacefully. Charles II had opened the door to them by entering into negotiations with them while Montrose was just beginning his campaign in the far north. In the name of Charles they hanged Montrose and congratulated themselves on a good job well done.

It was Charles II who destroyed *both* of these men whom history placed in opposition to one another. He destroyed Montrose quite surely by sending him back to Scotland with his commission and promising to do nothing to prejudice his chances in the north, and then going behind Montrose's back at once to negotiate with his sworn enemies. But he did not pardon Argyle either. It was Argyle who had him proclaimed King in Scotland on the death of his father. It was Argyle who personally placed the crown on his head at his Scottish coronation at Scone in 1651. But when Charles was finally restored in 1660, he was determined to destroy the chief trouble-makers in Scotland. On his instructions Argyle was arrested, and on 24 May 1661, aged fifty-seven, he was executed for having collaborated with Cromwell.

It was as feeble an excuse as Argyle's own excuse for executing Montrose—and Argyle at least had the saving grace that he probably could not have saved Montrose if he wished, for the other Covenanting leaders had lived for just that day. Many others, who had been far more actively involved in collaboration with Cromwell, were spared.

One thing is certain—Argyle was no coward. He has often been accused of cowardice—at Inverlochy, for example, when his army was overwhelmed and he made his escape to safety in his galley. But that was not cowardice. Argyle was never a military leader—he was a political one. To have thrown away his life then would have been to deprive the Covenant of its most powerful supporter for no purpose at all.

Always one comes back to the fact that Montrose was likeable and Argyle was not; that Montrose was a moderate, which modern historians tend to applaud although he lived at a time when moderates were regarded with intense suspicion, and Argyle was an extremist. Both men acted from conscience; both were loyal to their own Presbyterian beliefs; both were loyal to the King so long as the King did not take up arms against them in a matter of pure religion. The similarities are haunting; the differences led to tragedy.

Montrose has been accused of having unleashed an Irish Catholic horde on Scotland. But it was Charles who did that. In any event an army comprised of Catholics, Episcopalians and Presbyterians, as Montrose's was, was a miracle in itself. Nobody at the time seems to have grasped the lesson in it.

Objections to Montrose's reputation as a general, based on the fact that he never measured his skills against any of Europe's leading generals of the day, miss the point. Montrose did two remarkable things. He took an army of Highland clans into the field and kept it there for a year, which was up to that time regarded as impossible, even by the chiefs themselves. And he took that army all over the mountains in a series of lightning forced marches that must compel the awe of every student of military history who has studied the terrain. He was a very great man and a very unfortunate one.

Argyle was no less great and no less unfortunate. He put all the resources of his clan and all his prestige behind the drive to make the Scottish Church fully independent of interference from

England. He was personally loyal to Charles I and to Charles II, and the latter had him executed—which was not a very worthy thing to do to a man who had set the crown on his head at a time when his English subjects totally rejected him.

The obvious conclusion from all this is that both these men deserved better kings. Charles I is regarded by many as a martyr. If so, he brought about not only his own martyrdom but, infinitely worse, that of thousands of his subjects. He was badly advised, yes; but for that he must take responsibility for only the king can choose the king's advisers. He was unfeeling and uncaring about the religious sensibilities of others.

Charles II is a less pleasant figure than his rather sad father. He may have been a 'Merry Monarch' in the eyes of the English, but he was a stranger to Scotland. His reign was characterized by his one inflexible principle, which was that he was never going to 'go on his travels' again, and no matter what price had to be paid, he intended to remain on his throne till he died.

It is a pity that two of Scotland's leading men of the time, one a general of considerable status and the other with all the makings of a statesman, were sacrificed on such an unworthy altar. However much their families owed to the Stewarts and the House of Bruce, they had no cause to like the Stuarts.*

The Highlanders took the part of Charles II against Cromwell in 1650 and 1651 in the abortive attempt to effect a restoration. They fought and died at Inverkeithing and Worcester— MacLeans, MacDonalds, Frasers, Camerons, MacNeils, MacKinnons, Grants, Rosses, Sinclairs, Sutherlands, Macphersons, MacLeods, MacIntoshes, Murrays and Drummonds and others.

If Bruce had been the first to make use of the Highlanders, Montrose was the first to show just how effective they could become under the right sort of leadership. It is a pity William of Orange did not profit by the lesson. What he did will be discussed in the chapter that follows.

* Stewart was the name of the dynasty up to the time of Mary, Queen of Scots. Her son James VI and I was the son of Henry Stuart, Lord Darnley, and with him the dynasty changed. It involves more than a change of name, for the character of the Stuart kings is quite unlike that of the Stewarts, and although the theory that James VI and I was a changeling is discredited, one wishes that Mary, Queen of Scots, had married somebody else.

6

Life in the Highlands

So far, we have been concerned with the Highlanders outside their glens, with their appearances on the national scene, which is to say their appearances in various wars which were of national importance to Scotland.

It is time now to follow them into the mountains and to take a closer look at life there. Of necessity any such study must be a composite. Firstly a composite of time, because the fragments of first-hand knowledge that come to us prior to the eighteenth century *are* only fragments and refer to different periods. Putting them together therefore involves a certain amount of 'cheating' with regard to time. The alternative is no picture of life at all. Secondly it must be a composite of place, and for very obvious reasons. The way in which clansmen lived in Lochaber and Morven, in Argyll and the isles, differed from life close to the Highland-Lowland border. Even the characteristics of the people differ. The further west we go, the more pronounced is the Celtic influence, and in the far north and the isles the Norse influence is noticeable in the build and appearance of the people. The further east one goes, the greater the Anglo-Norman influence.

In the very far north there are small enclaves where the people do not regard themselves as living on clan territory at all. Thurso is a case in point, for, although it was surrounded by clans, the people of Thurso disclaim all connection with the clansmen. Also in the far north and in the east the Norse invaders preserved more of their identity than they did in the Hebrides, where they were absorbed into the Celto-Pictish society.

All composites, all generalizations are full of contradictions and exceptions. In the sketch of life which follows, the period is roughly valid from 1450 to the end of the 'closed' period in the Highlands. It is perhaps more characteristic of the west than the east. It is in no way representative of the *coastal* inhabitants of the east who, like the people of Thurso, disclaimed all Highland connections with varying degrees of intensity and generally disliked and feared the Highlanders.

The sketch is also not truly representative of the frontier clans who were half Highland, half Lowland. The Grahams, Drummonds, Ogilvies, Murrays and others had chiefs who were important Scottish noblemen, in constant contact with life outside the Highlands and who, during the life of the Auld Alliance, which began with John Balliol in 1295 and lasted till the Union of the Crowns in 1603 (and for a considerable time afterwards, in spirit if not in letter), had continual dealings with the French and other Continental European countries. They were much more exposed to the civilizing and cultural influence of such contacts than a chief living in the far west.

The civilizing influence did spread right across to the outer isles, of course, with the passage of time—but horn or glass windows, mirrors and French wines, for example, were rarer and much more prized the further one moved away from the trade routes. Architecture varied enormously, too, in exactly the same way.

By about 1450 a gradual change began to make itself felt in the Highlands. Cattle-raids gradually gave way to cattle-droving, sending cattle over the drove-roads to the great Lowland 'trysts'. There cattle sold for money, and hundreds of artefacts and geegaws were on sale at these trysts. Little luxuries made their way into remote glens, corn was purchased and grown, and the chiefs and chieftains, however petty, had at least some of the benefits of progress outside the Highlands; and this was witnessed by the clansmen. It would be easy to overdraw this picture. The change was gradual and spread over a very long period.

Cattle-raiding did not stop suddenly. Indeed, it did not stop completely *at all*.

The change was important. Scotland was much poorer in natural resources than England, with its great rolling agricultural lands—and the Highlands were poorer than the rest of Scotland. The contacts with the outside world were of considerable importance to the Highlanders.

Despite the relative poorness of the land, the life of the clansman was in many ways more enviable than that of any Lowland peasant. It was a better life than was later experienced by Robert Burns, for example—the life of grinding poverty of the Ayrshire tenant smallholder with, hanging over his head always, the grim threat of eviction and the iron hand of a cheerless Church.

The Highlander had a greater measure of security. The land belonged to the chief, but he held it for his clan, not for himself alone. It was not something he could sell in order to make off with the money (always assuming he could find anyone rash enough to buy). The chief kept his own chiefly portion of the land and divided the rest among his chieftains and tacksmen who were the 'officers' of the clan, and usually its privy councillors. Like the chief, the principal chieftains and tacksmen did not themselves farm the land. They divided it into lots for others to work.

The land supported the entire clan—the degree of comfort would depend on the amount of land and the population of the clan, among other things. But the clansmen were not merely tenants, they were members of the family. Eviction was a rare thing, especially in the west. Only somebody who posed a real threat to the rest of the clan, or who aroused universal disgust, would be driven out. Exile from the clan lands was the ultimate punishment for the ordinary Highlander, but it was not in the clan's interest to indulge in wholesale evictions.

The Highland clansmen therefore enjoyed a certain freedom, a certain degree of independence and of self-pride and self-respect, that was often denied to people of the peasant class outside the Highlands. Nor did the clansman live off a diet of thin brose—he ate meat, and usually a lot of it. Because of this, the entire clan, men, women and children, tended to be agile and strong. The men were very tough indeed, great hunters of considerable endurance.

The nature of the country made them herdsmen rather than cultivators. The clan lands would be populated by Highland cattle, Highland sheep which were nothing at all like the Cheviots which were responsible for the 'Clearances' discussed in Chapter 9, and shaggy mountain goats. The lochs and rivers abounded in fish, although there is some evidence that the Highlanders preferred meat and regarded fish as rather a poor substitute for it. Pork was detested, and pigs were not usually to be found.

The people were self-supporting. They made their own shoes, rawhide brogans, and the women wove the cloth, making attractive patterns by weaving exactly the same designs in warp as in weft and using locally available vegetable dyes. The history of Highland dress is a specialist subject and one on which not all experts agree. The women did not make neatly stitched short kilts for their men, with knife-edged pleats in which the pattern was exactly preserved by judicious cutting. The kilt of today is a work of art, a vastly superior garment to any short kilt ever worn prior to 1746.

The original dress of the man seems to have been the warm saffron shirt of the Irish, reaching to the knee and belted at the waist, and with it they wore warm woollen cloaks. They went bare-legged as a rule. If they wore brogans, they pierced them with a pattern of holes to let the water out, since they did not bother taking off their shoes before crossing streams.

To the shirt was later added the great tartan plaid, the 'great kilt'. This was laid on the ground and gathered into folds in the centre. The wearer lay down on top of it and gathered the loose ends across his stomach, fastened them there with a belt, and then stood up. He had now a short kilt reaching to above the knee and a great length of material hanging from the belt which he gathered up behind and fastened to his shoulder with a large metal brooch. The great kilt was kilt and plaid in one, and it was an excellent sleeping-bag at night.

Tartans were haphazard. Tartan was not a heraldic badge indicating name, as modern custom has tried to make it. Clan tartans as such were a late development and had a distinctly warlike purpose—one of easy identification in clan battle. But this also is easy to over-estimate. The system was at best embryonic when Highland dress was banned after 1746. There were district tartans, it is said, before clan tartans, but it is much more likely that the women, behaving exactly as one would expect, used their own ingenuity in devising tartan patterns which they wove for themselves, their menfolk and their children, competing with each other, no doubt, to see who could produce the nicest designs with the vegetable dyes available to them in their area. Indeed, district tartans, if they existed at all, were far more likely to be a matter of colour and shade than of actual design, since each district had its own plants from which the dyes were made.

The dress was primitive, of course—people outside the Highlands never quite got over the shock of seeing men bare-legged—but it was effective and suited to the life. It was extremely well adapted to their love of hunting in a country where the scenery tended to be more vertical than horizontal. Above all, it was ideal for men who at all times preferred outdoors to indoors and who regarded their huts and houses merely as sleeping-quarters.

The scenery incidentally must have been even more breathtaking before the road-builders, and the southern owners of so-called 'sporting' estates, committed environmental murder after the eighteenth century. The glens were beautiful, the blues and purples of the wooded mountains were a magnificent backdrop, and there were little lochs and streams and small waterfalls everywhere.

The clan was, of course, a tribe, and the most important events effecting the welfare of the tribe were births, which added to the population and, if the child was a male, would add to the fighting strength; marriages which ensured births; and deaths by which the tribe was diminished. Births had to cancel out deaths, and preferably to exceed them. This tribal heritage is to be seen everywhere today, not least in the births, marriages and deaths columns of the London *Times*, where everybody who is anybody in the social scale publishes news about their own tribal fluctuations and studies those of their friends.

Because marriage was designed to produce children, the custom of handfasting arose. It was widespread and must have varied from time to time and from place to place. The commonest account of it which remains is that, when a young man and a young woman wanted to marry, and assuming that the marriage had the approval of their elders, they lived together for a year and a day. If, at the end of that time, the woman was pregnant, they were regarded as being in every sense of the word fully and legally married. If not, they had the choice of staying married or of separating and trying again with somebody else. If during the year and a day the bond of love between them had grown strong, they would choose to remain together anyway, and the clan could not prevent this. People who had handfasted could not be separated unless that was what they wanted.

The usefulness of the system is obvious, and since men did not normally ill-treat women, it was rarely abused. Not everybody handfasted, of course, but it was a fairly common thing.

Another custom which was prevalent throughout the Highlands was that of fosterage of sons. A chief's son, for example, would live with foster-parents in the same glen and would be raised as a child of the foster-parents. The children of an ordinary clansman might be fostered with the chief. It did not only involve chiefs, of course; it involved everybody. One gave one's children to one's friends to foster. The purpose of this custom was simple, and its was remarkably efficacious. It gave a sense of unity, of belonging to one great family, and it bound the clan together just as much as, perhaps more than, their belief in their common descent from the ancestor who had founded the clan. Each Highland boy had not only his own parents and his own brothers and sisters but foster-parents and foster-brothers.

Fosterage away from the clan was rarer, but chiefs often used it as a way of forging friendships and alliances with neighbours. It became a diplomatic thing, and as such it was invaluable.

The bond of fosterage was extremely strong. Perhaps the best-known traditional story concerning it was that of Sir Hector MacLean, chief of the Clan MacLean, at the Battle of Inverkeithing in July 1651, when the Scots were attempting to overthrow Cromwell and restore Charles II. The clan MacLean was present in great strength under Sir Hector, who had seven foster-brothers, all of whom fought shoulder to shoulder with him. During the battle he became hard pressed by enemies, and his foster-brothers shielded him with their bodies. As each foster-brother died defending his chief, he called out 'Another For Hector', and one of his brothers stepped in to take his place, calling 'Death for Hector.' All seven of the foster-brothers were killed before Sir Hector himself was killed.

This story is almost certainly true, exactly as told in the clan tradition. Each clan bard was its historian, and he celebrated every detail of this sort in verse, as well as learning the verses of all his predecessors. And many of the clansmen could match the bards in remembering the verses themselves. Little or nothing was written down, and the bard's memory was his most important tool of his trade.

These oral traditions are extremely reliable, far more so than many of the extensive written histories which are the work of uncritical historians who accepted the monkish chronicles, which were sometimes based on very little but a rumour and the monk's strong imagination. The bard could not twist facts to suit himself. He was dramatizing real events, and there were too many eye-witnesses for him to be able to tamper with the truth.

The bard was the clan's daily newspaper. When anything interesting happened, he was bound to produce a poem or a song pretty smartly, else he would lose his hereditary office to somebody better equipped for the job. He might dramatize, but only within permitted limits.

Another Highland custom which acquired all the force of an absolute law was that of hospitality. If any person was admitted to a Highlander's home and sought and was offered protection, he was inviolate. It was a powerful variant of the southern law of sanctuary in church. There was no obligation to give shelter or to offer protection, but, once given, the rule was absolute and binding on everybody.

An example of this hospitality in action can be found in the history of the Clan MacGregor. Around 1600 their chief was Alexander MacGregor of Glenstrae. While he was at home, his son went out with a hunting party and they met the chief of clan Lamont. They dined together and a sudden quarrel broke out, and Lamont dirked the young MacGregor. He managed to get away but was closely pursued by furious MacGregors who had found their chief's son's body.

Lamont reached Glenstrae with the pursuit close behind, and, going to the MacGregor chief, he said he was fleeing from foes and asked for shelter. It was readily given with no questions asked, but soon afterwards the clansmen turned up and told MacGregor of the killing of his son. Alexander refused to hand his guest over to his angry clansmen. He had given hospitality, and he had to stand by his word. The following day he personally escorted Lamont back to safety in Cowal.

This particular story has a pleasing sequel, for soon afterwards the name MacGregor became proscribed by law, and the entire clan were declared outlaw. When that happened, the Lamonts came to their aid and gave them shelter on their lands in Cowal.

It was this same question of hospitality which finally made the name Campbell so unpopular in some parts of the Highlands.

Here we turn from the oral traditions to hard facts of history as recorded in documents.

William III (William of Orange) was determined to put an end to Jacobite unrest and insurrection, and in August 1691 an order went out that all clan chiefs must take an oath of allegiance to King William before 1 January. If not, troops would be sent to punish the clans.

Some of the chiefs decided to write to King James II (James VII of Scotland) in exile, asking for permission to take the oath. Among them was Alexander MacDonald of Glencoe. James readily gave his permission, and one by one the chiefs reported to take the oath of allegiance.

Unfortunately for him, Glencoe was the last to learn that he had been given permission. It was not till 29 December that he set out on foot, in severe winter weather, to take the oath at Fort William.

He arrived on time. He reported on 31 December to Colonel Hill, the governor of Fort William. But Hill refused to administer the oath on the grounds that he was disqualified from receiving it. He was a military governor, not a civil magistrate. What he did do, however, was to give MacDonald of Glencoe a letter to Sir Colin Campbell of Ardkinglass in Inverary, explaining the circumstances and asking Ardkinglass to administer the oath even although it would *appear* to be a few days late.

MacDonald was an old man, but he set off on foot for Inverary and arrived there on 6 January, having covered eighty miles across snow-clad mountains in terrible weather.

Sir Colin Campbell had no hesitation in administering the oath. He sent the certificate to Edinburgh plus Hill's letter dated Fort William, 31 December, and a letter of explanation. He told the elderly chief of the small clan to go home and not to worry. Everything was in order. There is no doubt whatever that, so far as Sir Colin Campbell was concerned, *it was*.

To diverge briefly here—one MacDonald chief did not ask permission from the exiled King James, for he did not intend to take the oath, and he did not take it. He defied King William, and King William did nothing about it. He was Macdonell of Glengarry.

MacDonald of Glencoe went home, satisfied that he had saved his small clan from government vengeance, and that should have been the end of the story.

It was in fact the beginning of as sordid a tale as British history has to show. Some Privy Councillors, prominent among them Sir John Dalrymple, the Master of Stair, were of the opinion that, to make the Glencoe certificate fully legal, a royal warrant would be needed. It was left to Stair, who was Secretary of State for Scotland, to see the King on the subject. Stair, however, deliberately misrepresented the matter to the King. Sir Colin Campbell's certificate was suppressed, and the King was apparently told that Glencoe had defied the order.

Stair obtained from the King a royal warrant for the extirpation of the MacDonalds of Glencoe for failing to comply. On 7 January 1692 he wrote to Sir Thomas Livingstone, the military commander in Scotland, saying that the MacDonalds must be made an example to the rest of the Highlands. He included in his letter the words, 'I hope the soldiers will not trouble the Government with prisoners.'

In a subsequent letter he wrote that he 'rejoiced' that MacDonald of Glencoe had not taken the oath—a bare-faced lie, for Stair certainly knew that MacDonald *had* taken it and had tried to take it in good time.

There is some evidence that Stair was hand in glove in the matter with the Campbell Earl of Breadalbane, who had some recent grudge against the Glencoe MacDonalds. This may well be true, but Stair was the moving force behind the plan to wipe out one small clan as an example to other chiefs. The wording of the royal warrant is highly unusual, the King's name appearing twice. A defence of William has been made on the grounds that he did not read what he signed. Even if he had failed to notice the unusual style of the warrant, he must accept full responsibility for his actions. But he was certainly not told the facts by Stair, and he signed in ignorance of what had really happened.

The job of destroying the Glencoe clan was given to a company of Scottish soldiers under the command of Captain Robert Campbell of Glenlyon. It must be emphasized that it was a party not of Campbell clansmen but of Scottish soldiers whose commanding officer was a Campbell.

It is what happened next that aroused such indignation all over Scotland when the story came out. Campbell went to Glencoe in friendliness, with a cover-story. Fort William, he said, was overcrowded, and he had been ordered to find alternative quarters nearby, from which to collect cess and hearth money for the Government. The MacDonald chief believed him, and the doors of the clan were opened to the Government soldiers. After all, the MacDonalds had taken the oath. They were, as it were, on the same side. More than that, Campbell of Glenlyon's niece was married to one of Glencoe's sons.

For several days the soldiers remained in Glencoe enjoying the hospitality of the clan, and at last, on 12 February, Glenlyon received his final orders which included a special warning not to let the chief or his sons escape. 'Old fox' was how the chief was described in the orders.

At 5 a.m. on 13 February, while everybody slept, Glenlyon murdered his host. The chief's wife was stripped naked, the rings were pulled off her fingers, and she was turned out into a blizzard which was raging outside. She died the following day of shock and exposure. Nevertheless, a warning was given and MacDonalds tumbled out of bed and ran off into the blizzard with their families. The massacre consisted of thirty-eight people murdered, including two women and two children. There were others who died during the trek through the blizzard to Appin, where they sought shelter and safety with the Stewarts.

There was an outcry when the facts came out, not merely from the clans but from people all over Scotland. King William waited three years before appointing a commission of enquiry, which found Stair culpable but exonerated Campbell of Glenlyon, who was obeying orders. One perhaps feels here the prickling of recognition—this was what the Nazi exterminators in the death camps claimed at the end of World War II. Nevertheless, it is true that, if Glenlyon had refused, somebody would have been found to take his place; and in that event the massacre might not have been so badly bungled, and many more than thirty-eight killed.

The Master of Stair was amazed by all the fuss. On 5 March 1692 he wrote, 'All I regret is that any of the sort got away, and there is a necessity to prosecute them to the utmost.'

As for William of Orange, his attitude can best be judged from the fact that he did not order Stair's arrest when the commission found him guilty. What happened was that Stair, who had succeeded to his father's viscounty, was promoted in the peerage to the rank of earl and rewarded with the teind duties of Glenluce. Campbell of Glenlyon was promoted Colonel. Sir Thomas

Livingstone, who had organized the massacre, was made Lord Teviot.

If William had been deceived by Stair, and he undoubtedly was, then he later knew it and he *did not care.*

The death of thirty-eight clansmen was not an unheard-of event in the Highlands. Some clan massacres involved upwards of two hundred people. What stuck in everybody's mind was the thought of the redcoats, hospitably received, fed and entertained, rising in the darkness to slaughter their hosts.

Campbell of Glenlyon received all the infamy. From that day on, in the Highlands the name Campbell was detested, despite the fact that the Marquis of Argyle knew nothing of what was going on and that a Campbell sheriff had actually administered the oath in good faith and sent an explanation to the Government—an explanation which was suppressed.

The popular story was that the rigid law of Highland hospitality had been broken by the Campbells. Certainly Glenlyon must have known and respected this custom in his private capacity, even if as an army captain he was under orders. His willingness to accept the task of killing an elderly Highland chieftain to whom he was linked by family ties was shameful.

In the great anti-Campbell smokescreen which went up, the name of Sir John Dalrymple was conveniently forgotten, yet he takes his place in Scottish history alongside two other detestable characters, Sir John de Menteith, who betrayed Wallace to Edward I of England, and MacLeod of Assynt, who betrayed Montrose to his Covenanting enemies who hanged him.

Such then was the power of the rule of hospitality.

Each year in the spring the Highlanders sent the young people and some of the elders up into the hill grazings, called shielings. There the cattle, sheep and goats had their summer feeding. Huts were built and all day was spent out in the open in the good weather, and in the evenings the old men told stories of the clan's prowess and might. The women made butter and cheese, and the lads looked after the herds, and life must have been pleasant, for the Highlanders always looked back on this part of the year with great nostalgia.

Back on the clan lands the small crops were tended and the young warriors indulged in various trials of strength which were the forerunners of modern Highland games. There would be hunting parties and probably cattle-lifting raids. Most clans had their hereditary friends and their hereditary enemies, who would of course change from century to century as alliances shifted. It was normal to try to steal cattle from enemy clans if there was any prospect of success.

After the summer was over, the harvest was gathered and the clan settled down to a winter routine in their township, or *clachan*. Jobs around the home and on the crofts were done, implements were repaired ready for the sowing after the winter, weapons were sharpened and oiled and carefully put aside; and *ceilidhs*, evenings of entertainment, were held. These were evenings of singing and poetry and story-telling and playing of the harp, which was the traditional Highland musical instrument for playing indoors.

Except for some of the chiefs or more important chieftains who lived in stone houses, most people lived in buildings not very different from the old 'black crofts' which have only recently disappeared from the Highland scene. The floors were of beaten earth, the walls were of mud and the roofs were thatched.

There were roughly three classes in a society which was not at all class-conscious. First there was the chief and his immediate family; then came the chieftains or the tacksmen, the principal landholders under the chief and the military leaders of the clan. Ranking with them were certain individuals such as the hereditary *seanachaidh*, or bard, who always stood high in the clan hierarchy, since he was the guardian of its history and tradition and of the chief's complicated genealogy. Finally came the ordinary clanspeople, who might be young warriors in the chief's 'tail' of retainers, or who might be crofters, or crippled or elderly members of the clan who did what work they could on the land.

Everybody had a part to play in the clan life, usually dictated by their abilities and not much else. Clansmen could and did rise to prominence by their warlike abilities; chiefs' sons and the sons of tacksmen descended in the social scale. There was a great mixing of social rank. It was essentially a mobile society, not a fossilized and stratified one.

All of them, of course, regarded themselves as being of the chiefly blood, which at any given time most of them undoubtedly were because of inter-marriage. The poorest, most infirm clansmen shared in the clan's ancient, proud, usually boastful heritage. There was no caste system, for a caste system was unworkable within the links that bound the clan together, and it is evident that the clansman had nothing in common with a Lowland peasant. He was proud, independent and at the same time interdependent, himself relied upon by others, and he was secure and relatively well fed. He lacked worldly goods; his life was essentially simple and pastoral; he certainly presented a peculiar appearance when he emerged into the Lowlands among his civilized 'betters'—whom he in any case despised, but on the whole he was a good deal more fortunate at any given time during the period under discussion than any peasant outside the Highlands.

There is a considerable amount of evidence, perhaps partisan perhaps not, that the Highlanders could recover quickly from wounds that would probably kill other people, from infection if nothing else. They were what some writers call 'clean-fleshed' and healed quickly and well. A number of observers have remarked with astonishment how quickly they recovered from hideous gaping gashes.

If this is true, it must have been very useful to them, because they were all accustomed to fighting with cold steel, and their swords did terrible damage. They lived at a time when men habitually carried weapons and knew how to use them. They did not carry them for ornament, but that was true of men every-where, not just in the Highlands.

To a great extent women have been discussed already. They were well treated and honoured by the men, as indeed were children of both sexes. The running of the clan was always a man's affair, but one suspects that, as is usually the case, the running of the men was a woman's affair. They may have had a good deal more influence than records show.

Their dress was similar to the men's. At no time in history did they ever dress up like the little girls in kilts, velvet doublets, tartan stockings and glittering sporrans who used to flock to various Highland games to compete in dancing. They did not wear the kilt at all, which was a man's garment. They wore a long tunic, not very different from the saffron shirt but much longer, and it was fastened round the waist with an ornamented belt—some of the belts being very beautiful. Over this they wore a small plaid or tartan *arisaid* which fastened on the breast with a large ornamental brooch and was gathered at the waist by the belt. Their hair was plaited and adorned with ribbons. Unmarried girls bound their hair in a snood. They frequently went barefooted and often bare-armed. When necessary, they would kirtle their skirts, i.e. gather them up between their legs, exposing their legs— another habit which to the outsider seemed like proof positive of barbarity.

Fashions were not fixed. They changed, but slowly. Women wore gowns of a mixture of wool and linen, sometimes with very beautiful sleeves. The *arisaid* might be replaced with a tartan plaid, smaller than a man's, not unlike a modern tartan stole.

Men wore the great kilt and then the little kilt, and began to wear short jackets. Men and women liked to wear silver adornments and semi-precious stones when they could afford them. However outlandish they may have seemed to the eyes of outsiders, accustomed to the latest fashions, they were not inadequately dressed. By the eighteenth century some of the women's costumes were very attractive, with gathered skirts, bodices, attractive sleeved undergarments and usually a tartan plaid which could be worn in a great variety of fashions.

It is impossible to generalize about chiefs. They were the leaders of their clans and they varied enormously in character, as people always do. The hallmark of the clan was its interdependence. Evidently some chiefs were far worse than others, just as some kings were, but there was a built-in system of checks and balances created by the self-interest and mutual dependence of the members of the clan. In Chapter 9, some of the less attractive chiefs will be described, men who did not scruple to betray their people, but this was long after 1746, and they were not at all representative of their ancestors. The bards who bemoaned their cruelties made that perfectly clear.

It is important to remember that no Highland chief ruled except by the consent of his clan. Chiefs who failed to please the clan could be deposed, even killed, and many instances of clan-power as opposed to chief-power will appear in Part Two, in the individual clan short histories.

It is possible to give brief portraits of two here, but they were no more 'average' than anybody else. In any case, the character of the chiefs varied enormously from west to east. The two chiefs described are both from the west, because so many of the eastern chiefs were peers and were not representative of clan chiefs at all but belonged to a special élite which had its base outside the Highlands.

Sir Ewen Cameron of Lochiel (1629–1719) was the grandfather of the 'Gentle' Lochiel who took part in the second Jacobite rising of 1745. He was raised at Inverary Castle by the 8th Earl and 1st Marquis of Argyle, but he seems to have imbibed none of his powerful protector's Covenanting enthusiasm.

At the age of eighteen he went back to lead his clan, by which time Montrose was already in exile. In 1650–1 he took his clan out in the attempt to restore Charles II, and he was present at the Battle of Worcester in 1651 which sent Charles back into exile for several years.

In 1652, when the Earl of Glencairn raised the standard of revolt against Cromwell's soldiers, Cameron joined him. The following is an extract from a letter written to him by Charles II at Chantilly on 3 November 1653: 'We are informed by the Earl of Glencairn with what courage, success and affection to us you have behaved yourself in this time of trial, when the honour and liberty of your country are at stake. Therefore we cannot but express our hearty sense of this your courage, and return you our thanks for the same.'

In 1654 Sir Ewen engaged in a guerrilla warfare against Generals Monk and Morgan, in the neighbourhood of Fort William, but eventually Royalist funds dried up and the war came to an end. Lochiel, however, refused to submit until he had secured a number of concessions for himself and his clan. When he did finally submit, he was merely asked to give his word to keep the peace and to return some prisoners. His men were permitted to keep their arms, and it is even said that he managed to get the authorities to remit all back-taxes and other dues.

He kept his word until the Restoration, but age had not dimmed his enthusiasm. In 1689, aged sixty, he joined Viscount Dundee in an attempt to restore the exiled James II. He refused the offer of money and a title from William of Orange and instead was personally present at the Battle of Killiecrankie at which Dundee was tragically killed, and with him died all hopes of a successful rising.

There are two interesting stories about Sir Ewen. One is that his second son was a captain in the Scots Fusiliers and was with General MacKay's Government army at Killiecrankie. MacKay, seeing the Highlanders on the hillsides, is said to have asked young Cameron, 'There is your father with his wild savages. How would you like to be with him?' Young Cameron replied, 'It signifies little what I would like, but my father and his wild savages may be nearer to you before night than *you* would like.' They were, of course. They routed MacKay's army, even though the victory proved to be a hollow one.

The other story refers to the days when Sir Ewen was conducting his guerrilla war against Monk and Morgan. During an ambush he was jumped on by an English soldier who flung him down and tried to throttle him. Lochiel kept his head. He grasped his opponent's collar, pulled his face down and bit out his throat. According to the popular account, he referred to it ever afterwards as the sweetest bite of his life.

He lived till 1719, dying at the age of ninety. He had lived through the reigns of Charles I, Cromwell's Commonwealth, Charles II, James II, William and Mary, and Queen Anne, and died in the reign of George I.

The other chief is Iain Dubh MacKinnon of MacKinnon who lived from 1682 till 1756. His grandfather Sir Lachlan Mor MacKinnon, the 28th MacKinnon chief, had been at Inverary Castle at the same time as Sir Ewen Cameron of Lochiel, also as a ward of the Campbell chief.

Iain Dubh was born on the day his father died, and when he was eighteen he succeeded his grandfather as 29th chief of the clan. He married a daughter or granddaughter of Archbishop James Sharpe of St Andrews and was a Jacobite intriguer from his earliest days—as his grandfather had been before him.

He was 'out' in 1715 and took part in the Battle of Sheriffmuir. The failure of that rising meant that his estates were put under Act of Attainder, but the chief of Clan Grant bought them and resold them to a MacKinnon clansman, and he in turn disposed of them to Iain Dubh's heirs, who were not included in the Act of Attainder. In effect, despite the Government's action against him, Iain Dubh never lost his lands at all!

After the death of his first wife, he married a daughter of MacLeod of Raasay in 1743 at the age of sixty-one. When the rising of 1745 broke out, he was well into his sixties and hemmed in on either side by the Skye MacLeods and MacDonalds, much more powerful neighbours who had refused to bring their men out for Prince Charles.

He was not able to join the clans who were present at the raising of the standard at Glenfinnan, but on 13 October 1745 he and about two hundred of his clan joined Charles in Edinburgh. The old man accompanied the army all the way to Derby and back. With MacDonald of Glencoe he shares the surprising honour of being one of the only two clan chiefs whose clan strength increased on the march south into England. All other clans suffered losses by desertion, which had been anticipated, for no Highlander enjoyed being so far from home.

Iain himself was at Culloden and took part in the meeting of chiefs on the following day to decide what they could do to re-rally the clans. Most of his clan, however, were off an on expedition with the Earl of Cromartie to recover some Jacobite gold.

He was active in various meetings to try to rally the clans again and went home to Skye only when it was obvious nothing could be done.

In July 1746 Charles finally reached MacKinnon country in Skye and was given shelter and entertained to a feast in a cave near Elgol on the evening before Iain and his nephew John were to convey him to safety on the mainland.

For twelve days the MacKinnons accompanied the Prince, finally delivering him into the safe-keeping of MacDonald of Morar. The following day Iain and John and their boatmen were taken prisoner and flogged when they refused to earn the reward of £30,000 for betraying the Prince's whereabouts. They were put aboard the notorious hell-ship *Furnace* and taken to Tilbury. The old man survived that infamous voyage and was imprisoned in the Tower of London for eighteen months.

At the end of 1747 he was put on trial for his life and was quite obviously guilty on all counts. In view of his advanced age and his 'mistaken sense of chivalry', he was pardoned. Before he left the court, the Attorney-General, Sir Dudley Ryder, asked him what he would do if Prince Charles were once again in his power. The old man drily replied that he would 'do as you have done this day to me. I would send him back to *his own* country.'

He returned to his home at Kilmorie in Skye. In 1753 his wife died, and he was childless because his son had also died. At the age of seventy-one he remarried and managed to father a son,

Charles, who succeeded him as chief, and another boy and a girl.

He died in his seventy-fifth year, on 7 May 1756, and at the time of his death a notice in the newspapers told how he used to love to go and sit in the cave where he and the Lady MacKinnon had entertained Prince Charles Edward Stuart to a feast, and daydream about his exciting past.

There is, of course, no evidence that Charles gave him a second thought after quitting him, any more than he appears ever to have mentioned the name of Flora MacDonald after he parted from her. Gratitude was never a hallmark of the Stuarts, and Highland loyalty could have been expended in a far better cause.

These two men are typical of nothing in their characters, but their devotion to the Stuarts was mirrored in many other chiefs. The accounts given are factual, and it is plain that they were men whose characters, properly harnessed, could have achieved great things. There was obviously much more to them than greedy self-interest.

The MacKinnons were always a small clan and, although independent, were never powerful. The Camerons belong somewhere in the middle spectrum, but Lochiel's prestige in the seventeenth and eighteenth centuries was far greater than his manpower. There were many larger clans, the four largest being MacDonald, Campbell, MacKenzie and Gordon. All of them produced from time to time chiefs who did not differ very greatly from the two mentioned.

Recreation in the Highlands has already been dealt with. Life was essentially simple, and the main excitements were hunting-parties and the endless feuds which were an inevitable consequence of the never-ending struggle to expand or merely to survive against expanding neighbours.

One favourite recreation, however, was the reciting of Gaelic poetry. At any *ceilidh* this was always a highlight of the evening, and the clansfolk could listen to it for hours. It did not merely consist of boastful accounts of the clan's prowess since its progenitor had founded it. The bards spoke also of the Gaelic greatness, of the days when the kings had lived in the Highlands. They fostered a belief, strong among the clans, that the long-gone greatness would return one day. There is evidence that their poetry encouraged a kind of messianic belief that one day a golden-haired young man would return to restore the fortunes of Gaeldom and become their High King, living among them.

Since the Stuarts were lineal descendants of Fergus Mor MacErc and of Alpin and Kenneth MacAlpin, it seems probable that they saw in the Stuarts their *only* hope of this Highland 'restoration'. And in Prince Charles Edward they undoubtedly saw the golden-haired youth of whom the bards had spoken for centuries. The importance of this tradition and its influence on the clans cannot be over-stated.

That they were mistaken about the Stuarts is easy to see with the hindsight of history. There is not a single scrap of evidence to support any belief that, if his cause had prevailed, even temporarily, Charles Edward would have been any more heedful of the Highlanders than any other monarch since James V. And of course his restoration would only have been temporary—neither Scotland nor England wished to be ruled over by Roman Catholics again, and just as Charles I, Charles II and James II had gone out of their way to arouse opposition among their subjects, so inevitably would the Young Pretender.

Jacobitism is properly the subject of the next chapter, but in Highland life the centuries-old beliefs that better days were just around the corner and that Gaeldom would one day come into its own again were rife.

The Highland culture was not only oral, it was musical. Highlanders seem to have expressed every mood in music, and also every activity. There were songs for reaping, for boatmen, for girls at the milking, for women waulking the cloth and for mothers rocking their children. They sang a great deal. The bagpipe was not a musical instrument but an instrument of war. Those who find bagpipe music unbearable should remember that it was intended to be listened to out of doors, in the glen or when on the march or in the heat of battle. Nobody would have dreamed of playing their bagpipes indoors, and when Highland dress was proscribed, so was the playing of the bagpipes, which was regarded as an incitement to violence.

One of the characteristics of the Celt is his ability to express his sorrow, his grief and his heartbreak in music more fluently than he expresses happiness. It may be this which gives so much Highland music a haunting undertone of pathos. In 1582 the celebrated Latin scholar George Buchanan, who was no lover of

Highlanders, grudgingly admitted that the songs of the Highlands were not inelegant. In 1187, for reasons best known to
himself, Giraldus Cambrensis went further and said that experienced judges regarded the Highlands as the fountainhead of the
art of music. That sounds far-fetched, but obviously the reputation for music was there.

We have seen that the *seanachaidh* or bard was a key figure in
the clan, ranking as a chieftain in the chief's household. Other
members of the chiefly household included the harper, the
standard-bearer, the piper and sometimes the servant who
carried the piper's pipes, the sword-bearer, the henchman who
remained close to the chief at all times to protect him, and the
bodyguard who were under the control of the henchman. The
bodyguard were the pick of the warriors and accompanied the
chief on all ceremonial occasions.

As has been said, the *seanachaidhs* were hereditary bards,
and the Vurichs were hereditary bards to the MacDonalds of
Clanranald for eighteen generations. Their job included inciting
the men to war by whipping up popular support for the cause of
the moment in rousing songs.

Many of the Gaelic poets were women, one of the most celebrated being Mairi nighean Alasdair Ruadh (Mary the daughter
of Red Alasdair), who died in 1674 aged 105. The oldest written
collection of Gaelic verse goes back to 1238, but it is believed to
enshrine subject matter infinitely older and contains the famous
lament of Deirdre. The first printed book in Gaelic was John
Knox's prayer book of 1567.

The Highlanders' attitude towards religion was uncomplicated.
They had been Christians long before they left Ireland to settle in
the inner Hebrides and in Argyll, where they founded their
Scottish kingdom of Dalriada. Their Christianity was grafted
onto older superstitions. No Highlander saw anything incom-
patible between being a baptized Christian and believing in
fairies, elves and sprites. Like the rest of Christendom, they were
nominal Roman Catholics for centuries, although the earlier
native Celtic Church had differed from Rome in some of its
customs, but not in beliefs. Rome, however, never figured greatly
in Scottish minds, and certainly not in Highland ones.

It is easy to dismiss the clansmen as a worthless lot, interested
only in booty. It is a wild overstatement to do so. In the first place,

they were no more worthless than any other race, and if they looked for booty, it was only because that was the only way in which they could be clothed, fed and paid. They accepted Montrose's discipline, even if grudgingly, and if they lifted cattle from the Campbells and others on their way home after the wars, that was only natural. *Somebody* had to foot the bill for the wars, and kings were miserable paymasters.

The Presbyterian Church did not become permanently established in Scotland till 1690, although there had been earlier establishments. The first Presbyterian minister was installed in Aberdeen in 1694, in Kirriemuir in 1713 and in Moy in 1727. In the far west they did not appear on the scene till after 1746, when it became a matter of Government policy. The Episcopalian Church had provided too many followers of the Stuart cause and went through a period of persecution from which it recovered only slowly. It is still called by many people 'the English Church', which it certainly is not, for it is a native Scottish growth in Scotland exactly as is the Presbyterian Church.

But in the glens all this counted for nothing. It was only when zealous missionaries were turned loose on clansmen, who lacked chiefs and chieftains and were leaderless in a world that had collapsed in ruins around them, that religion ceased to be a light-hearted, matter-of-fact affair.

It is impossible for a modern visitor to the Highlands to deny that the Highlander of the 1980s is infinitely better off than was his counterpart in 1480 or 1680. But of course that applies to everyone. The evidence of history, in so far as it enables us to reach any judgement, suggests that at any given time the clansmen in the Highlands were not noticeably worse off than their neighbours. Different, yes—but not worse off. They were certainly better off than the wretched people who went into grinding slavery during the Industrial Revolution.

Many of the clansmen emigrated, willingly or under pressure. Many others drifted south to the great cities. Whether they were any better off trying to scratch a living in the slums of the great industrial cities than their grandfathers and fathers had been in their native glens, is certainly open to debate.

7

The Jacobite Movement

The Jacobite disturbances in Britain were the last serious expressions of religious intolerance until 1968, when the civil war broke out in Northern Ireland.

Jacobitism began to all intents and purposes when James VII and II, the son of Charles I and the brother of Charles II, was deposed and went into exile in 1688. The mounting pressures which culminated in his short reign are too complicated to condense easily, but his own personal conversion to Roman Catholicism plus his desire to secure religious toleration of Catholics and Quakers aroused much of the opposition to him. The fact which set events in motion was the birth of a son to him in 1688. Britain as a whole was against the continuation of a Catholic dynasty on its throne.

By Act of Parliament dated 1689, it was made law that no Catholic nor any person married to a Catholic could ever succeed to the throne. This remains a cornerstone of the present constitutional monarchy.

James was replaced by his daughter Mary, who became Queen Mary II. Her husband, William of Orange, was himself a grandson of Charles I, so that both husband and wife were undeniably Stuarts. The dynasty had *not* been changed. James had been replaced by his own daughter, and the important consideration was that she was a Protestant Stuart.

From the moment of his flight, the Jacobite cause was born. James had an indisputable right to the throne and he had provided a male heir.

A Jacobite invasion was attempted some twenty years later when a French fleet sailed right into the mouth of the River Forth in 1708, carrying James's son (known to history as the Old Pretender) plus six thousand French troops. The prompt arrival of an English fleet, and the happy arrival of a severe storm, caused the French captains to scatter and run, and nobody set foot on land.

This attempt of 1708 was perhaps the one with the most chance of success, if it had been pressed home. There had been much discontent caused by the Union of Parliaments of 1707. The Scots claimed, with justice, that the English behaved as though they owned Scotland. Indeed, the English contempt for all things Scottish at this time, fed perhaps by a degree of resentment that the kingdoms had been united under the Scottish crown and not the English one, was a powerful spur to the Scots to support a Jacobite restoration. If the Pretender and his six thousand French troops had landed, there is no saying what might have happened. The union of the kingdoms might have been undone, and Scotland might have pursued a solitary course for a time. England would never have accepted a Catholic Stuart.

From then on, it is a sad tale of failure. When Queen Anne died in 1714, there was a moment when prompt action by the Old Pretender could have succeeded. It has been estimated that, if he had sailed at once for London and claimed his throne, he would have received popular support. Again one is forced to the conclusion that such a restoration of the Stuart dynasty would not have lasted. The most powerful English leaders wanted no Catholic, and the Scots wanted neither a Catholic nor bishops. In such a situation the Stuarts faced certain disaster. Nevertheless, there was a moment in time when the vacant throne could have been theirs, for Queen Anne had no heirs.

But James dithered until the following year, till George I had been settled on the throne, before launching the Jacobite uprising of 1715. There was a world of difference between claiming a vacant throne and trying to eject the occupant of the throne. In September 1715 the standard of revolt was raised in Scotland by John, 11th Earl of Mar, whose nickname of 'Bobbing John' was a yardstick of the flexibility of his loyalties. He was not the sort of leader to unite Scotland.

The Highlanders were easily recruited to the cause and formed a substantial part of the army which was defeated at the Battle of Sheriffmuir. The attempt was over. The following month, too late again, the Old Pretender arrived in Scotland. After idling indecisively for a few weeks, he left again for France and never returned to Scotland.

Two things demand attention here. The first is the nature of George I's claim to rule Britain, and the second is the motive behind the Highland support in 1715.

The claim to the throne of George I, nicknamed 'German Geordie' and known by that name to this day to Scottish schoolboys, is much better than is often realized by those who dwell in the romantic tartan twilight fostered by novelists. It compares very favourably with that of Balliol and Bruce in the fourteenth century.

After the death of Mary II, and of her husband William III, who was permitted to rule alone when his wife died, the crown went to Mary's younger sister, Anne. Anne is often misleadingly referred to as the last Stuart monarch. She was, like Mary, the daughter of the Catholic King James II, and the sister of the Old Pretender.

During Anne's reign the Act of Settlement was passed by Parliament, which said that when Anne died, if she had no heirs of her own, the crown was to pass to Sophia, the daughter of Elizabeth the 'Winter Queen' of Bohemia. Elizabeth was a daughter of James I, and the sister of Charles I.

Elizabeth of Bohemia had married Frederick V, the Elector Palatine. Her daughter Sophia was her only *Protestant* offspring with legitimate children, and had married Ernest, the Elector of Hanover. The descendants of Elizabeth were legally in line of succession to the throne had the direct male line failed—which it did not.

When Queen Anne died, Sophia was also dead, but she had a son, George Lewis, who had succeeded as Elector of Hanover. It was this George who became George I of Great Britain.

Obviously his claim was subordinate to that of the Old Pretender and his son, direct male descendants of James II and James I, but when genealogy has to give way to religion, and the best claimants are automatically disqualified on religious grounds, then a certain amount of genealogical nonsense results.

Nevertheless, George I was the great-grandson of James I through his daughter, and only three generations removed from the throne. In the fourteenth century John Balliol was the great-great-great grandson of King David I, through the daughter of his granddaughter! Robert I (Robert Bruce) was six generations removed from the throne, being great-great-great-great-grandson of David I, through a younger daughter.

Compared with these two men who became kings, German Geordie had a much closer link with the royal dynasty. His Stuart blood is unquestionable. Anne was the last of the Stuart *dynasty*, for George's father was not a Stuart at all, but George represented the Protestant branch of the Stuart family. He was invited to rule because of his Stuart blood as much as his Protestant religion. The Act of Settlement is quite specific that it is the Protestant heirs of *James I*, the first Stuart monarch, who are to succeed to the throne.

On the male side, of course, George was German and spoke little or no English. He did not much care for England and never tried to understand his new subjects. If he had been turned loose in the south of England, he could never have found his way to Scotland unless he had found a German to give him directions. Genealogy, like statistics, can be used to prove just about anything, and when the senior line has been arbitrarily debarred, such a situation is bound to arise. But the senior line was not the 'rightful' line unless it is argued that Parliament itself had no right to make the laws, for it was Parliament which passed the Act debarring the succession from all but Protestant descendants of James I, and which specifically named Sophia at the time of passing the Act. To infer that the present royal House is illegal is to miss the whole point, which is that in a Catholic country they would be, but in Britain they most certainly are not. In Protestant Britain they are legal, and they represent the Stuarts, and if it were not for their Stuart blood, they would not be here at all.

But how much of this concerned the Highlanders? Probably not a word of it. The Highlanders saw in the Stuarts their only hope of a revival of Gaeldom, that much is certain. But they were not naïve enough to imagine that such a revival stood any chance under the Hanoverian line now called on to rule.

At this late date, too, the importance of Campbell politics counted for a lot. The Marquis of Argyll, true to his family tradition, supported the *de facto* ruling House. He had every reason to do so. Not only were his family dedicated Presbyterians, opposed to any Catholic restoration, but the first and second Marquises of Argyll had both been executed, one by Charles II and the other by his brother James II. They had no cause whatever to like the Catholic Stuarts who had been debarred from succession by constitutional means.

Many of the clans preferred to oppose Argyll. They were fed not only by the MacDonald hatred but by memory of the Campbell persecution of the MacGregors and others, and of course the great Glencoe scandal. No doubt many chiefs remembered, with a good deal of false nostalgia, the 'good old days' when the MacDonalds had been Lords of the Isles.

The Highland chiefs had therefore two powerful reasons to support the Jacobite cause, both of them connected with self-interest, and they did not share the common suspicion of Catholics. It probably made little difference to any Highland chief *what* religion the king followed. The English Protestants and Scottish Presbyterians were just as much influenced by self-interest, of course, when they opposed the direct line of Stuarts.

The old Highland-Lowland antagonism was still rife, of course, and the Highlanders still despised everybody who was not Highland. The clergymen who accompanied the Darien expedition wrote most contemptuously of the Highlanders, describing them as savages. The fact that they spoke Gaelic instead of English was held up as certain evidence that they were barbarians and not to be considered as human beings. One finds that same attitude persisting right up into the time of the clearances when, in one of the most shameful episodes in history of any *soi-disant* civilized nation, the Highlanders were treated as worse than beasts.

There were therefore strong, almost compelling reasons for the Highland participation on which the Stuarts relied so heavily. If they did not do something to restore the heir to their rightful kings, all chance of recovering their former greatness was gone for ever, and they would remain barbarous savages to be treated with cruelty by their own countrymen as well as by the distant English.

It was during the rising of 1715 that one of the most widely quoted remarks was made, which has provided ammunition for those who even today want to show the chiefs as primitive savages. Bobbing John, the Earl of Mar, dissatisfied with the way recruiting was going on in his lands, wrote to his bailie: 'Jocke, ye was in the right not to come with the 100 men ye sent up tonight, for I expected four times the number.' He then warns that, if more recruits do not arrive promptly, he will send a party to burn the roofs over their heads.

This letter enjoys a wide currency because there is so little else to support the barbarian view of the chiefs. Much has been made of the fact that they had the powers of pit and gallows over their clansmen, that they held their lives in their hands. The story is trotted out of the Clanranald chief who once punished a female thief by tying her hair to seaweed and leaving her to drown in the incoming tide. It is a fact that later on, in 1745, Atholl recruits had to be whipped up vigorously, for many of them were reluctant. Much later on, a few of the chiefs disgraced themselves and their names by the savagery with which they evicted their own clansmen to make way for sheep. These are all facts.

Power of pit and gallows—it sends a chill into the stomach. Until one remembers that during the Jacobite risings the civilized English would hang a hungry man for stealing a crust of bread, and the public would turn out to enjoy the entertainment. Somebody always has power of life and death, except in these countries which have recently abolished the death sentence and where somebody instead has the power of life or living death. If not an absolute monarch ruling by divine right, or a haughty nobleman ruling by the same power of pit and gallows, or a Highland chief ruling by the consent of his clan and not by any divine right or the right of any peerage title, then it is a judge and a jury of twelve 'good men and true' who are neither more good nor more true than any other twelve citizens chosen at random.

In both the '15 and the '45 it is currently fashionable to represent the clansmen—especially at Culloden, for some curious reason—as half-starved, terrified children, driven by ruthless chieftains. It is time to put this into perspective too, by putting it into some sort of reasonable context.

During the 1914–18 war, it was the practice to execute any man who lost his nerve under fire. The word 'coward' was used because nobody was prepared to admit that shell-shock could be a reason for anything. The wretches were tried on the spot by their own regimental officers and put up against a wall and shot by their comrades. *This happened.* It is to be inferred from this that the British soldiers in the Great War all went in fear of being shot by their officers? Many of them mere boys of seventeen and eighteen? The question answers itself by its own absurdity.

So far as Culloden is concerned, the picture painted overlooks the widely reported fact that all during the '15 and the '45, Highland clans suffered from constant drainage of manpower by desertion. By the time of Culloden a great many experienced warriors had simply gone home. Why therefore would any frightened boy stay to be pulverized by Cumberland's cannon when he could simply join his comrades and go back to the clan land? What sort of savage authority did the chieftains really have, when all through clan history clansmen were in the habit of going home when they felt like it?

Historians and journalists alike tend to follow the rule of the negative imperative. Only things which horrify or astonish, only things which are *not* ordinary, are worthy of record. When things are normal, that is not news and is not worth recording. In a ship's log one records changes—change of course, change of speed, change of weather, change of watch—not the long uneventful hours in between.

Of course, the debunkers have been provoked endlessly by those who like to present the Highlander as a gay, gallant Highland laddie in his neat little clan tartan kilt, who cannot wait to die for Bonnie Prince Charlie. Any serious-minded historian wishes to destroy this myth.

The basic facts are unquestionable, and the brief histories in Part Two of this book uphold them. The clan chiefs were by nature responsible leaders. It was their self-interest, which was bound up with the interest of the clan, that gave their lives any meaning. Some were better than others, but none could keep their men in the field for long periods of time. Even Montrose accepted desertions, and he was the finest of all leaders of Highlanders.

The Highland chiefs were not essentially different from the various Governments, with their powers of death and imprisonment. There is no record of the chiefs holding drumhead courts-martial or treating their men the way Cumberland did. As for Mar—who was no Highlander himself—burning roofs: that was a less serious matter than it appears in modern eyes, for the thatched-roofed huts were fairly easily rebuilt. It was not the burning of the roofs which made the later clearances so terrible—

it was the cold-blooded murder, the senseless brutality and above all the eviction from the land that were terrible.

No doubt the Highland leaders had the same problems with recruitment as anybody else, but to single them out for one-sided attention in an effort to prove that they were men who did not know where their own self-interest lay, is to misunderstand the whole situation.

After 1715 the tale of bungled attempts continues. In 1743 a proposed invasion, with ample French support this time, aborted. The following year, 1744, Marshal de Saxe and several thousand French troops attempted to invade England from Dunkirk, to place young Prince Charles (the Young Pretender) on his father's throne. With almost tragic inevitability, a storm sprang up. It wrecked many transports and caused the loss of lives of soldiers and sailors and the loss of valuable stores. The invasion fleet scattered and put back into port, and the last effort properly backed by the French came to nothing, as had others before it. It was the third time the French kings had provided considerable bodies of troops to help the Stuarts. Thereafter they grew decidedly cool about the whole project. King James, as the Jacobites called the Old Pretender, had already gloomily surrendered himself to personal failure.

At this point, history takes a decidedly strange turn. In the summer of 1745 Prince Charles set out with no troops, no money, no arms, with only two ships, the *Elizabeth* and the *du Teillay*. He had decided to stake everything on one throw of the dice. He did so without informing his father, who would certainly have forbidden the stupidity; and he did so without the knowledge of Louis XV of France, who would certainly have prevented the ships from leaving France.

In 1740 seven leading Jacobite supporters had formed what has become known as the Edinburgh Association. They met in Edinburgh and pledged themselves to support the Stuart cause with their lives and their fortunes. But they stipulated that no rising was to be attempted without substantial support in the way of French troops and arms. Indeed, prior to 1745 no attempt without outside support had ever been considered. The Edinburgh seven did not speak only for themselves: they represented all the clans whose chiefs were likely to support the Jacobite cause.

The names of the seven were Lord Lovat (Fraser), the Duke of Perth (Drummond), the Earl of Traquair (Stuart), Sir James Campbell of Auchinbreck, Cameron of Lochiel, Lord Traquair's brother John Stuart, and Lord John Drummond, the Duke of Perth's uncle. Their messenger to the exiled James VIII and III was Drummond of Balhady.

At this time, although it was not recognized as such by the Jacobites themselves, the Jacobite cause was already a lost cause. People wanted peace and stability. Even if they sympathized with James, and it is not clear just how many did, they did not want to embark on a civil war on his behalf.

The Jacobites believed that, once a rising began, thousands of people would flock to their side. It was particularly believed that there would be considerable support from English Jacobites.

They existed, the English Jacobites. They drank to the health of the king over the water, and liked to drink toasts with a glass of water on the table in front of them, so that when they gravely toasted 'The King', it would be 'over the water', but no eavesdropper would know that they meant another king. It makes good reading for *Boys' Own Paper*, but it is hardly suitable for the serious business of unseating the British government.

The French King obviously had his own sources of information and did not believe in this English support (the real English Jacobites were loyal to the death, but they were very few in number compared with those who liked to fancy themselves Jacobites). Louis demanded evidence of this support before he would send troops, and the Jacobites kept pointing out that, until the troops came, nobody would declare their support. It was a stalemate.

The Jacobites were in fact gambling with a hand containing no cards, and if Prince Charles had not rashly taken matters into his own hands, it seems fairly certain that France would have shelved the whole project for ever.

The popular version of the '45 is that Charles was determined to break the stalemate and that he had unbounded confidence in the Highlanders. Yet it is difficult to know how he could have looked confidently for support when all the messages from Scotland insisted on the one *sine qua non*—substantial French support. At no time did the chiefs ever consider bringing their clans into the field in support of an empty-handed prince. Their leaders were not fools.

The chiefs indeed knew very well how the country was divided on the issue, and they did not want an army of occupation in the Highlands. Many of them must have had secret fears that the present-day Stuarts would be no more sympathetic towards the Highlanders than their predecessors James I, Charles I, Charles II and James II had been. The good old days of the early Stewart kings were gone. The later Stuarts represented a last hope, but it was not a hope for which anybody wished to commit suicide.

So Charles set out with two ships, secretly he believed. He had not gone far before the British warship *Lion* intercepted them. The *Elizabeth* engaged it, while the *du Teillay*, with Charles and his suite, stood off. Charles, of course, was furious to be an onlooker, but the others sensibly realized that there was no point in having the Prince killed before the attempt even started. Even in his heroism he is too much the schoolboy, not enough the calculating, shrewd leader of men.

The *Lion* was defeated but the *Elizabeth* was so badly damaged that she had to put back into Brest, with her handful of French soldiers and her stores. Charles sailed on alone in the *du Teillay*, heading for the west coast of Scotland. On 22 July they sighted land.

They anchored off the coast of Barra, the clan possession of the MacNeils, whose chief was the brother-in-law of one of Charles's suite, Aeneas MacDonald, a banker. They managed to recruit MacNeil of Barra's piper but nobody else. They also learned that the chief of Clan MacLean had been arrested by the Government. He was a prominent Jacobite plotter, and this news alarmed the Prince's companions, who wanted to call the whole thing off there and then and sail back.

Charles was obstinate, so they sailed on to Eriskay, owned by Alexander MacDonald of Boisdale, and here the Prince first set foot on Scottish soil. Messages were sent to the chief of Clanranald, an infirm man of fifty-three, whose son was believed to have great influence among the MacDonalds.

Clanranald and MacDonald of Boisdale arrived to meet the Prince; but they were not all helpful and advised him to go home. Here begin some rather theatrical sayings. The Prince is supposed to have replied haughtily, 'I *am* come home, sir, and I will entertain no notion at all of returning from where I came, for I am persuaded that my faithful Highlanders will stand by me.'

This is the first of such remarks to be considered, which have all the hallmarks of later additions. The phraseology rings false. Why not just say he would not return to France? Or to Rome, where his father was? Why his 'faithful Highlanders', when so far they had refused to join him?

In any event, he asked Boisale to approach the Skye MacLeods and MacDonalds. Boisdale flatly refused. He said that MacDonald of Sleat and MacLeod of Dunvegan had both told him that under no circumstances would they take part in any rising which did not have considerable outside support. They, too, would only advise the Prince to go back.

So far all this has the ring of probability. It is exactly the sort of reaction one would expect in view of the messages exchanged between the plotters and the court in exile. Charles was behaving like a naughty child.

Charles left Eriskay as empty-handed as he had arrived, and the *du Teillay* finally sailed into Loch nan Uamh, in the heart of MacDonald country. From here it was hoped that Young Clanranald would ignore his father's advice and persuade the MacDonalds to declare for the Prince.

The events at Loch nan Uamh make no sense. The story runs something as follows:

Young Clanranald, MacDonald of Kinlochmoidart and his brother came to visit the Prince aboard the *du Teillay*. The Prince gave Young Clanranald an audience in his cabin, which lasted for two hours or more. When they came back on deck, the Prince and Kinlochmoidart were seen pacing it and arguing with Clanranald, who refused to join the rising. Kinlochmoidart's brother was standing watching and overheard some of the argument, enough to know that Clanranald was *refusing* to call out his own clan, exactly as his father had done. He stepped forward and offered to follow the Prince.

'Will you assist me?' the Prince asked.

'I will, I will. Though no other man should draw a sword, I am ready to die for you.'

The Prince then said that he wished all Highlanders were like this—one may reasonably ask if he meant all his faithful Highlanders of whom he had been so sure shortly before.

Clanranald, moved by the example of this man, promptly changed his mind and declared that he would support the Prince.

Really? We move on . . .

Soon afterwards Donald Cameron, younger of Lochiel, known as the 'Gentle' Lochiel, arrived at Loch nan Uamh. His brother Dr Archibald Cameron had already been sent to answer the Prince's summons and had said that Lochiel would not raise his clan if the Prince had arrived without support—the support which had always been accepted by both sides as being crucial to the cause. Now Lochiel had come in person *to persuade the Prince to return to France.*

Lochiel was adamant. He was a member of the Edinburgh Association, and he told the Prince to go back and wait till the French King had provided troops, arms and money and then to return to Scotland, when all the loyal clans would rise for him.

Charles speaks:

'Soon, with the few friends I have, I will raise the royal standard and proclaim to the people that Charles Stuart is come over to claim the crown of his ancestors, to win it or die in the attempt. Lochiel, whom my father has often told me was our firmest friend, may stay at home and from the newspapers learn the fate of his prince.'

Even Mackie, the historiographer royal, quotes Lochiel's reply to this childish taunt: 'No, I'll share the fate of my prince and so shall every man over whom nature or fortune hath given me any power.'

These two stories are repeated endlessly by historians, yet their unlikeliness is staggering. Of course the facts are not in dispute. Young Clanranald and Lochiel, who were both initially opposed to the venture, did change their minds. Although they were both the sons of living chiefs, they were responsible for their clansmen. Had they refused to support the Prince, it is difficult to believe that there would have been a rising at all. If Lochiel and the Clanranald and Skye MacDonalds and the MacLeods all refused to join the rising, not many other clans would have done so.

It is true to say therefore that it was crucial, imperative to the attempt to win over these two men, both opposed to Charles's plans—Charles who was accompanied only by the Seven Men of Moidart, famous in Jacobite history, and who, as Professor Mackie points out, included one Englishman, three Irishmen and one MacDonald from Northern Ireland.

We are asked to believe that one was shamed into committing

his own and his clan's future by the flowery speech of an ordinary Highlander and that the other was similarly shamed by a 'smart-alec' remark about newspapers. What newspapers, one wonders? There was no daily delivery at Achnacarry in 1745.

Here is a mystery which nobody seems to have considered. Although the rising of 1745 was never intended to be a purely Highland rising, it needed initial Highland support to become a rising at all. We are being asked to believe that Charles sailed empty-handed, trusting only in his own boyish enthusiasm to overcome the objections of responsible men to something which their native common sense had told them instantly was utter rashness.

We know it worked, but the question is *how*? Not in the way told, surely.

There is one fact which seems to have been consistently over-looked by historians. If anyone had a vested interest in tempting Prince Charles into a rash act, *it was the English Government*. Charles, alive in France or in Rome, a centre of trouble and intrigue, would be for so long as he lived a thorn in the flesh of the Government. And if he had sons, there was no knowing how much trouble that would cause in time.

But Charles's father was resigned to personal failure. Charles's brother had gone into the Church and would not produce heirs. The death of Charles would kill the Jacobite cause totally.

During the entire Jacobite era there was a network of spies on both sides. The government in London were kept very well informed indeed of all that was going on in France and in Rome. A detailed study of the doings of these agents and double-agents is very reminiscent of the world of espionage of modern times.

If the Duke of Newcastle could tempt Charles out of France and could fall on him and destroy him, the government could forget about Jacobites. The attempt by the *Lion*, conveniently handy to intercept the Prince's two ships, had been foiled. Yet if there was one man in Europe who must have rejoiced when the standard of revolt was raised at Glenfinnan on 19 August 1745, it was Newcastle. He certainly had too realistic a picture of the pseudo-Jacobites in England to fear that ultimate victory would go to Charles. Indeed, he probably expected that the rising would be nipped in the bud in the Highlands, and the Prince taken prisoner in an act of open warfare. Charles at the head of a

Highland army was exactly what the government needed, provided they did not let him escape. After Culloden they were so frantic that they put the unheard-of reward of £30,000 on his head.

It is not beyond the bounds of possibility that there was some connection between the government's desire to tempt Charles into something foolhardy, and Charles's apparent foolhardiness. It was an era of agents and double-agents. It was not beyond the ingenuity of Newcastle to 'leak' some sort of false message to Charles, saying that if he sailed Louis would promptly send the necessary support hard on his heels. If Charles believed this, it would explain much that is otherwise inexplicable, for, although Charles had considerable boyish impulsiveness and tended to believe what he wanted to believe, he was not a complete fool.

It would explain the initial dismay of the Highlanders when they encountered him with only his small personal suite, but if he had something concrete to show them, something suggesting that help was definitely promised, say on the raising of the standard, they might have swallowed their first fears and been persuaded to do what initially they did not want to do at all.

There is no evidence one way or the other, nor is it likely now that any will appear to answer our doubts. But such an explanation puts all three men in a far more probable light, particularly that level-headed Jacobite Lochiel, whose character was such that he must have weighed carefully the terrible consequences of failure should a premature rising take place.

What happened thereafter is too well known to be repeated in detail. The standard was raised, some of the clans flocked to join it, others did not. The Skye MacDonalds and MacLeods never did rise for the Prince. Some of the Campbells did! There were some spectacular victories, but not against either Wade or Cumberland.

The lightning thrust which took the Prince's army as far south as Derby is a remarkable exploit, but it cannot be termed an invasion of England. Lord George Murray was perfectly correct in advising the Prince to turn back to Scotland, and in this he had the support of the chiefs. The Jacobite army which crossed into England consisted of some five thousand men, and on the march southwards they were *not* joined by thousands of eager English supporters. The loyal English Jacobites were few in number, and some of their men were quite definitely dragged out after them, most unwillingly.

At Derby the Prince was in a desperate situation, with Cumberland and Wade converging on him with over twenty thousand seasoned troops. The Jacobites were in hostile territory, surrounded by enemies and about to be caught and crushed.

They won through, back to Scotland. Even in Scotland there was no widespread support for the Stuart cause. Yet it is possible that they could have won Scotland and held it for a time—it is debatable for how long they would have held it.

There is a terrible sense of fatality about the rising, a tragic air of impending doom which is associated to some extent with all the Jacobite attempts. The Prince ignored the advice of the only general of any substance in his entire army—Lord George Murray. He clung to the assurances of his favourites, allowing Sheridan and that most un-military of colonels, O'Sullivan, to poison his mind against Lord George. His secretary, Murray of Broughton, was another intriguer against Lord George—the Prince was surrounded by intrigue which he himself fostered.

The end came at Culloden, a battle that should never have been fought—which *would* never have been fought if they had listened to Lord George. For the first time the Highlanders found themselves fighting a battle on highly unsuitable ground, when they were bone-weary and hungry, when many of their army were absent—and the man facing them, Cumberland, was an excellent general whose troops were well fed and rested.

It could have only one ending, and it came quickly on that grim day. Among the prisoners were fifty or more Campbells.

Following Culloden, Charles showed for a few months a courage and a stamina which made his defeat the prelude to the finest episode in his unhappy life. With a reward the equivalent of roughly £750,000 today on his head, he dodged Government troops. The clans gave him shelter, and no man could be found to betray him. Not one. It was a remarkable tribute to the loyalty of his friends.

He finally made his escape back to France to become one of history's forgotten men, forgotten except for the fact that he was 'Bonnie' and that Flora MacDonald helped him on the run, which gave a misleading air of 'romance' to his escape.

All his later dreary despair and his drunkenness may easily be explained by the fact that he would far rather have died at the head of the Highlanders in whom he had so much faith. Life in exile is not a bed of roses for a man who believes himself to be a divinely appointed king.

But the final bill was footed by the unfortunate Highlanders. Cumberland earned the name 'Butcher', and the flower Sweet William, called after him, is known as 'Stinking Billy' in Scotland.

The powers of the clan chiefs were taken from them. It was not the clan system which died at Culloden, for the system exists today. It was the powers of the chiefs and their place as the fathers, the leaders, of their clanspeople. The clans were left without anyone to direct them and became prey to grim missionaries determined to teach them a relentless Presbyterianism which would bind them forever to the Government. Roads were driven into the Highlands, and they were policed; tartan, Highland dress, their weapons, even the bagpipes were all made illegal.

1746 has often been described as the end of the *separate* history of the Highlands. But for more than a century that separate history went on, as the following chapters will show. It was, on the other hand, the end of the Jacobite cause, the end of all hope for that legitimate but unfortunately Catholic family whose history can be said to have begun with Mary, Queen of Scots.

It was also the beginning of the legends, of the great smoke-screen of nonsense, of high-flown sentiment and downright bad history. What follows is history that everyone would prefer to forget.

8

The Highland Donation—
the Highland Regiments

After Culloden there was no immediate danger from the clans, who were leaderless. The clansmen themselves were bewildered and broken in spirit, for the great dream of Gaeldom had been shattered. Nevertheless, during those first years the Government must have been aware that Prince Charles, who was the rightful heir to the throne on grounds of primogeniture, was very much alive on the Continent and that the Highlands contained many thousands of fit men who had recently displayed Jacobite sympathies.

It was not a situation which the Government would want to allow to remain static for long. The threat posed by the Prince had diminished with the changing European political situation, but one never knew. The Scots and the English were not the best of friends, and Cumberland had left behind a bitter legacy which disgusted many Scots who had no love for the Jacobites either. Cumberland of course did not like *any* Scotsmen, and he did not much care if everybody knew it.

As early as 1738, Lord President Forbes of Culloden had put up a scheme to the Government for the raising of Highland regiments, to be officered by 'loyal Englishmen'—there is something touchingly naïve about this proviso. His aim was to channel the energies of the possible Jacobite supporters into activities which would leave them no time for plotting.

The scheme was in the end vetoed by the Cabinet, but out of it there came in 1739 the Black Watch Regiment. In 1745, prior to the Jacobite rising, the Black Watch had fought with Cumberland at Fontenoy, and he had been impressed. He was not an easily impressed man, nor did he have any regard at all for the private soldier. He would have been the first to agree with the Duke of Wellington that they were the scum of the earth.

It was after Fontenoy that he is credited with having worked out a method of withstanding the famous Highland charge. The Highlander went in with his targe high to protect his head and chest, and his point low. The Lowland soldiers feared that terrible belly-thrust, and repeatedly they broke before such furious charges. Illustrations of the time show Lowland soldiers using their bayonets in a downward thrust, their rifles held above their heads, which left their bodies entirely uncovered.

Cumberland is said to have drilled his men to ignore the Highlander in front and to bayonet the man on their right. Of course it took nerve. It was necessary to trust that the man on one's left was doing the same thing and killing the savage Highlander in front. It was not tactics such as those which won Culloden in any case—it was the combination of stupidities and petty jealousies at work which undid all the advice offered by Lord George Murray, who did not want to fight at all that day, who chose different ground and was overruled and who finally suggested the forced night-march which, if it had succeeded, would have put the Highlanders in among Cumberland's army before they awoke at dawn. It did not succeed because the main body did not keep up with the van of the army, with the result that they did not come up with Cumberland till too late, when the redcoats were fully awake and standing to.

The Black Watch experiment had been successful enough to warrant the raising of another regiment in 1745, Loudoun's Highlanders, who also formed part of the Government army during the rising. They did not distinguish themselves in the '45, however, for it was this regiment which was routed at Moy by a handful of MacIntoshes who frightened them into thinking that a great force was lying in wait for them. They turned and ran! They were employed in Flanders in 1747 and 1748 and were finally disbanded in 1748 when peace came.

It was left to William Pitt to propose the raising of regiments from among the 'disaffected' clans, to serve overseas with the British Army. In 1757 he raised Montgomery's Highlanders and Fraser's Highlanders from among the Jacobite clans, officered by their own chiefs, chieftains and leaders. Both regiments served in North America, and Montgomery's also served in West Indies. In

1763, with the signing of the peace, they were disbanded. The men were allowed to settle in the USA and in Canada if they wished, and were given small grants of land.

Between 1757 and 1761 ten Highland regiments were raised and disbanded. They were:

Montgomery's Highlanders	1757–63	North America and the West Indies
Fraser's Highlanders	1757–63	North America
Keith's Highlanders	1757–63	Germany
Campbell's Highlanders	1759–63	Germany
The Duke of Gordon's Highlanders	1759–65	India (this was the original Gordon Highlanders)
The 100th Regiment (raised by Colin Campbell of Kilberrie)	1761–3	Martinique
The Queen's Highlanders	1761–3	Ireland
The Royal Highland Volunteers	1761–3	Home Service (used to feed other regiments in Germany)
Johnstone's Highlanders	1760–3	Used to feed Keith's and Campbell's
MacLean's Highlanders	1761–3	Drafted to other regiments

The experiment was a resounding success, and in 1766 William Pitt was able to say to Parliament: 'I sought for merit wherever it was to be found, and it is my boast that I was the first minister who looked for it and found it in the mountains of the north. I called it forth and drew into your service a hardy and intrepid race of men, who when left by your jealousy became a prey to the artifice of your enemies, and had gone nigh to have overturned the State in the war before the last. These men in the last war were brought to combat on your side; they served with fidelity as they fought with valour, and conquered for you in every part of the world.'

This is indeed stirring stuff coming from the lips of an Englishman. Unfortunately he was a politician and does not mention the interesting fact that, when he first commended his scheme in 1757, he had been at pains to point out the obvious advantage that, in sending them off to war, 'not many' of the Highlanders would return. Nevertheless, whatever his motives in the beginning, and however much he might like to take all the credit to himself, it was Pitt who finally implemented the idea of employing the Highlanders legitimately as fighting soldiers in the service of their country.

Up to 1780, which is to say in less than thirty-five years from Culloden, some twenty Highland regiments were called into existence, including three famous ones who were not disbanded but became part of the permanent establishment—the Black Watch, the Highland Light Infantry and the Seaforth Highlanders.

In the forty years from 1797 to 1837, the island of Skye, alone, provided the British Army with 21 lieutenant- and major-generals, 48 lieutenant-colonels, 600 majors and captains and subalterns, 120 pipers and 10,000 soldiers and non-commissioned officers. The island also provided four colonial governors, one governor-general, a Chief Baron of England and a Judge of the Supreme Court of Scotland.

How was it accomplished? The groundwork for the answer to this has already been laid. In the first place, the new House of Hanover was a Protestant branch of the old House of Stuart and ruled by virtue of its Stuart blood rather than its Hanoverian connection. In the second place, the chiefs who might have opposed the scheme were in exile or dead, and those who remained on their clan lands had no wish to repeat the futile performance of 1745 with its savage repercussions. Then again, the power of the Campbells no longer threatened the other clans. The days of feuding and fighting among themselves were now over. In the first years after Culloden, the only way in which an Highlander could legally wear Highland dress, carry weapons and play the bagpipes was to join one of the new Highland regiments. And since the regiments were officered by men he knew and included men from his own glens, it was just like the clan days all over again except that now the Government fed and clothed them and paid them money, and they had no retribution to fear. And, of course, mostly they were not Catholics; they had no religious loyalty to the Stuarts.

All these considerations acted together to make the prospect of army service very attractive to fit men—the very men who, left to their own devices, might just conceivably become the spearhead for another Jacobite attempt. It was not likely, but the Government preferred to pre-empt the possibility.

If anything put the final seal on the fate of the Stuarts, it was these Highland regiments.

Not only did they do good service—Pitt was not exaggerating about that even if he did rather give the impression that all the achievements of the British Army in North America and Germany were due to the Highlanders—but they provided good, hardy settlers for the USA and Canada. In the clearances, which follow, they were joined by thousands more.

It is quite impossible to deal in one chapter with the detailed stories of any of the Highland regiments, but they quickly acquired a fine reputation of their own in the army. They were crack infantry regiments. Those who survived, and were not disbanded, were:

The Black Watch	Raised 1739
The Highland Light Infantry	Raised 1777
The Seaforth Highlanders	Raised 1778
The Gordon Highlanders	Raised 1787
The Queen's Own Cameron Highlanders	Raised 1793
The Argyll & Sutherland Highlanders	Raised 1794

In 1900 the Lovat Scouts were raised, and in the Second World War they were a commando battalion. They were disbanded in 1945 and are now a part of the Royal Armoured Corps (TAVR).

Three Scottish regiments were raised in England, all with Highland affiliations:

The London Scottish	1859	affiliated with the Gordon Highlanders
The Liverpool Scottish	1900	affiliated with the Queen's Own Cameron Highlanders
The Tyneside Scottish	1914	affiliated with the Royal Highland Regiment, the Black Watch

In Canada, Australia, New Zealand and South Africa, Highland regiments were raised from the descendants of Highland immigrants and distinguished themselves in two world wars.

One of the most striking features of the Highland regiments from their inception in 1739 was the lack of discipline necessary to impose by normal means—that is to say, by savage floggings. This was mainly because of the territorial nature of the regiments. The territorial link is a feature of the entire British army, but it was unusually strong in the Highland regiments between 1739 and 1914 (at which time the expansion of the regiments into dozens of battalions meant drafting recruits from anywhere).

There was no greater threat to any Highland soldier who showed signs of misbehaving than a stern warning that, if he did not behave, his name would be sent back to his village. That was quite literally enough. A Highlander would accept any discipline willingly rather than undergo the terrible humiliation of being disgraced in the eyes of his family, his clansmen, his neighbours. He would also accept any discipline rather than risk corporal punishment, which was particularly offensive to the Highlanders. At a time, therefore, when savage and brutal punishments were considered the only effective way of maintaining discipline, even in the best of British regiments, they were virtually unknown among the Highland regiments. This characteristic of the troops made them particularly popular with various generals and commanders-in-chief.

They were not angels, of course—but they were extremely well disciplined. And of course they were excellent fighters—had they not been, their reputation would never have been earned.

At the present time the fate of the British Army is uncertain. The whole nature of warfare has changed drastically since 1945, and this is reflected in the defence estimates and how the money is to be used. The whole of Scottish command at present consists of one division, and the Highland regiments are a shadow of their former selves. The HLI has been amalgamated with the Royal Scots Fusiliers, which is not a Highland regiment at all, to form the Royal Highland Fusiliers. The Queen's Own Cameron Highlanders have been amalgamated with the Seaforths to make the Queen's Own Highlanders. The Argylls came perilously close to extinction, and only a desperate last-ditch battle with the Ministry of Defence saved them for the moment.

The role of the army and of the infantry battalions in the twenty-first century has yet to be decided. One day, the Highland regiments which served Britain so well for two and a half centuries may become a memory, their uniforms to be found only in military museums. But the memory is likely to persist for a long time.

In the heading to this chapter, the Highland regiments are referred to as 'the Highland Donation'. Indeed they were. They helped to keep alive the clan spirit in far-off lands, so that the

Highland clans of today exist mainly outside Scotland and are to be found in the USA, Canada, Australia, New Zealand and South Africa.

In the chapter which follows, it will be related how the clearances added to this traffic from the Highlands to what were once called the 'Colonies'. This pouring-out of men to take root abroad, strengthened by the pride in their own regiments and the great military tradition they created, has ensured that, even if the ancient kingdom of Scotland were to disappear entirely from the map of the world, the Scottish people would live on, and with them the Highland clans.

It is no mean achievement. As it stands, without romanticizing about it or getting it out of proportions, in its starkest simplicity, it is no mean achievement. It is matched, of course, by the achievements of other Scottish emigrants and other Scottish regiments; but this is a book about the Highlanders.

After 1746 the Highlander really becomes for the first time a Scotsman rather than a Highlander, no longer one of a different race to be hated, feared and consequentially despised, in turn hating and despising others.

It is a great tragedy therefore that, just when this had been achieved, the Highlanders should have fallen prey to the greatest cruelty and savagery, the most humiliating indignity that has ever been inflicted on them—and this in modern times by their fellow Scots, even by their own erstwhile chiefs.

The final chapter in the separate history of the Highlands is the most astonishing and the most shocking.

9

Murder Most Foul

Had the Highland story really ended in 1746, to be followed by the stirring history of the Highland regiments over two and a half centuries, it would indeed be easy to overlook much of the hypocrisy that lurks menacingly behind the tartan smoke screen raised by Sir Walter Scott, fanned by King George IV and finally given the royal warrant by Queen Victoria.

It did not end then.

Evictions had been heard of in the Highlands prior to 1745, but rarely. In 1739 both MacDonald of Sleat and MacLeod of Dunvegan, the principal Skye chiefs, *sold* some of their followers as indentured servants in the Carolinas. Such examples were rare, however, and have no connection with the exercise in cruelty known as 'the Highland Clearances'.

The clearances proper fall roughly into two periods: A long period from 1785 to 1820, and a shorter one from 1842 to 1854.

During the entire period covered by the clearances, i.e. from 1785 to 1854, Highland regiments were serving with distinction in the USA, in the French revolutionary wars, in the Napoleonic and Peninsular Wars and in other campaigns. In 1854, the year of the disgraceful slaughter of Ross women at Greenyards, the 93rd Sutherland Highlanders won everlasting fame at Balaclava when their Thin Red Line broke a cavalry charge.

Also during this shameful period, Queen Victoria and Prince Albert, from 1848 onwards, were living in a sentimental day-dream at Balmoral, talking about their beloved Highlanders, covering the floors and windows with tartan and discovering a very genuine love for the Highlands that continues to this day in some of their descendants. Yet not a hundred miles away, these same Highlanders were being evicted, reduced to poverty and cruelly beaten and murdered by police constables acting for the factors of landlords who placed sheep above men.

It is not even remotely possible to give a full account of the clearances in a chapter, or half-a-dozen chapters. All one can do is to look at the cause and to consider some of those who were principally responsible, and the cruelties that resulted.

The chiefs who remained on their lands after Culloden soon realized that they had become landlords rather than fathers of the clan family, and very uneconomical landlords at that. Their clan lands were divided, sub-divided and further sub-divided into small lots scarcely sufficient to support their tenants, who were in no position to pay rents. Under the clan system this had not been serious for the clan functioned as a whole unit, and the chief, who might not have £50 Scots to his name at any given time, had a thriving economy and an invaluable manpower to guard it.

Now, however, the clan lands were *his* lands; he began to acquire expensive tastes, and his clansmen had to pay him in cash rents, which were insufficient for the chief's new conception of his place in outside society. Rents were raised and raised again, till finally they could not be paid. It became more profitable for the landlords (they were by no means all ex-chiefs and chieftains, for many of the chiefly estates hand been forfeit) to get rid of their tenants and let the land in larger lots to southerners who could work it better.

There was an economical squeeze, and thousands of Highlanders were forced to emigrate. They were not evicted—not at this point. They emigrated. They did so in large numbers as early as 1772. Between 1772 and 1791 over 6,500 persons emigrated from Inverness and Ross alone, unable to withstand the economic pressures on them.

The clearances, that is to say forcible evictions, began in 1785, when one of the better-known Highland chiefs, Macdonell of Glengarry, allowed his wife Marjorie to evict five hundred tenants from Glen Quoich to make room for a sheep-walk. (It is significant that this Marjorie was the mother of Elizabeth Chisholm, wife of the 24th Chisholm, whom we shall be studying shortly.) There had been widespread emigrations from the Glengarry lands during the preceding twenty years, but now economical pressures gave way to legal evictions. Marjorie continued to evict Glengarry tenants in 1787 and 1788, when her docile husband Duncan finally died.

He was succeeded as heir to the title and the lands of Glengarry by his son Alisdair Ranaldson Macdonell, whose portrait in Highland dress by Raeburn is one of the most famous and seems to epitomize the proud, honourable father of a Highland clan. Nothing could be further from the truth.

Alisdair loved to play at being a Highland chief, and he inspired Sir Walter Scott with some of his least accurate ideas on Highlanders. For a start, he killed Flora MacDonald's grandson in a duel but managed to get himself acquitted at his trial. He strutted proudly in full Highland dress, wearing broadsword, dirk and pistols, and was followed by his 'tail' of henchman, bard, piper and bodyguard.

He was very splendid and he ran up a lot of bills. Money had to come from somewhere to finance his mad play-acting, and so he leased more and more land, very profitably, to southern sheepmen. To do so, he evicted more and more of his clansmen to make way for the sheep. It has been estimated that his income from rents was over £5,000 a year, which was totally insufficient. This gives some idea of the scale on which he existed, for £5,000 a year then must represent around £100,000 a year today, free of tax. It was a bold man who would have dared to ask Glengarry in his lair to pay taxes or other dues.

The earlier portrait of a Highland chief as a man who, from self-interest as much as self-preservation, was genuinely concerned about the welfare of his clansmen, gives way now to the portrait of a man who felt no sense of responsibility to anyone but himself. There were now no dangerous neighbours to rob him of his lands if he did not have loyal and faithful clan to protect them. The law protected him.

It is significant that Walter Scott admired Alisdair Ranaldson Macdonell enormously and that Robert Burns called him a cold-hearted tyrant.

His whole life is astonishing. He evicted clansmen and then fell into fury when he learned that they were emigrating—although what he expected them to do has never been discovered. He detested the sheepmen who were making him rich. He hated the Caledonian Canal which was being constructed to link the three lochs of the Great Glen, making it possible to sail from Inverness to Fort William. He blandly stole timber and bricks from the canal, and when confronted, he brazened it out. A Highland gentleman was not accustomed to make a fuss about a few bits of brick and wood left lying about! He was inevitably involved in a number of court cases, but he always avoided the hand of justice.

He died in debt up to his ears and was buried in a thunderstorm. Within a generation of his death, there were no Glengarry chiefs and no Glengarry clansmen left on Glengarry lands.

It was in 1790 that a new and sturdy strain of Cheviot sheep was introduced into the Highlands. They were so successful that landowners realized that they had real wealth within their grasp. But first one had to get rid of the people. Glengarry, for one, had shown the way.

In 1801 William, the 24th Chisholm, whose wife was the daughter of Marjorie Macdonell of Glengarry mentioned above, began the clearances in Strathglass. In that year half of the clan were evicted and sailed for Canada and Nova Scotia.

When William died, his son was a minor; but his wife Elizabeth carried on the good work with a will. She evicted clansmen to pay for her son's education at Cambridge.

Alexander, the 25th Chisholm, followed in the footsteps of his mother and father. He totally depopulated Strathglass. Only one Chisholm, it was said, remained. One of his bards described him as a man who wanted nothing so much as to replace his people, 'his family from the beginning of time', with sheep. And, of course, it was true.

Not everybody was like Glengarry and Chisholm. The most notable exceptions were the chiefs of Clan MacLeod, who went to enormous lengths to improve the lives of their clanspeople in Skye and who were brilliantly successful. They were in dazzling contrast to the 'improvers'.

But the greatest 'improver' of them all was undoubtedly the Englishman George Granville Leveson-Gower, Marquess of Stafford, born in 1758. He was the richest landowner in Britain, possessing huge estates in England. His wife was Elizabeth Gordon, Countess of Sutherland in her own right, eight years younger and her dowry was two-thirds of the county of Sutherland. The rent-roll, however, produced a beggarly £15,000 a year, which must have seemed ridiculously trifling to Britain's richest landowner. In 1807 the Most Noble Marquess began to evict his Scottish Highland tenants beginning with a modest ninety families, men, women and children. His aim was, of course, the laudable one of improving his estates. Improving the lives of other people was not within his self-imposed terms of reference.

In the following twenty years he moved more and more people off their lands to make way for sheep. He lived in the princely splendour of Dunrobin Castle when he was in Scotland, and his Countess could wax sentimental over her clanspeople, but always from a safe distance. She was more English than Scottish in her outlook and, although she had a resounding Gaelic title which meant 'Great Lady of Sutherland', she spoke not a word of the language so many of her people spoke.

Lord Stafford's agents carried out the first Strathnaver clearance in 1814. Their method was simple but effective. The occupants were ordered out of their homes, and the torch was put to their roof-timbers. If anyone was slow in getting out of doors, then the fire was started with them inside. Furniture and possessions all went up in flames. Women and children, old men and animals, stood in huddled, frightened groups while the cruel work went on. Their houses were levelled to the ground so that the Cheviots could browse contentedly on nice empty rolling straths devoid of human habitation.

The evicted lost their clothing and their furniture and cooking-utensils. They had no place to go, and nobody thought to provide them with one. They were, as was said at the time, driven out like dogs.

The story is told of one woman too old to be moved. The agent is said to have commented callously, 'Damn her, the old witch. She has lived too long. Let her burn'. And her house was put to the torch. She died five days later, as surely murdered as anybody could be.

The eyewitness stories told about the evictions are blood-curdling. One man who tried to save some bits of wood was discovered, and the wood was burned so that he should have nothing. People died of fatigue, cold and sheer fright. The factors and constables seemed to take a perverse pleasure in maltreating the old and the frail—they were so easy to deal with. Pregnant women were mistreated, and there were premature labours as a result.

Not even animals were spared. One account tells how a terrified cat, which tried to escape the flames of a burning croft, was thrown back again and again until it finally perished.

Homeless people were left destitute in wind and rain, to survive as best they could without food or shelter. The crying of terrified children and the groans of the elderly made an edifying accompaniment to the important work of improving the Most Noble Marquess's estates.

No compensation was paid in respect of homes destroyed, far less the personal possessions destroyed with them. No help was given to resettle. Stafford could easily have cleared his estates in a far more humane way, for his possessions were vast. People could have been given help to resettle on the coast, time to move their few possessions. Of course their new land might have been useless, but it would have been at least an attempt to grapple with the problem. No attempt appears to have been made.

All this was happening in the year or two before Waterloo. The sons, brothers and fathers of some of these defenceless people were serving with the Duke of Wellington in Britain's war. Their regiments acquired renown, but their families were being treated with all cruelty one would look for in Romanov Russia of that time.

Glengarry, Chisholm, the Great Lady of Sutherland—how times had changed.

The Strathnaver clearances were repeated in Upper Strathnaver in 1819, and at Kildonan. The story is told of an old man in his nineties, who could remember the Jacobite days and who had already been evicted once. His wife had died as the result. When he heard he was to be evicted again, he went to the churchyard, stood over her grave and is reported to have said, 'Well, Janet, the Countess of Sutherland can never flit* you again.' His words could well serve as an epitaph for the whole of the clearances.

The same man was finally turned out again, from the house where his wife had died, and he walked to Wick where he died alone, unmourned.

The first, long period of clearances came to an end when Hugh Munro of Novar cleared Culrain and Oykel in 1820.

The Sutherland clearances are probably the most notorious.

---

* In this usage, 'flit' means 'evict'.

They were widely reported in the Press at the time, in great detail, but all that resulted was that well-intentioned gentlefolk in the south began to raise charitable funds for the relief of the destitute. Later on, during the Skye clearances, Prince Albert lent his name to a scheme for helping the Skye people emigrate. But at no time does anybody seem to have challenged the work of butchery and brutality going on in the glens. That was left to historians to do later, when the power that protected people in high places was no longer able to protect them.

And yet Sutherland was one of the counties that supplied thousands of men for the Highland regiments.

People resisted, of course, sometimes. But the clearances were usually carried out by law-officers so the resistance was useless. There do not seem to have been many fit and able young men in the cleared areas, and a lot of the resistance was put up by the women, whose sex did not protect them from retribution.

In 1842 the clearances began all over again, when William Robertson of Kindeace authorized the removal of all the tenants of Glencalvie in Strathcarron. In 1849, by which time the Balmoral tradition had begun to take root with Queen Victoria, there were clearances in Glenelg, and Lord MacDonald ordered clearances at Sollas in South Uist. In 1851 the MacKinnons were cleared from Strathaird in Skye—first the rack-renting by alien absentee landlords, then the burning-down of their homes and the orders to quit the land where their forefathers had lived for a thousand years.

It was not the MacKinnon chief who cleared Strathaird. The clan lands had been sold to MacAlister of Skirrinish in 1791, and the last chief of the main line died in Leith in 1808, where he was working for a living as an exciseman. Many other chiefs were powerless to do anything about what was happening on their ancient possessions.

The story reaches a blood-thirsty climax in 1854, the year of the great killing of the women of the Rosses, which again had nothing to do with the clan chiefs. That year it was decided to clear Greenyards in Strathcarron. The landlord was Alexander Munro, and rumours began to spread that he intended to evict his tenants. When questioned directly by some of them, he emphatically denied it and said that no warrants would ever be applied for in his name.

On 31 March constables from Ross and Inverness, after a few drinks to fortify them, set off to clear Greenyards. They were met by the women, who protested that their landlord had given them assurances that they would not be cleared. The procurator fiscal ignored them and curtly told the police to knock down the women and get on with the job. In the nineteenth year of Queen Victoria's reign the police, armed with truncheons, set about the Ross women. A woman of fifty was beaten up by three constables, kicked on the head and kicked again on the breasts. She became completely insane.

A woman of forty was beaten to the ground and knocked senseless. A younger woman who tried to help her was driven off. She tried to hide in a bush but was kicked in the head till she crawled out. The police knelt on her breasts in order to handcuff her.

Another woman was so terribly beaten on the head that in prison it was discovered she had lost all her faculties. Yet another was beaten, knocked down and then kicked on the breasts. Her scalp was torn away, the frontal and parietal bones shattered. Marks of hobnails remained on her breasts for days afterwards.

A woman of forty-seven the mother of seven children, was clubbed to death on the spot, and a young girl was kicked savagely on the breasts and then in the crotch. An elderly man of sixty-eight, a veteran of Waterloo, who tried to help was knocked down and kicked on the ground. Two young boys were chased and attacked, and one was clubbed into insensibility.

The police, having done their work and burned down the houses, took prisoners back to Tain where they were charged with rioting and disorderly behaviour!

The whole story of the clearances fills a book. What is important is that these were *crimes*, cloaked by the authority of the law, supported and enforced by the law, committed by Scotsmen against Scotsmen, often at the instigation of other Scotsmen.

Parliament did nothing about it, although it was widely reported in the Press. All that happened was that in 1854, the year of the killing of the Ross women, a cry went up when it was learned that only three Highland regiments were fighting in the Crimea.

'Where are the Highlanders?' Parliament and country demanded.

Old William MacKay, whose wife Janet would never be flitted again, could have told them. They had been driven out of their glens and out of Scotland. Those who remained were reluctant to serve a country which treated their families as worse than vermin. The young men of Sutherland, anxious not to be considered cowards, sent an address to the newspapers in which they said: 'We have no country to fight for'. Yet, they added, they were as willing to serve queen and country as anybody in Britain, if the wrongs they and their fathers had suffered would only be redressed. They were never redressed. The whole episode was swept under the carpet, the glens remained desolate, and sheep bleated where once a proud race had spoken and sung in Gaelic.

In 1856, only two years after the slaughter of the Ross women, Harriet Beecher Stowe wrote *Sunny Memories*. She had been twice the honoured guest of the Duke and Duchess of Sutherland. Yes, the Marquess of Stafford had been rewarded for his philanthropy by being given a dukedom and was insensitive enough to take the name of a county where his own name was cursed.

In *Sunny Memories* Harriet Beecher Stowe comes hotly to the defence of her friend the 2nd Duchess of Sutherland. This was the woman who wrote *Uncle Tom's Cabin* because the plight of American Negroes had aroused her anger. Like Queen Victoria, who also visited Dunrobin but failed to see the significance of the empty glens, she could find nothing but good to say about the Duke and his Duchess.

One of the Highlanders, from the safety of Canada, responded with *Gloomy Memories*. In it he agreed that the Duchess of Sutherland would never have dreamed of doing harm to any person, any more than her mother the 1st Duchess. Nevertheless, he pointed out, it had all been done in their names and with their knowledge. The fact that they had others willing to dirty their hands in the grim work did not exonerate those who employed them.

The whole thing was quite simply about money. A man like Glengarry with a rent-roll of £5,000 could no longer live on it. The Countess of Sutherland's £15,000 a year did not satisfy her wealthy husband. 'Improving' the Highlands meant improving the rents, the yield from the land. It had nothing to do with improving the ecology and least of all with improving the lot of the people.

The end of the Highland story comes, then, in 1854, after which the Highlanders were regarded somewhat contemptuously as simpletons, when not serving in the army. Thereafter they became British, and in theory the law would protect them—the same law which evicted them.

The Highland clan was an institution. As such we are entitled to enquire sceptically if it was defensible by human reason. We are entitled to ask if it contributed to the happiness of the people and if it respected the dignity and worth of the individual. It is against these three unrelenting standards that *all* institutions must finally be judged—indeed all human behaviour.

The clan was certainly defensible on the grounds of reason, taking into account the geography of the Highlands and the time at which they flourished. The clan was the reasonable answer to time, place and the general lack of national coherence. Indeed, we have seen that Glengarry, when he did not have to worry about neighbouring clans, ceased to worry about his own clan's welfare.

The clan seems to have contributed more, rather than less, to the happiness of the people, if we make direct comparisons with the plight of cottars in the south. Much will always depend on which century is being discussed, as well as which corner of the Highlands, but overall the clan was not behind other human institutions of its time.

As for respect for individual dignity, again there seems to have been rather more than less of this. At the height of the clan system, every clansman, however humble, had his part to play in the clan's life. Others depended on him just as he did on others. The system, the institution, made this essential.

The institution was certainly not perfect. Men are not perfect, and their institutions cannot hope to be. But the clan stands up well against the institutions of the civilized, prejudiced, ignorant, supercilious and careless people who despised all things Highland—whether they were Scottish Lowlanders, foreign English or visitors from other countries.

The lasting memorial to the clans is the fact that they exist all over the world, and that Canada, Australia, the United States, South Africa and New Zealand have all benefited considerably from the infusion of Highlanders, along with other Scotsmen, into their society.

The clans are bigger by far than they ever were in the past, and they have become international. Few other British institutions of such antiquity can boast of such a remarkable continuing success.

PART TWO

The Clans

The Clans

In the clan histories which follow, every attempt is made to link them, where possible, to the mainstream of events outlined in Part One, involving the Highlanders—the Wars of Independence, the Lordship of the Isles, the Campbell-MacDonald power struggle and its effect on life in the Highlands and indeed on Scottish history, the wars of religion and the Jacobite cause. Where any interesting story from the clan tradition is known, it has been given.

It must be re-stressed that the clans which did not follow Robert Bruce were not traitors to Scotland. Bruce was a baron engaged in a fight for the vacant throne. There were other contenders and other options. The Campbells were not newcomers usurping MacDonald power by underhand tricks. The Lords of the Isles were all rebels, and it was their own ambition which brought down the wrath of the government. They were neither right nor wrong—they merely chose that way of behaviour.

Montrose is neither better nor worse than Argyle. He is different. He supported a king whom he had initially opposed. In his own way, Argyle also supported that king and crowned his son.

The Jacobites supported the rightful king in the purely hereditary sense, but that king and his children had been disqualified on religious grounds by the British Parliament.

The larger issues frequently do not divide neatly into right or wrong—which is one of history's main attractions as well as one of its more important lessons for us today. No clan is to be despised because it chose the losing side or the less romantic or less 'rightful' side. This is the story of a people in which every clan played its part.

1.   Buchanan

The progenitor of the clan was Auslan or Anselan, son of a king of Ulster, who came to Argyll in 1016 and who received from King Malcolm II the lands of Buchanan which lie on the eastern shore of Loch Lomond.

The patronymic of the chiefs was MacAuslan, and their territorial designation 'of Buchanan' was added later, and it was not till the use of surnames was imposed on the clansmen that they took the surname Buchanan from their chief, as happened so often. The name MacAuslan is, however, synonymous with Buchanan.

In 1282 Sir Maurice MacAuslan of Buchanan was confirmed in his ownership of the Buchanan lands by the Earl of Lennox. The district called Buchanan is in West Stirlingshire and was also known as Inch Caileach—the Old Woman's Island—after one of the islands in Loch Lomond. The clan's war-cry of 'Clar Innis' derives from another island in Loch Lomond belonging to them, which they received from the 1st Earl of Lennox in 1225.

The Buchanans supported Bruce during the Scottish Wars of Independence, and Bruce's son King David II confirmed the chief in his possession of all the Buchanan lands. The clan also fought with King James IV at Flodden in 1542. The chief's eldest son, Patrick, who was married to a daughter of the Earl of Argyle, fell at Flodden with many of the clansmen. They supported the Regent, Mary of Guise, at the Battle of Pinkie in 1547, when the Protector Somerset invaded Scotland, following Henry VIII's 'Rough Wooing' of 1544 and 1545.

The Buchanans were also active in the Scottish attempt to restore Charles II in 1650 and 1651, and the chief, Sir George Buchanan, was taken prisoner at the Battle of Inverkeithing. His son George was the last proprietor, and when he died in 1682, his estate was sold.

Perhaps the most amusing clan story is that of John Buchanan, younger son of Walter Buchanan of that Ilk, who was killed at Pinkie five years after his elder brother was killed at Flodden.

King James V of Scotland had the habit of going about among his people incognito, using the name of 'the Gudeman of

George IV in Highland dress by Wilkie: the King's visit to Scotland in 1822 was stagemanaged by Sir Walter Scott as though it had been a pageant

The MacNab by Raeburn

Macdonell of Glengarry, a close friend of Walter Scott

Invergarry Castle, ruined stronghold of the Macdonell of Glengarry

Dunvegan Castle in the western Highlands, home of the Clan Macleod of Macleod since 1200

Achnacarry Castle, home of Cameron of Locheil. Little now remains of the chief's wooden house, burnt by Government troops in 1746

George, 5th Duke of Gordon, chief of Clan Gordon 1827–1836, in full Highland dress as worn in the early nineteenth century, from an engraving by John Lucas after the painting by George Sanders

Loch Eck, Strathclyde

Inverary Castle. Princess Louise, fourth daughter of Victoria and Albert, lived here as Duchess of Argyll

Prince Albert in Highland dress, a preparatory study for Carl Haag's painting 'Evening at Balmoral', painted in 1853 towards the end of the Highland Clearances

The Black Watch memorial in Dunkeld Cathedral

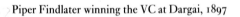

Piper Findlater winning the VC at Dargai, 1897

The thin red line at Balaclava, 1854

Scottish pipers at Brodick, Isle of Arran

Winter scene at Loch Morlich in the Cairngorms

Skiers on the northern flank of Meall a' Bhuiridh, the highest of the Black Mount peaks

Ballengeich' (i.e. the laird of Ballengeich). On one occasion when the court was at Stirling, the King sent for venison from the neighbouring hills. His men hunted and killed the deer and were taking it back to Stirling, past the gates of Arnprior Castle, when John of Arnprior saw them.

He and his men seized the venison for themselves, and when the King's servants warned him that he was stealing the King's property, he replied haughtily that, if James was King of Scotland, *he* was King in Kippen—Kippen being the name of the district around Arnprior.

The men returned to Stirling empty-handed, and the King, when he was told, at once rode to Arnprior alone. His way was barred by an armed clansman who refused to let him pass, saying that the laird was at dinner. James told him to go to the laird and tell him that the Gudeman of Ballengeich had come to dine with the King of Kippen.

Of course, when Arnprior heard, he knew that it was the King who was at his door, and he must have feared the worst; but James V had only come to give him a fright, and the affair ended amicably with the King joining the company for dinner and finally getting a meal from his own venison.

From that day onwards the Buchanans of Arnprior have been known as the Kings of Kippen.

The main line of the Buchanans of that Ilk became extinct in 1762 when the 22nd chief of Clan Buchanan died.

2.   Cameron

There can be few names more closely or gallantly identified with all things Highland (and Jacobite) than that of Cameron of Lochiel. It is a name like a flag, and it is all the more startling therefore to discover that this clan is almost certainly of Lowland origin. Sir Iain Moncreiffe of that Ilk attributes their name to a place-name in Fife, and not to the Gaelic '*cam-shron*' or 'wry nose'. The clan is believed to be a branch of the ancient and royal House of MacDuff, and the Cameron coat of arms is a differenced version of the arms of the MacDuff Earls of Fife (the vertical stripes are turned on their side to become horizontal, which was a well-known method of differencing the arms of cadets).

The original Cameron lands were in Fife and in the Carse of Gowrie and in the Lowland area of Perthshire. Sir Robert Cambron was Sheriff of Atholl in 1296, and his seat was Ballegarno Castle near Dunsinane. The earliest version of the name was Cambrun or Cambroun, and Sir John of Cambrun was a signatory of the Arbroath Declaration of 1320.

It was not till the start of the fifteenth century that the Camerons acquired their Highland lands in Lochaber when Donald Dhu, 11th of his line, married the heiress of the MacGillonies. The MacMartins of Letterfinlay were a sept of the MacGillonies, and both these clans became part of Clan Cameron.

Although Donald Dhu was the eleventh of his line, he was in fact the first *Highland chief* of Clan Cameron, as they now became. The patronymic of the Camerons of Lochiel, MacDhomnuill Dubh derives from him. In the beginning he followed the Lords of the Isles and fought for them against the King's forces at Harlaw in 1411. Later on, in 1429, the Camerons and Clan Chattan both defected from the MacDonald cause.

Ewen, the 13th chief, was the first to take the territorial designation 'of Lochiel'. The clan's war-cry, which translated is, 'Sons of the hounds come here and get flesh', is one of the most ferocious and has the double significance that they will feed their enemies' flesh to their hounds and also summon the clansmen (the 'hounds') to come and kill.

Almost from the start of their Lochaber days, the clan feuded bitterly with the MacIntosh chiefs of Clan Chattan, a feud which continued well into the seventeenth century.

In 1546 the Camerons, together with the MacDonalds, inflicted a terrible defeat on the Frasers at Kinlochlochy, in the course of which Fraser of Lovat and his son were killed along with a great number of their clansmen. The Earl of Huntly, with the help of the MacIntoshes, took prisoner the chiefs, Ewen Cameron of Lochiel and Ronald MacDonald of Keppoch. They were taken to Elgin and beheaded, and a number of their followers were hanged.

It is a clan which has provided a number of outstanding chiefs—Donald Dhu, his son Allan, but above all Sir Ewen Cameron of Lochiel who has already been subject of a portrait in Part One and who successfully defied Cromwell, among many other remarkable feats. It was his grandson Donald, Younger of Lochiel, 'the Gentle Lochiel', who made the Jacobite rising of 1745 possible and whose name shot forever associated with gallantry and loyalty to the Jacobite cause. He was shot in both ankles at Culloden and died in France, in exile, in 1748.

Perhaps one of the most interesting of the clan stories illustrates yet again the tremendous bond with existed in the Highlands between foster-brothers. It occurred at the Battle of Killiecrankie on 27 July 1689, when the Highlanders under John Graham of Claverhouse, Viscount Dundee, routed General Hugh MacKay of Scourie, the commander of William III's army in Scotland. MacKay's men were trapped in the Pass of Killiecrankie and utterly defeated.

The legendary Sir Ewen Cameron of Lochiel was present with his clan. He was aged sixty at the time, and thanks to his foster-brother he had another thirty years to live.

His foster-brother followed him everywhere in battle, as the custom was, remaining always at his side. Suddenly Lochiel missed him, and turning he saw him lying on his back, his chest pierced by an arrow. Just before he died, the faithful man told Lochiel that somebody had fired on the chief from behind. There was no time to do anything except to jump behind the chief and shield him with his own body, which he did.

General Stewart of Garth, relating the incident, makes the dry comment, 'This is a species of duty not often practised, perhaps, by an aide-de-camp of the present day'.

During the Second World War, Achnacarry, which has been the home of the Camerons of Lochiel for some centuries, became a commando training centre—very aptly perhaps in view of the fact that clan Cameron has been described graphically as 'Fiercer than Fierceness itself'.

3.   Campbell

The progenitor of this ancient Celtic clan has already been mentioned in Part One. He was Sir Colin Mor Campbell of Lochow (Cailein Mor), who was killed in 1294. The ancestor of Sir Colin seems to have been Diarmid O'Duin, and the clan's Gaelic name is Clan Duibhne. In English they are usually known as Clan Diarmid.

The surname Campbell is said to derive from a Gaelic nickname of one of their chiefs, '*cam-beul*', meaning wry or twisted mouth. The chiefs, however, are all known as MacCailein Mor, and the clan is Clan Duibhne of very ancient Celtic origin.

Their lands were and are widespread, and there are many branches of the clan, the principal among them being the Campbells of Breadalbane and the Campbells of Cawdor. The Campbells of Glenlyon were related to Rob Roy MacGregor by marriage, provided the luckless officer in charge of the massacre of Glencoe and were Jacobites in 1745 and fought against the rest of their clan at Culloden!

The chiefly lands are in Argyll, and the seat of the chiefs is Inverary Castle on Loch Fyne.

The Campbells supported Bruce in the fight for Scottish independence, and their spectacular rise over the MacDonalds is said to stem from this; but in fact the MacDonald Lords of the Isles were treacherous, and the Campbells made clever use of royal favour instead of consistently abusing and flouting it. The great Campbell-MacDonald feud certainly springs from the aftermath of Bannockburn, but the Campbell rise was certainly based on MacDonald intransigence.

The clan fought for James IV at Flodden, where the 2nd Earl was killed commanding the right wing of the Scottish army.

The 4th Earl adopted the reformed faith, but the Campbells remained constant supporters of the Stewart dynasty. The 5th Earl commanded the army of Mary, Queen of Scots, at the Battle of Langside—where he distinguished himself by fainting!

The Campbells were always to be found on the side of law and order and in support of the central authority, and few families have such an unswerving tradition of this as they do. When, during the Wars of the Covenant, the 8th Earl and 1st Marquis became one of the extreme Covenanters, he was following the same general line of conduct as Montrose—a Scots king who came in arms against his own people in order to force religion on them had to be resisted by force. The two men were briefly on the same side. Montrose later claimed that the extremists led by Argyle sought to turn the King into a puppet king by wresting his power from him and establishing a theocracy in Scotland.

Possibly this is true, for the 1st Marquis of Argyle was something very close to a religious fanatic. But it was this same Marquis who, when Charles I was beheaded in London, and Cromwell's Commonwealth was inaugurated, immediately had his son Charles II proclaimed king and who personally placed the crown on Charles II's head at this Scottish coronation at Scone. It is obvious therefore that, whatever his strong religious views, he was not opposed either to the Stuart dynasty or to the person of the King.

He was rewarded by being beheaded shortly after the Restoration—on the grounds that he had intrigued with Cromwell: grounds that were farcical. His son, the 9th Earl and 2nd Marquis, was beheaded in 1685 by Charles's brother, James II. He had supported Monmouth's rebellion but he was not beheaded for that, but for his earlier failures to take the oath of obedience to the Test Act of 1681—another religious infringement.

This 2nd Marquis had had a most romantic escape from death in December 1681, when he was condemned to death for failing to take the test. He lay in Edinburgh Castle awaiting execution. On 20 December his stepdaughter, Lady Sophia Lindsay, visited him with her page, whose head was bandaged. The Marquis and the page exchanged clothes and wigs, the Marquis donned the bandages, and Sophia left with her stepfather. The Marquis successfully escaped to Holland.

The Glencoe affair is recounted in detail in Part One but it has a curious sequel. The Campbell chieftains of Glenlyon seem to have believed that a curse lay on their family as a result of it, and the grandson of the Campbell of Glenlyon who commanded the massacre believed it implicitly.

He was an officer in the Marines, and apparently he was

ordered to execute a Marine private who had been sentenced by a court-martial. A last-minute reprieve was sent, but with provisos. The miserable private was to be led out to his execution, and only at the last minute was the order for his reprieve to be read—instead of the signal for his execution.

The wretch was led out and made to kneel blindfold before his open grave. The signal to fire was the dropping of a handkerchief. When Colonel Campbell of Glenlyon pulled the reprieve from his pocket to read it out, his handkerchief fell to the ground. The firing-party, who knew nothing about what was going on, fired, and the man was killed. Colonel Campbell retired immediately from the service, convinced that he was the victim of the curse of God and Glencoe.

The whole story of alleged Campbell infamy which has been fostered so carefully among some of the other clans is built on very bad history indeed. Of course no clan's record is spotless, and the Campbells became ruthless towards the MacGregors—but no more ruthless than the MacDonalds towards the Campbells!

Of the four great Highland clans—Campbell, MacDonald, Gordon and MacKenzie, none has a more unequivocal record of loyalty to the government of their country. That they should have supported the Protestant Stuarts after James II was deposed was inevitable given their religious convictions, their distrust of Stuart kings in all religious matters and the fact that both the 1st and 2nd Marquises had been beheaded by the Stuarts on flimsy pretexts.

Thereafter they supported the Protestant monarchy during the Jacobite rising and afterwards, and the clan has provided some of Scotland's most outstanding soldiers.

4.   Chisholm

The Chisholms are best known to many people for having convincingly spread the totally fictitious story that the only people entitled to be called THE are The King, The Pope and The Chisholm. Other clan chiefs in Scotland have used the same style (it is only a style) and some still do—and any *can*, if he is the head of a whole name. There are those (not Chisholms, obviously) who have turned the phrase into 'The King, The *Devil* and The Chisholm'! In fact, the title officially recognized at court is Chisholm of Chisholm. The chief's Gaelic patronymic is An Siosalach.

The clan is definitely of Anglo-Norman origin, and their first Scottish lands were not in the Highlands at all but on the borders in Roxburghshire and Berwickshire. They made their first appearance in the Highlands in 1359, when Robert Chisholm, a cadet of the main Roxburgh line, became Constable of Urquhart Castle on the north shore of Loch Ness not far from Inverness. His son, Alexander de Chisholm, married the Lady of Erchless, thus bringing the principal clan possession to the family, and their son Thomas, born in 1403, is commonly held to be the progenitor of the Chisholms of Strathglass.

The Border Chisholms continued their independent existence, of course, so that the name Chisholm does not necessarily indicate Highland descent at all: but it does indicate descent from the first Chisholms to come to Scotland, who were the ancestors of both the Border and Highland branches.

When Alexander de Chisholm married the heiress to Erchless and acquired, as it were, 'instant clan', it was not many generations before blood lines must have been established with the earlier clansmen in Strathglass and Glen Affric, so that, although the Chisholm chief was originally a 'stranger' in his clan, a close bond would soon have been forged in the usual Highland fashion.

Within a short time of their arrival in the Highlands, the Chisholms claimed the earldom of Caithness, but apparently the claim was abandoned in 1375. The shifting nature of Highland alliances is demonstrated by the fact that in 1513 the Chisholms assisted the MacDonalds of Glengarry in an attack on Urquhart

Castle—of which they had once been constables. In 1587, like many other clans from time to time, they had to give security to the Government for their 'peaceful' behaviour.

The Chisholms were staunch Roman Catholics, and it was therefore natural that they should have been devoted Jacobites, and the clan was out with Prince Charles in 1715 and 1745. In 1746 a Chisholm was one of the seven men who sheltered the Prince in Glenmoriston and helped him to escape from Scotland.

In the earlier chapter on the Highland Clearances, mention was made of William Chisholm, the Chisholm who began the evictions of his clansmen in Strathglass and who was bitterly commemorated in verse by his bards. The present chief of the clan, however, is not a descendant of William at all. When the old chief Alexander died in 1793, it was his brother William who succeeded him and whose line eventually failed. Alexander, however, had a daughter Mary, who married James Gooden.

This Mary Chisholm is as celebrated in the north as her uncle William was cursed. She was completely opposed to any evictions of any sort, and it was not till after her death that it was possible to complete the 'good' work of improving Strathglass and the Chisholm lands by getting rid of all the clansmen (except one, the story goes). When the main line failed, it was the Gooden-Chisholm family, descendants of Mary, who succeeded and who are present chiefs. Unfortunately Erchless Castle, the seat of the chiefs, had to be sold in 1857.

It was a great pity that Alexander Chisholm had a daughter instead of a son, and an even greater pity that she did not succeed him to the chiefship, as is the general Scottish custom. Had she succeeded instead of William, the evictions would not have taken place. The attachment of the Chisholms to Strathglass and Glen Affric was very strong, for they are among the most attractive places in the entire Highlands, and the feeling of the people thrown out to make way for sheep must have been very bitter.

Like the Frasers and Gordons, the Chisholms—although of unquestionable Anglo-Norman descent—were as Highland as anybody else. Their clans were on the clan lands before the Norman chiefs arrived, and as for the chiefs, they have seven centuries of Highland ancestry now! Curiously, most of those chiefs who were given grants of land in Scotland by David I were

Jacobites when the time came, and they are among the most widely known clan names.

5. Colquhoun

The Colquhoun lands are in Dumbartonshire on the west bank of Loch Lomond, facing the Buchanan lands on the opposite of the Loch. Their slogan or war-cry, 'Cnoc Ealachain', refers to a mountain near Rossdhu, the seat of the chiefs.

The progenitor of this clan was Humphrey Kilpatrick, who obtained a charter for the barony of Colquhoun from the Earl of Lennox early in the thirteenth century. His son Ingram styled himself 'de Colquhoun'. The origin of the word 'Colquhoun' is obscure. It has been conjecturally related to the Gaelic '*Gillen-an-con*' which means 'Keepers of the Dogs', but it was a place-name by the time the Kilpatricks adopted it as their territorial designation—as a result of which it became the clan surname.

The laird of Colquhoun supported Robert Bruce in his struggle to win the crown and free Scotland from English interference, and as a result he was confirmed in his lands and his castle of Dunglass, near Dumbarton.

In 1424 Iain Colquhoun, the 10th of Luss, became Governor of Dumbarton Castle. The story of his family motto *Si Je Puis* ('If I can') is connected with this episode. James II asked him to capture the castle, and he is said to have replied 'If I can'. He could. He used a clever ruse, setting a stag free near it and then chasing after it with his hounds. The garrison, seeing it, joined in the chase, and while the gates were open, the Colquhoun clansmen rushed them and captured the castle of the King.

The Colquhouns made themselves unpopular by resisting some of their more unruly neighbours, and Iain was finally killed when he was invited by Lachlan MacLean of Duart to a conference to settle their differences and reach some sort of peace. Iain agreed, and the various leaders met on the island of Inchmurren in Loch Lomond, in 1493, and Iain was treacherously killed.

He was succeeded by his grandson Sir John, one of the

outstanding chiefs in an outstanding family. He extended the clan possessions into Stirlingshire and acquired Rossdhu (which became the chiefly seat) and Glenmachome. He was Comptroller of the Exchequer and Sheriff Principal of Dumbartonshire, received further grants of land at Roseneath and Strone and in 1474 became the Lord High Chamberlain. He was killed at the siege of Dumbarton Castle in 1478.

The Colquhouns were always troubled by aggressive neighbours, and in particular by the MacGregors. In 1592 their territory was ravaged by MacGregors and MacFarlanes acting together. Sir Humphrey Colquhoun, 16th of Luss, had certainly given ample provocation—he was having an affair with the wife of the chief of the MacFarlanes!

He tried to eject the intruders but was beaten by them and pursued. He took refuge in Bannachra Castle, one of his possessions, but was besieged there. The legend is that a treacherous servant deliberately shone a flaring torch full on him when he was passing a loophole in the castle walls, and an archer who was waiting outside, by arrangement, saw his target lit up in the dark, fired and killed him. An alternative version is that it was his younger brother, who wanted the chiefship for himself, who shot Sir Humphrey during the confusion of the night siege.

The most widely known story of the Colquhouns is probably the affair at Glen Fruin. In 1602 the MacGregors had raided Glenfinlas and killed a number of Colquhouns and driven off some cattle. Alexander, the 17th Colquhoun chief, furious because he was given no protection against such incursions, decided to obtain letters of fire and sword against the MacGregors. He thought up a clever scheme to convince the King, and he and a number of his womenfolk presented themselves at Stirling before the King (James VI of Scotland who very soon became James I of Great Britain). The keening women each carried a blood-stained shirt, reputedly the shirt of their murdered husband.

James VI was notoriously terrified by the sight of blood (not long before he was born, his mother, Mary, Queen of Scots, had to stand by and watch Rizzio cut to pieces before her eyes, and was locked up for the night in the small chamber where it happened).

The King issued the necessary authority to Sir Alexander to rout out the MacGregors.

On 7 February 1603, when the MacGregors were again occupied with what must have been a favourite sport by now— raiding the Colquhoun territories, Alexander set out with his clan to destroy them. The MacGregors, who were assisted this time by the Camerons, apparently got word of it. They laid a trap in Glen Fruin, setting ambushes at both ends. When the Colquhoun force entered the glen, in a hurry to get through, they found their exit blocked by a strong force, and at the same time the other half of the raiding force had followed them into the glen and now fell on them from behind. They were trapped with enemies in front and at the rear, and steep slopes on either side, and were entirely routed. The slaughter is said to have been deadly, and Alexander of Colquhoun barely managed to escape with his life.

What happened to the MacGregor chief, also called Alexander, can be found in that clan's history.

The Colquhouns do not seem to have been involved in the Covenanting wars or the Jacobite risings. The chiefs have a tradition of public service dating from the Union of the Crowns in 1603. Rossdhu, on its peninsula on Loch Lomond-side, remains the seat of the chiefs—the present chiefs being descended from a younger son of James Grant of Pluscarden, who became heir to the chiefship and took the name Colquhoun.

6. Comyn (Cumming)

This is another clan of undoubted Norman descent, and the first Comyn to appear on the pages of Scotland's history was William, Chancellor to King Henry I of England, Bishop of Durham and, in 1133, Chancellor of Scotland under King David I.

This powerful figure was succeeded by his nephew and heir, Richard, who is the real founder of the Scottish Comyns—whose surname derives from Comines near Lille in France. In addition to being Lord of Northallerton in England, Richard received a grant of lands in Roxburghshire in Scotland, and he married Hexilda, the granddaughter of the Scottish King Donald III (Donald Ban, who had been deposed and blinded in 1097).

Richard's son William, who died in 1182, was the first to take the name of Comyn into the Highlands, when he married Marjory, Countess of Buchan. Thereafter the Comyns were known as the Lords of Badenoch and of Lochaber, and their power grew very quickly.

During the reign of King Alexander III, who ruled from 1249 to 1286, the Comyns acquired the earldoms of Buchan, Monteith and Atholl and the Lordship of Strathbogie. They acted as princes and made treaties, one still in existence being with Llewellyn of Wales. During this same period of their greatness, they were, from 1270 to 1308, Hereditary Constables of Scotland.

The House of Cumming of Altyre, on whom the chiefship of the clan ultimately devolved, are descended from Robert, the younger son of John, Lord of Badenoch. Robert's elder brother, John, was the famous 'Black Comyn'. He was a contender for the Scottish throne in 1290 to 1291—and when the crown went to King John Balliol, he promptly married Balliol's sister.

In this way the position of his son, another John and this time known as the 'Red Comyn', was strengthened, for he now had a double claim to the throne, and he seems to have disputed Bruce's claim, for it was he whom Robert Bruce stabbed to death in the church at Dumfries in 1306.

The Red Comyn's son, the last of his line, was killed at the Battle of Bannockburn in 1314, fighting against Bruce.

Sir Iain Moncreiffe, Scotland's leading Highland historian, has pointed out amusingly that the daughters of this last of the Comyns took the family's claim to the Scottish throne to France, when they fled there from the wrath of Robert Bruce. This eventually passed, by a series of marriages, to King Louis XIV of France! When later the exiled Stuarts, who were of course heirs to Robert Bruce, sought refuge at Louis XIV's court, they were placing themselves under the protection of the French heir to King John Balliol!

Bruce harried the Comyns ruthlessly after his own power was secure, and devastated the lands of Buchanan. Devastation in the fourteenth century was a grim and bloody affair, and the Comyns paid the price for their lord's claim to the Scottish throne. The Lordship of Badenoch passed to the MacPhersons, and the princely family disappears from Scottish history.

Not, however, the clan or the name, for to the north of
Badenoch the Comyns of Altyre (now the Cummings of Altyre)
were seemingly spared by Bruce. The family received grants of
land from Bruce's successors, kings David II and Robert II. They
flourished as a Highland clan in Morayshire up to and beyond the
end of the Jacobite era, and the present chief of the clan still lives
at Altyre.

7. Davidson

The chief's patronymic of MacDaibhidh
(MacDavid) is taken from the clan's progenitor, Black David of Invernahaven, who
was a son of one of the Clan Chattan chiefs.
The origins of the Davidsons are thus those
of Clan Chattan itself, which are very ancient
indeed and are said to go back to an early St
Catan.

The Davidsons are therefore one of the
great Clan Chattan confederation which consisted of a number of
different clans, all usually united under the MacIntoshes. The
confederation consisted of the MacIntoshes, MacPhersons,
Davidsons, Shaws, Farquharsons, MacGillivrays, MacBeans,
MacQueens, MacPhails and others.

This subordination to the MacIntoshes is undoubtedly the
reason why so many of these clans are omitted from the lists of
clans with their fighting strengths which were sent to the
Government from time to time from the seventeenth century
onwards. In some of these lists only the MacIntoshes are mentioned, and in others only the MacIntoshes, MacPhersons and
Farquharsons.

The most celebrated story of the Davidsons is that of the clan
battle which was fought on the North Inch of Perth on 23 October
1396, in front of King Robert III and his court—much as a
football match might be played in the present time!

The origins of the battle go back to a feud between the
MacPhersons and the Davidsons. During a clan battle between
the Clan Chattan, commanded by The MacIntosh, and the
Camerons, at Invernahaven in Badenoch, the MacPhersons and

the Davidsons quarrelled bitterly over who was to command the right wing of the Clan Chattan army. The MacPhersons seem to have had a better claim—at any rate in their own eyes it was better—and as a result Cluny MacPherson stood by and did not join in the battle until the Davidsons had been badly savaged by the Camerons.

For ten years thereafter the MacPhersons and the Davidsons kept their part of the Highlands in a constant state of uproar with their feuding and fighting, and it was finally decided to stage the clan battle.

Sir Walter Scott, as usual in Highland affairs, has got an entirely wrong idea of the whole thing. There was nothing chivalrous about it, nothing noble. None of the chiefs or gentry of the two clans took part at all—and it was far more in the nature of a Roman spectacle in which ordinary clansmen were turned loose on one another with the order to kill or be killed.

The teams consisted of thirty a side, and they gathered on the North Inch of Perth on the Monday before Michaelmas, in front of the King, Robert III, and his Queen, Annabella Drummond, and members of the royal court. The MacPhersons were one man short—it is said that one of them very sensibly decided to absent himself from the débâcle—and there is a story that a Perth burgher took his place for a fee. This is the story which Walter Scott has embroidered on in his account of how Henry Gow, the Perth smith, when he had killed his man, stood by and, when challenged by the leader of the MacPherson 'team' as to why he was not fighting, said he had done what he had been paid for!

The basic fact is that the Davidsons were all killed apart from one man. The story of him throwing himself into the Tay and swimming to safety may or not be true. In any event, he would have been mad to have tried to fight the nineteen surviving MacPhersons, merely to amuse the King.

The battle, which certainly took place, did not settle anything, but both the MacPhersons and the Davidsons stayed quiet for a long time afterwards, having lost a good many of their swordsmen in what was the culmination of ten years of bitter fighting. No doubt both were badly denuded of fighting men.

Robert III has the dubious distinction of being the only person in history who had a private clan battle staged for his amusement.

Today the Davidsons exist as a separate clan in their own

right. Their chief, known as Davidson of Davidson, is hereditary Keeper of the Royal Castle of Dingwall. Their ancient seat was Invernahaven of Speyside, where the clan battle against the Camerons was fought, which led eventually to the confrontation on the North Inch of Perth. The present seat of the chiefs is Tulloch Castle, near Dingwall.

8. Drummond

 The name Drummond is believed to derive from the place-name Drymen in Stirlingshire, but in fact the earliest recorded member of this clan, Malcolm Beg, who became Steward of the Lennox in 1225, is believed to have been of west Highland descent, and the clan's distant origins may therefore have been Celtic and not Hungarian, as some of the old chroniclers insist.

Malcolm Beg's eldest son used the name 'de Drummond', and the family also seems to have been called Drummond of Drymen (which is repetitious, since Drummond equates with Drymen). Malcolm de Drummond was captured twice by the English, in 1296 and 1301.

His son, the third Sir Malcolm, was one of the heroes of Bannockburn in 1314. He and his men were facing the English heavy cavalry, and a heavy cavalry charge was something foot soldiers could not survive. So he scattered caltrops on the ground in front of his men. These were iron gadgets with four arms each coming to a long, wicked point, and no matter how they were thrown, one spike was always upwards, resting on a firm tripod of the three others. This broke the heavy cavalry charge very effectively, and the feat is remembered in the coat of arms of the Earl of Perth to this day.

Bruce rewarded the Drummonds with lands in Perthshire which became their permanent home, and in 1345 the chief acquired Stobhall by marriage, which has been the chief's seat ever since. The clan was a 'frontier' clan, being half Highland and half Lowland, with possessions on both sides of the Highland Line.

The Drummond women must have been fascinating, for no fewer than three Scottish kings loved them. King David II married Margaret Drummond in 1363, and King Robert III married her niece, Annabella Drummond. A century later King James IV rejected an offer of the hand of Margaret Tudor, daughter of the English King Henry VII, because he was in love with and wanted to marry another Margaret Drummond. The unfortunate Margaret was mysteriously poisoned 'by a person or persons unknown' in 1500, and three years later the English marriage went through!

Queen Annabella's eldest brother, Sir Malcolm Drummond, was a tragic figure. He had married Lady Isabel Douglas and through her succeeded to the earldom of Mar. Alexander Stewart, son of the famous Wolf of Badenoch, wanted the Mar lands, and so he had Sir Malcolm kidnapped and kept in prison till he died of neglect and maltreatment.

Sir Malcolm's brother Sir John was Justiciar of Scotland, and in 1488 he became Lord Drummond. His younger son was executed in 1450 following an affair with the Clan Murray. The Drummonds and Murrays had been feuding, and a Murray had been unsporting enough to shoot a Drummond from a window of the church at Monzievaird. The young Drummond decided to teach the Murrays a lesson, and he and his men cornered a number of them in the church and set fire to it and burned them to death.

The 3rd Lord Drummond embraced the reformed faith, and his son, the 4th lord, became the 1st Earl of Perth in 1605, a title still held by the chief of the clan. Later on, the Earls of Perth became Dukes of Perth in the Jacobite peerage, but the dukedom remained a 'titular' one only.

The clan were attached to the Stuart cause and supported it in 1715 and 1745, the 2nd Duke commanding the cavalry at the Battle of Sheriffmuir in 1715.

When the 9th Earl died in 1692, the chiefship passed to a cousin from whom the present Earls of Perth are descended. The Earl of Perth's Gaelic patronymic is An Drumanach Mor.

9. Farquharson

The Clan Farquharson are an offshoot of the Shaws, their progenitor being Farquhar, son of Alexander Shaw, 3rd Laird of Rothie-murchus. They are, with the Shaws and others, part of the great Clan Chattan confederation, but they seem always to have been a very independent clan in their own right.

Clan Fearchar, as it was originally called, acquired Invercauld when Farquhar's son Donald married the Stewart heiress of Invercauld. Their son Finlay Mor, who was the royal standard-bearer at the Battle of Pinkie in 1547, gave his Christian name to the clan, which became known in Gaelic as Clann Fionnlaigh. The chief's Highland patronymic is still MacFionnlaigh.

The names MacKinlay and Finlayson derive from Finlay Mor, and are properly Farquharson names. The names MacErracher and MacKerracher are variations of MacFarquhar, and the Atholl Farquharsons used this form. One can see here, excellently illustrated, how, when surnames were forced on the Highlanders, there was a proliferation of names *not* indicating different clans but different versions of the clan name—Farquharson, MacFarquhar, Finlayson, Finlay, MacFinlay, MacKinley, MacErracher and so on.

The clan did not lack shrewdness, for the City of Aberdeen entered into an agreement with the Farquharson chiefs to maintain a clan 'army' of three hundred to protect the landward side of the city, in return for a payment or tribute!

The Farquharsons were one of the clans who were consistently in support of the Stuart kings. Donald Farquharson of Monaltrie joined Montrose and took part in his campaigns. The clan also took part in the unsuccessful Scottish attempt to restore Charles II in 1650–1 and fought at Inverkeithing and Worcester. Later they supported Dundee against the Covenanters and must have been among the clans who savagely defeated the Government army in the narrow pass of Killiecrankie in 1689.

The Farquharsons have the distinction of having been the first clan to muster when the standard of revolt was raised in 1715, and they fought at Preston and Sheriffmuir.

In 1745 the clan raised two battalions, one under Farquharson of Invercauld and the other under Farquharson of Balmoral. They fought at Falkirk and Culloden, although they were not with the army when it marched into England and had to turn back from Derby. The celebrated Lady Anne MacIntosh of the '45, who raised her clan while her husband Aeneas, the chief, was serving as an officer in a Government regiment, and who chased off Loudon's Regiment at the Rout of Moy, was the daughter of John Farquharson, 9th of Invercauld, by his wife Margaret Murray.

The clan lands are mainly in Aberdeenshire, although they also possessed land in Perthshire, and today the chief is perhaps best known for his association with the Royal Highland Gathering held at Balmoral every year.

The clan war-cry 'Cairn na Chuimne' is the name of a cairn of remembrance which was their rallying-point in time of war.

10. Forbes

The name Forbes is another clan-name deriving from a place—in Aberdeenshire. The clan, however, is almost certainly of Irish/Dalriadic origin, and their presence in north-eastern Scotland may have been part of the early Dalriadic policy to 'police' the Picts.

The boars' heads on the Forbes coat of arms commemorate the exploit of a distant ancestor who rid their part of Aberdeenshire of a wild boar which was terrorizing it, and their gathering-cry of 'Lonach' is the name of a hill in Strathdon, where the clan assembled in times of trouble. The March of the Forbes men at the annual Lonach Gathering is now an established part of modern Highland life.

The ancient seat of the chiefs was Druminor Castle, but later it became Castle Forbes. The present chief's seat is Balforbes near Craigievar Castle, which is another Forbes castle belonging to the Forbes chieftains who became Lords Sempill.

John of Forbes is known to have possessed the Forbes lands in Aberdeenshire as early as the reign of King William the Lion

(1165–1213). In 1236 Fergus of Forbes received a charter for these lands from the Earl of Buchan. Alexander de Forbes was made Governor of Urquhart Castle near Inverness and defended it against Edward I of England in 1304. He was forced to surrender with his garrison, but the English put every man alive to the sword after having accepted their surrender.

His son, also named Alexander, supported Robert Bruce and Bruce's son King David II. He was killed in 1332 at Duplin, fighting at King David's side.

Robert Bruce gave the family further lands in Aberdeen, and Sir Alexander de Forbes, who died in 1405, was Justiciar and Coroner of Aberdeenshire. Another Alexander Forbes, chief of the clan, became Lord Forbes around the year 1436, and he married a granddaughter of King Robert III.

The Forbeses seem to have pursued a policy not unlike that of the Argyll Campbells, in supporting law and order and the established government. In 1488 yet another Alexander, Lord Forbes, furious over the treacherous murder of King James III, who was stabbed to death by a false priest after the Battle of Sauchieburn on 11 June of that year, raised an army to revenge the King. He carried the dead King's blood-soaked shirt on the point of his spear and was only persuaded to disband his army by the direct intervention of the new King, James IV.

The principal enemies of the Forbeses seem to have been the Gordons—who were Catholic and rebellious by nature. The Forbeses had accepted the reformed faith. The 8th Lord Forbes married Lady Margaret Gordon, eldest daughter of the 4th Earl of Huntly. Their son turned Catholic and entered a religious order, and Forbes disowned his wife. This led to a clan battle in 1572 at Catt in Aberdeenshire, in which the Gordons had the better of the day, killing Lord Forbes's brother.

Lord Forbes, however, subsequently married Janet Seton of Touch, and not surprisingly in 1595 he was one of the lieutenants of the northern counties created by the King in order to suppress the 'Popish' Earls of Huntly (Gordon) and Erroll (Hay).

Thereafter the chiefs pursued the Protestant line faithfully and were opposed to Mary, Queen of Scots, and the Catholic Stuarts. Nevertheless, questions of religion and of 'rightful' kings cut across ordinary loyalties, and we find the Forbeses of Pitsligo on the Jacobite side in 1745. After Culloden their chieftain was able to remain a fugitive on Forbes lands until his death fifteen years later.

The Forbeses of Culloden produced Lord President Forbes, who exerted a powerful influence on many of the clans who were undecided which side to take in 1745. His success in keeping many of them at home, neutral, is said to have contributed considerably to the Government victory at Culloden in 1746. His name, it is nice to be able to say, was and is respected generally throughout the Highlands, even by the most hard-line Jacobites.

The chief of Clan Forbes, Lord Forbes of Forbes, is the premier baron of Scotland.

11. Fraser

The Frasers are undoubtedly of French origin, their name deriving from la Fresilière in Anjou. Three sons of this French house, which presumably followed in the wake of the Conqueror after 1066, appear in Scotland before 1160, by which year they held lands at Olivercastle in Tweeddale, Keith in East Lothian, and Touch in Stirlingshire.

The Tweeddale branch became Sheriffs of Peebles, and the head of it, Sir Alexander Fraser, Chamberlain of Scotland, was a hero of Bannockburn and married Robert Bruce's sister, who had been kept in a cage on public display by the English. From him descend the Frasers of Saltoun, now Lords Saltoun, who are counted as head of the whole name of Fraser but who are *not* the chiefs of the Highland Clan Fraser.

Sir Alexander's younger brother was the famous Sir Simon Fraser who, while fighting for Sir William Wallace, defeated the English three times in one day in 1302—a veritable Hammer of the English. He fought at Bannockburn in 1314, and Froissart says that afterwards he chased the English for three days. He was finally taken prisoner at the Battle of Halidon Hill in 1333, much to the delight of the English, who had him barbarously executed.

Sir Simon had married the heiress of John Bisset of Lovat, and his son or grandson, Hugh, is the first Fraser of Lovat and also the first MacShimi, taking his Highland patronymic from the celebrated Sir Simon. Hugh inherited from his mother both Highland lands and a Celtic Highland clan. His grandson, also named Hugh, who was Sheriff of Inverness in 1431, was raised to the peerage as the 1st Lord Lovat.

Whatever their distant origins, the Lovat Frasers became as Highland as anybody in Scotland. They also rose to prominence, the 3rd Lord Lovat, who died in 1524, being Justiciar of the North of Scotland under James IV. His son Thomas, Master (i.e. heir to the barony) of Lovat, died fighting at Flodden in 1513.

Hugh, the 4th Lord Lovat, was also Justiciar of the North, and in 1539 James V gave him a new charter, incorporating all the Lovat estates in the barony and ensuring the succession of the title through heirs of the body if heirs-male failed. (This is normal *clan* succession but not normal *peerage* succession.)

The 4th Lord Lovat's son, yet another Hugh, Master of Lovat was killed at Blar-na-Leine (the Field of the Shirts) in 1544, in the curious affair of the Clanranald 'Hen Chief' (see MacDonald of Clanranald).

The Frasers were among the clans who opposed Montrose in 1645–6, preferring to follow the MacKenzie Earls of Seaforth, but in 1650 the clan formed part of the Scottish army which opposed Cromwell and attempted to restore King Charles II.

In 1715 the clan were on the Government side under their celebrated chief Sir Simon Fraser, 11th Lord Lovat, who later became titular Duke of Fraser in the Jacobite peerage. He again supported the Government in 1719 when some Spanish troops landed in Scotland in a futile attempt to start a Jacobite rising.

In 1745 he changed his views, and his clan were mustered on the Jacobite side. Sir Simon himself was an old man, but his son, Simon, Master of Lovat, commanded the Frasers and they fought at Culloden. The young Simon was pardoned for his part in the rising, but the Government took a hard line against his father, and the old Lord Lovat (he was eighty at the time) was taken and beheaded in 1747, being the last British peer to die under the axe.

The son Simon, who had been pardoned but whose estates were forfeit, became an outstanding British general. In 1757 he was asked to raise a regiment (the 78th or Fraser's Highlanders) which saw service in North America and was with Wolfe at the storming of Quebec.

The list of officers sounds like a Jacobite roll-call, for they included John, brother of Cluny MacPherson, Donald, brother of MacDonald of Clanranald, Ronald, son of Macdonell of Keppoch, Archibald, son of Campbell of Glenlyon, Allan, son of Stewart of Invernahyle, Charles, the son of the Jacobite commander Colonel John Roy Stewart, Donald, the son of Cameron of Fassifern, plus Fraser of Inverallochy, Fraser of Struy, Fraser of Culduthel, Fraser of Balladrum and Fraser of Balnain.

The regiment was disbanded in 1763, and many of the men decided to stay in North America as settlers and were given grants of land. In 1775 Simon Fraser was asked a second time to raise a regiment for service in North America, and so Fraser's Highlanders were recreated as the 71st Regiment of Foot. In addition to its chiefly colonel, its roll of officers included Duncan MacPherson of Cluny, Duncan Chisholm of Chisholm, Norman MacLeod of MacLeod, Charles Cameron of Lochiel, Lamont of Lamont, and Aeneas MacIntosh of MacIntosh, all clan chiefs, and the two sons of Lord Nairne, William and John (William later succeeding to his father's title).

The 71st was disbanded in 1783. Simon Fraser became a major-general in 1771 and was allowed to purchase back his forfeited family estates in the neighbourhood of Beauly. He died in 1782.

The military tradition has remained strong among the Frasers. The 16th Lord Lovat raised the Lovat Scouts from among his clansmen and employees, for service in the Boer War and in the First World War. His son the 17th Lord Lovat and 22nd MacShimi, re-raised the regiment as a commando battalion which he commanded with distinction in the Second World War.

12. Gordon

The names of both Gordon and Huntly are Berwickshire place-names, and the first members of this family to come to Scotland were Anglo-Norman. The Sir Adam Gordon who was the first to obtain lands at Strathbogie in the Highlands was originally a supporter of John the 'Red Comyn', whom Bruce stabbed to death in church. Thereafter Sir Adam supported Edward I against Bruce until the English stupidly devastated his lands and even put him in prison for a time. When he came out, he joined Bruce and fought at Bannockburn. Thereafter he had the great distinction of being chosen as Scotland's ambassador to Rome to carry the Arbroath Declaration of Independence to the Pope. Bruce rewarded him with enormous tracts of land in the north, and he was killed at Halidon Hill in 1333.

His great-grandson was killed at Homildon in 1402 also in the service of the Scottish king.

The nickname of 'Gay Gordons' does not mean that they were frivolous or light-hearted but derives from 'Gey', meaning 'head-strong' and 'reckless'. Nevertheless, they have acquired a reputation for light-hearted gallantry that is enviable.

For a time the Highlands were policed for the king by the Campbells in the west and the Gordons in the north, and it may be from this that the Gordon chiefs are known as 'Cocks o' the North'.

Alexander, the son of Elizabeth Gordon, was created Earl of Huntly in 1449, the 6th Earl, George, was created Marquis of Huntly in 1599, and the 4th Marquis became Duke of Gordon in 1684. The dukedom lapsed when the 5th Duke died without issue in 1836, and the present clan chiefs are Marquises of Huntly and descendants of the Earls of Aboyne on whom the chiefship devolved after 1836.

Such a powerful clan played its important part in Scottish national affairs. The Gordons fought at Flodden, and afterwards, during the minority of James V, they and the Campbells held the other clans in check—not without building up a good many enmities in the process!

The Gordons were eager to serve Mary, Queen of Scots, but, being hot-headed Catholics, they could not help becoming embroiled with the unlovely group of Scottish nobles known as the Lords of the Congregation. Mary had to play a deep political game, and the Gordons never understood fully why she treated them as she did. They were branded as rebels, and Mary herself took an army against them, and in the inevitable battle which followed, the Earl of Huntly died of a stroke, while his unfortunate son was captured and beheaded in the Queen's presence.

In 1592 the Gordons murdered the 'Bonnie' Earl of Moray, son-in-law of the Regent Moray, who was shot by a Hamilton laird in 1570. It was James VI himself who sent Huntly to 'arrest' the Bonnie Earl, knowing full well that Huntly and Moray were deadly enemies. Evidently Huntly decided against bringing his prisoner back alive. The Gordons cornered him in a house and set fire to it, and when Moray rushed out with his hair in flames, they stabbed him to death. Huntly is said to have struck first, slashing his face, and Moray, according to popular legend, told him as he lay dying, 'Ye have spoiled a bonnier face than your ain'.

The Lords of the Congregation were not the sort to endure Huntly and his friends meekly. They alleged a conspiracy between the Spanish government and the Earls of Huntly, Erroll and Angus, aimed at overthrowing the Protestant monarchy and government.

James was persuaded to send an expedition against the Catholic earls in 1594 and ordered the 7th Earl of Argyle north with an army to bring Huntly to trial for having murdered Moray. Argyle raised a Highland force which included the Earl of Atholl's men, Sir Lauchlan MacLean and his clan, MacIntoshes, Grants, MacGregors, MacNeils of Barra, his own Campbells and some of the western clans. On 27 September they attempted the siege of Ruthven Castle, but it failed thanks to the MacPhersons who defended it.

In October Huntly, with a very much smaller force, gave battle to Argyle and his army at Glenlivet. It is said that he knew some of Argyle's army planned treachery. In any event, Argyle evidently thought Huntly had lost his senses, and he refused advice to wait for reinforcement of Frasers, MacKenzies, Forbeses and others.

Huntly's cavalry were commanded by the Earl of Erroll, Gordon of Auchindun and Gordon of Gight. The MacPhersons held the right wing, and Huntly himself the centre. There is a story that Campbell of Lochnell planned to change sides when the battle started and had arranged secretly that Huntly would use his three pieces of field artillery to fire at Argyle's standard, whereupon Lochnell would desert the King's army. He was, needless to say, Argyle's nearest heir! The plan miscarried, for the opening salvo of cannon killed not Argyle but Lochnell himself.

It was a hotly contested battle, the MacLeans putting up a remarkable fight against the cavalry. It was Argyle himself who finally called the retreat when the Gartinbeg Grants and the Lochnell Campbells deserted, weakening his left and centre.

James VI prudently decided to forgive Huntly, confirmed him, Erroll and Angus in their honours and shortly afterwards created Huntly a marquis.

When the first Bishop's War broke out, Montrose commanded the Covenant army and defeated Lord Aboyne and the Gordons at Bridge of Dee in 1639. Later, when Montrose refused to fight for the second Covenant (the Solemn League and Covenant) and fought instead for the King, the Gordons under Lord Lewis Gordon were among the flower of his Highland army—but Huntly himself never became reconciled to Montrose.

The Duke of Gordon, as he had now become, was not 'out' in 1745, but his clan were and provided two regiments which fought for Prince Charles at Culloden.

Later, in 1794, the 4th Duke of Gordon raised the Gordon Highlanders, and his beautiful wife Jane is said to have whipped up recruiting by giving every recruit a kiss along with his guinea bounty when he joined up—a story in the best Gordon high tradition.

There had been an earlier Duke of Gordon's Highlanders, the old 89th Regiment, which was raised in 1759 and served in India until it was disbanded in 1765. Later the Gordon Highlanders served with much distinction in India and their name is still remembered with respect on the North-West Frontier.

Perhaps the best Gordon story is the one about the minister of Alvie, who was summoned to appear before the Duke of Cumberland to explain his conduct in sheltering Highland rebels. Cumberland did not like Scotsmen and detested Highlanders, no matter which side they had fought on. Undismayed, the intrepid *Gordonach* man of God turned up armed with a broadsword and pistols. Believing that attack is the best defence, he promptly demanded of Cumberland whether he, the minister, was to serve his heavenly king or his earthly one! He then proceeded to plead for leniency for the defeated Jacobites, a plea which unfortunately fell on deaf ears—but the whole story is a typical piece of Gordon daring.

13.　Graham

The origin of the name Graham has been variously attributed to the Gaelic '*Grumach*' ('a stern person'), the old British word '*Grym*' ('strength') from which the Antonine Wall became nicknamed Grime's Dyke, and an English manor, Graegham (Grey Home), which is mentioned in the Domesday Book!

The Grahams, however, were Anglo-Norman barons, wherever their name came from and the earliest of whom any definite account is known was William de Graham, a companion of King David I, who witnessed a royal charter to the monks of Holyrood in 1128 and who received the lands of Abercorn and Dalkeith in Midlothian from the King.

Henry de Graham married the daughter of Roger Avenel (who died in 1243) and so acquired the Avenel estates in Eskdale. Sir David de Graham, Sheriff of Berwick, acquired the lands of Kincardine from Malise, Earl of Strathearn. He died in 1270, and his son, Sir John Graham, was a friend of Sir William Wallace, fought for him and was killed at Falkirk in 1298.

Sir Patrick Graham of Kincardine was killed at Dunbar 28 April 1296, carrying the King's banner into battle against the English, and his brother Sir David de Graham of Kincardine was a devoted follower of Robert Bruce. In 1325 he received the lordships of Kinnaber and Montrose, from which later district the Grahams took their peerage titles. Sir David died in 1327.

His great-grandson Sir William Graham of Kincardine was greatly in favour with King James I, as the result of having led the negotiations with the English to obtain the King's liberty in 1423. The English had held him hostage from the age of eleven till he was twenty-nine, frequently shutting him up in the Tower of London, and coolly charged 60,000 merks for his board and lodging before they would release him!

Sir William's second wife was the Princess Mary Stewart, second daughter of King Robert II, the first Stewart king, who died in 1390 aged seventy-four. From a younger son of his royal marriage descended Graham of Claverhouse ('Bonnie Dundee') who, as Viscount Dundee, led the troops of James VII (James II of Great Britain) and who died tragically at the Battle of Killie-crankie in 1689.

Patrick Graham of Kincardine was created a peer of Parlia-ment as Lord Graham in 1455. William, the 3rd Lord Graham, was created Earl of Montrose in 1504, his title being taken from the lands of Auld Montrose which were erected into a free barony and earldom. The title is not taken from the town of Montrose on the coast. William, like so many of the leading Scottish nobility, was killed at Flodden in 1513.

It was James Graham, the 5th Earl and 20th in direct descent from King David's old companion Sir William de Graham, who was created Marquis of Montrose in 1644, who was the cele-brated 'Montrose' of Scottish history and who has been discussed in detail in Part One of this book. Although the Marquis of Argyle was his bitter foe and was among the Covenanting leaders who had Montrose executed, both men came from families who had always supported law and order and a strong central authority and who had supported Bruce and the later Stewart Kings. Curiously they were both staunch Presbyterians all their lives!

The 'Great Marquis' overshadows all others, but it was a cruel twist of fate when John Graham of Claverhouse was killed in the very moment of victory at Killiecrankie, for had he lived, he might have accomplished as much as his famous relative, and the path of British history would have followed a different road.

There is an amusing story about one of the Graham septs, the Grahams of Menteith, who became known as '*Gramoch an Geric*' ('the Grahams of the Hens'). In 1547 a party of Stewarts, retreat-ing from the defeat at Pinkie, came to the house of the Earl of Menteith, where a marriage feast was being prepared which consisted mainly of poultry. The Stewarts broke up the party, grabbed all the food and made off with it. They were pursued by furious Grahams, but in a gorge at Wolf's Cliff the Earl of

Monteith and most of his followers were killed while the leader of the Stewarts made his escape.

The Grahams were among that very prominent handful of 'frontier' clans who held the marches between Highlands and Lowlands and who usually had possessions on both sides of the Highland Line. Certainly they had little in common with the more remote west Highland clans; yet it was their Highland connection which served Montrose so well, for the Highlanders followed him as they had never followed any other military leader. The same was true too of Claverhouse. Indeed, the Grahams provided two of the only three military commanders who were able to command the respect of the Highlanders, the third one being Lord George Murray whom Bonnie Prince Charlie was stupid enough to ignore during the '45. Had he listened to Lord George, Culloden would never have happened.

In 1782 the Grahams again acquired permanent Highland fame and admiration, for in that year the Duke of Montrose, supported by General Simon Fraser of Lovat, succeeded in having repealed the Act of Parliament of 1747 which made it illegal to wear Highland dress.

14. Grant

Despite efforts to show that the Grants are Anglo-Norman (because of the similarity between Grant and le Grand) the Grants are part of the Siol Alpin. The Siol Alpin is the subject of Appendix I and consisted of seven Highland clans whose chiefs were all closely descended from King Alpin, father of Kenneth MacAlpin, first King of Picts and Scots. These seven clans all wear the same plant-badge, the pine, and share a very strong clan oral tradition about their origins.

The Grants are said to descend from Gregor Mor MacGregor who lived in the twelfth century. Their clan lands were in Strathspey, and the name Grant may derive from a moor called Griantach, which would explain the early surname of de Grant which so many earlier historians tried to relate to the le Grands of Anglo-Norman England!

The first recorded Grant is Gregory de Grant who was Sheriff of Inverness in the reign of Alexander II (1214–49). Gregory married a daughter of Bisset of Lovat (the clansmen of Lovat were Bissets before the Frasers became their chiefs and gave them the Fraser surname).

Gregory's son, Sir Lawrence de Grant, obtained lands in Strathspey by marriage, and his son, Sir John, supported both Wallace and Bruce against the English.

The Grants feuded with the Gordons, who may well have been jealous of the rising importance of this clan, which reached its zenith in 1694 when their barony of Freuchie was made into a 'regality'.

This was a considerable honour and meant that the Grants legally ruled over what was in effect their own kingdom—subordinate only to the Crown but in most day-to-day affairs entirely independent. Sir Iain Moncreiffe has described it as 'Home Rule for the Grants', which in fact it was, the chief ruling through a council exactly as the king in council did. Not only did he have powers of punishment, but he was allowed to regulate his own weights and measures. The regality lasted until after Culloden when the Government in London abolished it.

The Grants were adherents of Mary, Queen of Scots, and the clan fought with Montrose as well as for James VII at Killie-crankie and Cromdale. In 1715 and in 1745, although the chief of the clan was not 'out', the Grants of Glenmoriston fought for the Stuarts and provided a considerable clan army of about eight hundred on both occasions.

The chiefs of Clan Grant are Lords Strathspey. In 1633 the lordship was to have been advanced to an earldom, but the chief died before the warrant could be signed, and the earldom never came to pass.

Clan Grant is subdivided into a number of branches which often pursued quite separate and independent policies, when it suited them. The chiefly branch is Freuchie, but other important branches were Glenmoriston, Ballindalloch, Tullochgorum, Monymusk and Dalvey.

The clan's slogan 'Stand Fast Craigellachie' refers to the clan's rallying-place, a projecting rock on a hillside in Rothiemurchus.

15.   Gunn

The Gunns are of Norse descent, and the progenitor from whom they take their name was Guin or Gunni, the second son of Olav the Black, the Norwegian King of Man and the Isles, who died in 1237. Another tradition places Guin a century earlier as the son of Olav who lived in the Orkneys. The clan has an early connection with the Orkneys as well as with Norway. Their clan lands were always in the far north of Scotland, where they were hemmed in by larger neighbours, the Sinclairs, Sutherlands and MacKays.

It is hardly surprising that the Gunns acquired the reputation of being aggressive and warlike, being described sometimes as the northern counterparts of the MacGregors.

The traditional enemies of this clan of Gunns, descended from the ancient Norse sea-kings, were the Keiths, a prominent Celtic family belonging within the Clan Chattan confederation. The Gunns and Keiths quarrelled over land for centuries, but of course the Gunns were usually embroiled with one or other of the three great clans who were their neighbours, the Sutherlands, the Sinclairs and the MacKays. They were frequently beaten in battle by more powerful armies, but nobody ever succeeded in keeping them down! They were what in modern terms would be termed 'survivors'—against heavy odds.

As early as 1438 the Keiths and MacKays forced the Gunns to battle near Wick and defeated them. Again in 1464 the Keiths overcame them at Dirlot. At this time the Gunn chief was a prominent figure in Caithness, George Gunn the Coroner of Caithness. His nickname was '*Am Braisteach Mor*' because of a great silver badge of office which he wore as a plaid brooch. George Gunn and George Keith of Ackergill decided to settle their disputes for once and all on the outcome of a twelve-a-side cavalry battle. This is quite unlike the clan battle fought at the

North Inch of Perth which was a spectacle for king and court and in which no chiefs or chieftains took part.

The Gunns and Keiths turned up to the contest led by their chiefs, who were accompanied by their sons. The Keiths played a dirty trick, mounting two men on a horse, and inevitably they had the better of the battle, killing George Gunn and many of his followers. Some of George Gunn's sons survived, however, and followed the few remaining Keiths to Dalraid, where they killed George Keith of Ackergill and made their escape.

It was George's son James, who succeeded him as chief, who gave to the Gunn chiefs their Gaelic patronymic of MacSeumas Chataich.

In 1517 the Gunns took part in the Battle of Torran Dubh, which was the result of a dispute between the MacKays and the Sutherlands, and in which the Gunns particularly distinguished themselves.

Later in the same century there appears to have been a serious attempt to 'liquidate' the Gunns entirely, their enemies in this case being a branch of the Clan MacKay which acted independently of the MacKay chief who was brother-in-law to the Gunn chief. The Caithness Sinclairs and the Sutherlands became involved, and in 1586 the Gunns inflicted a decisive defeat on the Sinclairs, assisted by some of the chief of MacKay's men.

This complicated feuding went on for years, with considerable loss of lives all round, but Gunns survived it all, holding on to their clan lands which were a buffer state between Sinclairs to the north and Sutherlands to the south.

It was not surprising that, in their geographical position and engaged in a continual struggle for survival, the Gunns did not play any notable part in national affairs. In 1745 a few Gunns joined the Earls of Loudoun on the Government side, but the clan cannot truly be said to have been involved in the Jacobite risings.

The early seat of the Gunn chiefs was Hallburg, but later on it became Killearnan Castle, and the chiefs used the designation Gunn of Killearnan. Killearnan was destroyed by fire in 1690.

16. Lamont (Lamond)

The Lamonts were not only the original pro-prietors of Cowal but were almost certainly descended from ancient Irish kings. The founder of the clan is usually described as Fearchar who must have been born about the end of the twelfth century, as his sons Malcolm and Duncan were alive in 1238 and granting charters. Tradition has it that Fearchar was descended from Lachlan, son of Rory the Lord of Bute.

Laomainn, who gave the clan his name, was the son of Malcolm and the grandson of Fearchar. Prior to his time the clan were known as MacFarquhar or MacKerracher—names which are now associated with the Aberdeenshire Farquharsons who have no connection whatever with the Lamonts. The chiefly title was Lamont of Inveryne, and later Lamont of Lamont, and at least one of their chiefs, perhaps John Lamont who was the Baillie of Cowall in 1456, was known as 'the Great Lamont of all Cowall'.

The clan, according to the historian Skene, were able to prove their ancestry by charters at a very early time when most chiefly genealogies were based on the oral tradition of the bards. Oral traditions are not at all less accurate for being oral—rather the opposite—but the early use of charters is unusual.

The Lamont castles were Ascog and Toward, at which latter castle the chief of the clan, Sir John Lamont, entertained Mary, Queen of Scots. The clan also has an interesting connection with a much celebrated castle—Glamis. According to Sir Iain Moncrieffe of that Ilk, Sir John Lyon, who became Thane of Glamis in 1372, was a descendant of the Clan Lamont chiefs. The Lamont arms were a silver lion on a blue shield, and the descen-dants of Sir John Lyon bore a blue lion on a silver shield, a reversal of colours which was a well-known way of indicating a cadet or junior House. It seems probable therefore that HM Queen Elizabeth the Queen Mother and her descendants are Lamont descendants.

The story has been told in Part One of the Lamont chief who claimed the hospitality of Alexander MacGregor of Glenstrae, after having killed his son in an argument. Glenstrae gave him protection from his own furious clansmen and escorted him safely home to Cowal. Later the Lamonts repaid this punctilious observance of the sacred laws of hospitality by sheltering the MacGregors when they were outlaws and their name was proscribed by Act of Parliament.

The Lamont possessions, which were considerable and included a large part of Argyll, were encroached on by the Bute Stewarts, the MacLauchlans and the Campbells, all of whom acquired Lamont lands by marriage ties with the great family of the chiefs of Cowal.

Tragedy struck the clan in 1646. Sir James Lamont of Lamont, who was a Royalist supporter during the conflict between King Charles I and the Scottish Covenanters, joined Sir Alasdair MacDonald (Colkitto) and his MacDonald and Irish followers in raiding Campbell territory. Apparently the MacDonalds and their Irish kinsmen were brutally savage in settling old scores with the Campbells. The Lamonts, of course, were implicated, and eventually Sir Colin Campbell of Ardkinglass forced Sir James Lamont of Lamont to surrender Ascog and Toward Castles.

The Campbells, having seemingly granted terms to the Lamonts, then paid off the score of atrocities which had been committed on Campbell lands by massacring over two hundred Lamonts including women and children, in the most blood-curdling fashion. Ascog and Toward were reduced to ruins, and the Lamont lands were 'devastated' in the same way as Robert Bruce, three centuries earlier, had devastated the Buchan lands.

It was obviously not a wise thing to become involved in the age-old MacDonald-Campbell feud, and the Lamonts paid heavily for joining forces with the wild Irish. The Lamont power never recovered from the massacre, which is commemorated by a Celtic memorial stone at Dunoon. Their power in Cowal was broken and their possessions were reduced, and thereafter the chief had his seat at Ardlamont.

17. MacAlister

The MacAlisters (the name can be spelled in a number of ways) are the descendants of Alisdair, the younger son of Donald of Islay, the first Lord of the Isles. He supported Bruce in his struggle and was killed in 1299.

The clan originally inhabited Knapdale where their chiefs were Constables of Tarbet Castle. After the forfeiture of the Lordship of the Isles, to whom the MacAlisters were a vassal clan, they became totally independent under their own chiefs, and the chief's seat was at Ardpatrick in South Knapdale.

In 1481 Charles MacAlister was Steward of Kintyre, an office of great local importance, and Iain Dubh, who was the chief of the clan in 1493, gave the subsequent MacAlister chiefs their patronymic of MacIain Dubh.

In 1587 James VI passed an Act called 'the Black Band' which made the clan chiefs directly responsible to the Government for the peaceful behaviour of their clansmen and the 'broken men' (chiefless men) who had attached themselves to the clan for protection. One of the chiefs mentioned in the Act was Alexander MacAlister of the Loup, so that obviously by this date the chiefs had adopted the style which remains the chiefly title. There are cadet branches of MacAlester of Tarbet and MacAlister of Glenbarr.

In 1618 the Laird of the Loup is named among the principal nobility of Argyll and made responsible for the government of the county during the absence of the 8th Earl (later 1st Marquis). This MacAlister chief, Godfrey, married a daughter of Campbell of Kilkerry, and because of his connection with the Campbells he took no part in the wars of religion, although his clan joined Montrose.

Alexander MacAlister of the Loup took the side of the exiled King James VII and was present at the Battles of Killiecrankie and the Boyne, fighting on the Stuart side. His younger son Charles, who eventually succeeded to the chiefship, was married to the daughter of the Lamont of Lamont.

Field Marshal Earl Alexander, who won fame in the desert campaign of the Second World War, is said to belong to a family of Alexanders descended from the MacAlisters and so, through them, was descended from Somerled, King of the Isles, the common ancestor of both the MacDonalds and the MacAlisters.

18. MacArthur

The antiquity of this ancient clan from Loch Awe is enshrined in the old Gaelic verse which, translated, runs:

> The hills and streams and MacAlpin—
> But whence came forth MacArthur?

meaning that the MacArthur origins are lost in antiquity and, more important, that they were always there—i.e. that they were believed to be original settlers on their land.

The clan is claimed by some to be the senior branch of the great Campbell clan, Arthur being the elder brother of Sir Colin Campbell of Lochow, the Campbell progenitor. Certainly they were closely linked with the Campbells. There is, however, a counter-theory that there were two distinct MacArthur clans, the MacArthurs of Loch Awe who were the 'ancient' Clan MacArthur, and the MacArthur Campbells of Strachur, a Campbell branch clan who disputed the leadership of the clan with the 'Sons of Colin'—i.e. the present Campbell line of chiefs.

Whatever the truth of the exact early relationship with the Campbells, we are here plainly dealing with some of the oldest known settlers in the west Highlands. Their supposed descent from King Arthur Pendragon and his knights of the round table is largely fanciful, and the probable fact is that both the Campbells and the MacArthurs are descended from original settlers whose blood was fused with that of the Irish-Celtic invaders who established the old kingdom of Dalriada at the start of the sixth century.

The MacArthurs supported Bruce (as did Sir Colin Campbell of Lochow), were rewarded with the estates of the MacDougalls and were made Captains of Dunstaffnage Castle. Subsequently the MacDougalls got back most of their lands, and the Campbells became proprietors of the Loch Awe estates and Captains of Dunstaffnage following the breaking of the MacArthur power.

The clan flourished until 1427, when King James I had the chief, Iain MacArthur beheaded and deprived that family of their lands, thereby turning the clansmen into 'broken men'. At the time of his execution Iain was described as a 'prince' who could bring a thousand warriors into battle, which gives some idea of the MacArthur importance at the height of their power. It is more than probable that jealousy played a part in their downfall, and since the Campbells were the main clan to benefit by it, obtaining the MacArthur lands, it seems probable that they were glad to be rid of a clan which claimed to be senior to their own.

After the dispersion of the clan, the family of the beheaded chief finally obtained lands at Strachur in Cowal, and from that time on the chiefs of the clan were called MacArthur of Strachur.

The clan also possessed lands in Glenfalloch and Glendochart, but it ceased to function as a distinct clan under its hereditary chiefs, and the great tragedy of the MacArthurs is their disappearance from clan history, following the forfeiture of their estates.

Indeed, there is a great deal of mystery about the early history of the MacArthurs, who were princes, and the most haunting clan slogan of all is perhaps theirs: '*Eisd, O Eisd* . . . Listen, oh listen'.

19. MacAulay

The origins of the MacAulays are discussed more fully in Appendix I, for they are part of the Siol Alpin 'family' of seven clans, being an offshoot of the MacGregors, as the MacAulay bonds of manrent of 1591 and 1694 explicitly state.

The clan's seat from early times was Ardincaple in Dumbartonshire, and many of the early clan historians found difficulty in reconciling the clan's claims to MacGregor (and thus Alpinian) descent with its connections with the Earls of Lennox. The two things are by no means irreconcilable, for the MacAulays were always vassals of the Earls of Lennox (other Alpinian clans were vassal clans of the Lords of the Isles) and were probably related to them by marriage.

The son of Aulay de Ardincaple, who lived during the reign of James V (1513–42), was Alexander de Ardincaple and seems to have been the first to assume the surname 'Mac Aulay', which subsequent chiefs used instead of 'de Ardincaple'. There is a theory that the name Aulay is a version of the Norse 'Olla' and that the MacAulays are therefore linked at an early time with Dunolly Castle in Argyllshire which is the MacDougall seat.

Sir Aulay MacAulay, who died in 1617, started the gradual decline of the family. He and his successors lived in great extravagance, and bit by bit they had to sell their possessions to keep up their style of living.

In 1689 the MacAulay chief raised a fencible regiment in support of William and Mary, so they do not seem to have had any enthusiasm for the Stuart cause. The 12th chief, Aulay MacAulay, sold the last of the clan lands and died in 1767 'having seen the patrimony of his house sold, and his castle roofless'. Ardincaple had been sold to the 4th Duke of Argyll.

There was an entirely separate clan by the same name of MacAulay in Lewis, descended from Olav the Black, the brother of Magnus, last King of Man and the Isles. This Hebridean clan has apparently no connection at all with any of the Siol Alpin clans, and certainly none with the MacGregors from whom the Ardincaple MacAulays were descended. They were settled at Uig in Lewis and followed the Lewis MacLeods, frequently feuding with the Morrisons. A branch of this clan lived on the mainland and followed the MacKenzie Earls of Seaforth.

The name Aulay MacAulay seems to have been popular with them too, for there was a minister in Harris by that name, whose father, '*Fear Bhreinis*', 'the Man of Brenish', was renowned for his feats of strength and who was the subject of many songs and stories.

This Reverend Aulay MacAulay was the great-grandfather of the famous historian Thomas Babbington MacAulay, Lord MacAulay.

20. MacBain

The MacBains or MacBeans were a branch of Clan Chattan, and the Gaelic version of their name, MacBeathain, suggests that they were members of the same clan as the MacBeths. Little is known of their early history except that they probably inhabited Lochaber before migrating to eastern Inverness to join the MacIntosh chiefs—which explains why the name MacBeth is to be found among the followers of the MacDonalds and the MacLeans, both western clans, and why some of the MacBeans fought under Lochiel at the Battle of Culloden.

At one time the MacBeans were a numerous clan, and their chiefs took the style MacBean of Kinchoil or Kinchyle. One of their chiefs obtained a charter for the Kinchyle lands from Campbell of Cawdor in 1609.

Of the clan's early history, tradition says that a MacBean and his four sons killed the Steward of the Red Comyn—the celebrated John Comyn, stabbed to death in a church by Robert Bruce in 1306. The MacBeans were evidently on Bruce's side. On 24 July 1411 the clan fought at the Battle of Harlaw, when Donald, Lord of the Isles, with the western clans, swept down on Dingwall and then thrust along the Lowland plain bordering the sea till he almost reached Aberdeen. There he was successfully halted by Duncan Stewart, the Earl of Mar. Although the battle is usually depicted as undecisive, effectively the western clans were defeated, for next morning they had all gone home either with booty or else to lick their wounds, and Aberdeen was spared. At this battle the MacBeans fought with the rest of Clan Chattan, in support of the MacDonalds, and greatly distinguished themselves, suffering heavy losses.

Most of the MacBean stories, however, concern the Battle of Culloden, where once again they distinguished themselves. The most celebrated warrior in this battle must undoubtedly have been Golice or Gillies MacBean of Kinchyle, a giant of a man, six feet four in height, who was a major in the MacIntosh battalion.

After the battle he was set on by a troop of dragoons and, being alone, put his back to a wall and defended himself with his broadsword. He cut down and killed thirteen or fourteen dragoons in a desperate hand-to-hand encounter and wounded others, and an officer of Cumberland's army, seeing his bravery, called to the dragoons to spare him. Unfortunately it was too late for, covered in wounds, Gillies MacBean fell dead.

James Logan also tells of another Gillies MacBean at Culloden who served under the banner of Lochiel. When Cameron of Lochiel fell wounded in both ankles, Gillies helped him to escape from the battlefield and was instrumental in sending the Cameron chief to safety, from which he eventually made his way to France where he died about two years later.

Yet another of the clan, Aeneas MacBean, also pursued by dragoons after the battle, saved himself by his agility. He ran along the banks of a stream, and every time the dragoons got too close, he leaped over it. The dragoons followed and then Aeneas would leap back, and in this hair-raising zigzag fashion he finally shook off the pursuit and escaped.

Later, after the power of the chiefs was broken and the Highlanders found an outlet for their energies in the British Army, one of the clan, William MacBean, succeeded in performing the extremely rare feat of rising from the rank of private soldier in the 93rd Sutherland Highlanders to become a major-general. He won the Victoria Cross at Lucknow in 1858.

While much of the MacBean history is that of Clan Chattan itself, the clan always enjoyed a reputation for great bravery and skill at arms, a reputation which it seems they richly earned.

21. MacDonald

At one time the greatest and most numerous of all the clans, the MacDonalds, had it not been for the incredible foolishness of all four Lords of the Isles in challenging the power of the Scottish kings, might easily have been princes or sub-kings of a virtually independent west Highland state. The Lordship of the Isles has been discussed at some length in Part One. Here it is necessary to study the clan in its various branches.

MacDonald—Clan Donald

The senior branch of the great MacDonald confederation is the main stem of the great race of Somerled and takes its name from Donald of Islay, son of Reginald King of the Isles, whose father was Somerled, Lord of Argyll. Somerled who was killed in 1164 had married Princess Ragnhildis, the daughter of a Norwegian King of the Isles, and was the real founder of the clan's power.

The clan has the distinction of being commanded by a *high* chief, and its chieftains rank as clan chiefs in their own right, although they were subordinate to their high chief.

The early history of the main branch is that of the Lordship of the Isles itself. After the forfeiture of the lordship, the chiefship devolved on Hugh of Sleat, from whose name the MacDonalds of Sleat take the name Clan Huisdean. It was the chief of this Clan Huisdean, in Skye, who was MacDonald of MacDonald in 1745 and who understandably refused to support Prince Charles, who had arrived in the Highlands empty-handed, having been frequently advised not to attempt any sort of rising without considerable support in the form of French troops, arms and money.

Subsequently the chiefship of Sleat became separated from the high chiefship of Clan Donald, the former becoming baronets of Sleat and the latter Lords MacDonald and chiefs of the whole name of MacDonald.

Despite their early rebellious nature when they were Lords of the Isles, the MacDonalds subsequently became supporters of the Stuart cause during the wars of religion and the Jacobite risings. They were always, of course, to be found in opposite to the Campbells, who had profited enormously from earlier MacDonald indiscretions and who had become a challenging power.

Before the Lordship was forfeited, many of the western and island clans were followers of the MacDonald high chiefs and were in fact vassal clans, among them being MacLean, MacKinnon, Cameron, MacNeil and MacLeod, and even clans from the east such as Clan Chattan, the MacKenzies and the Rosses were often MacDonald supporters. When the MacDonald power was curtailed, and with it all chance of Home Rule for the Highlands perished, these clans naturally pursued their own independent ways under their own chiefs, but although they were no longer subservient to the MacDonalds, they frequently allied themselves with them.

The great Celtic dream of glory, of a return to their former greatness of the days when the Dalriadic kings were the rulers of Scotland and lived in the Highlands, died with the MacDonald downfall. It is by no means safe to assume that Scotland in general or the Highlands in particular gained by this downfall. If two states had existed side by side in Scotland and had become merged by marriage, as would almost certainly have happened, it is possible that centuries of bloodshed might have been avoided. One can only speculate—but the MacDonald power put to proper use could have been a most powerful influence for peace and stability. One can only regret that it was not.

MacDonald of Glencoe

This small clan would appear to be the senior of the branch clans, since its descent is from Iain Fraoch who is said to have been the *brother* of John, 1st Lord of the Isles. Iain Fraoch is said to have acquired Glencoe by marriage to an heiress, something that was very common and which suggests strongly that there may have been an entirely *different* set of clans in the Highlands before the clans we now know (cf. the Bissets of Lovat, whose name as a Highland clan has disappeared but who were chiefs of Lovat before the Frasers came in by marriage).

The Glencoe people seem to have been on the whole, viewed over the centuries, a fairly peaceful small clan. They supported their kinsmen and friends, of course, but they do not seem to have had any expansionist ambitions of their own.

They followed the general MacDonald policy of supporting Montrose against the Covenanters led by Argyle, and they fought for the Stuarts in Jacobite times. It was their chief's sense of honour and his loyalty to his pledged word that was directly responsible for the tragic affair known as the Massacre of Glencoe. When the chiefs were forced to take an oath of loyalty to William and Mary, Glencoe among others asked permission from the exiled James VII. He was the last to receive word that permission had been granted and, owing to a genuine mistake, was a few days late in taking the oath.

Logan gives the text of the order for the destruction of the MacIains of Glencoe as follows: 'William Rex—as for MacIain of

Glencoe, and that tribe, if they can be well distinguished from the rest of the Highlanders, it will be proper for the vindication of public justice to extirpate that sett of thieves. W.R.' It is about as vicious an order as one can imagine for what was a highly technical breach of the law, Glencoe having submitted himself as required.

Luckily the alarm was given and only thirty-eight members of the clan were killed, although others died of exposure during their flight into the safety of Appin. As massacres go in the Highlands, it was a small one, but the manner of it had a profound effect on public opinion.

The clan survived this misfortune to fight in the '15 and the '45, but today there is no chief of Glencoe, and the glen itself, once filled with Highland cattle supporting an entire clan in a state of contentment if not riches, is bleak and empty, the object of tourist curiosity.

The massacre had one curious result—the nine of diamonds in an ordinary deck of playing-cards is known to this day as the Curse of Scotland. This seemingly is because the coat of arms of the Dalrymple Earls of Stair displayed nine lozenges or diamonds. It was Dalrymple of Stair who persuaded William III to sign the order for the wiping out of the clan—a fact well masked by the widespread but mistaken belief that the massacre was some sort of Campbell-MacDonald feud.

C51

MacDonald of Clanranald

The Clanranald branch of Clan Donald descends from Ranald, a younger son of John, 1st Lord of the Isles. From them in turn descend the Macdonells of Glengarry as well as the lesser branches of Moidart, Knoidart and Morar. The Clanranald war-cry is the well-known 'Gainsay Who Dare', and their chief's title is Captain of Clanranald.

The clan provides at least two examples of clan-power against chiefly power which contradict the modern idea that the chiefs were petty tyrants who tyrannized a following of subservient serfs. Dougal the 6th chief was put to death by the clan because of his cruelties, and his sons were deprived of their rights of succession.

This may have been the chief who is said to have punished a woman who stole something by tying her hair to seaweed and leaving her to drown with the incoming tide.

Dougal's brother, Ranald Galda, was the heir male of the chiefship. He had been fostered away from the clan by his uncle, Lord Lovat, the Fraser clan chief. When he succeeded his brother as chief, the clan gave a great feast in honour of the occasion and boasted to their new chief that they had killed and roasted fifty bullocks, no doubt hoping to please and flatter him by this exhibition of loyalty. Instead Ranald replied tartly that this was a great extravagance and depletion of the clan's wealth and asked if chickens would not have done as well.

The outraged clansmen promptly dubbed him the 'Hen Chief' and drove him out, as being unfit to be the Captain of Clanranald. Lord Lovat quite naturally took the part of his foster-son and tried to re-establish him but was unsuccessful. Eventually this led to a savage battle at Loch Lochie on 3 July 1544, popularly remembered as '*Blar-na-Leine*', or 'the battle of shirts', because it was a very hot day and the clansmen threw off their belted plaids and fought in their shirt tails.

Lord Lovat and his eldest son, together with the luckless Ranald Galda, were all killed, and the killing on both sides was extensive. The story is that, as he lay dying, Lovat told Ranald to escape from the field of battle while he could, but the young chief refused and stayed to die beside his foster-father.

The Clanranald chiefs were lairds of Moidart and had their seat at Castle Tirim. The clan fought for Montrose and Dundee and for the Jacobite Stuarts, although in 1745 their chief did not support Prince Charles, and it was his son who led the clan.

Macdonell of Glengarry

This branch of Clan Donald descends from Donald of Knoydart a son of the first Clanranald chief. For a long time the Glengarry chiefs also claimed the Clanranald chiefship, and Aeneas or Angus the 9th chief of Glengarry, actually became high chief of Clan Donald as Lord MacDonald, but the title expired with him in 1682.

The Gaelic patronymic of the Glengarry chieftains is the well-known Mac-'ic-Alasdair, which refers to Alasdair the 4th chief of Glengarry. The clan gave good support to Montrose, as a result of which Cromwell deprived them of their estates, but they got them back again at the restoration of Charles II. Not surprisingly, the clan fought for James VII and II at Killiecrankie and for his son and grandson during the Jacobite risings.

It was the 15th chief of the clan who was a close friend of Sir Walter Scott and whose portrait by Raeburn is one of the best-known portraits of a Highland chief, seeming to epitomize all that is popularly conjured up by the images painted by Walter Scott in words. Alas, he was a wildly extravagant man who suffered from quite remarkable delusions of grandeur and certainly believed himself to be above the law. Much of his money was spent in lawsuits and the rest on maintaining a state of feudal splendour. His rents (put at £5,000 a year) were insufficient for his needs, and he began by rack-renting his clansmen and finally evicted them to make way for the more profitable pursuit of sheep-farming.

His son, the 16th chief, had to part with all the clan lands and finally emigrated to New Zealand, so that in the end not only were there no clansmen on the Glengarry lands but no chiefs either. It was a sad ending to a proud story.

Macdonell of Keppoch

This branch of Clan Donald are descended from Alistair the youngest son of John, 1st Lord of the Isles. In 1398 they became Lords of Lochaber, but after the Battle of Inverlochy in 1431 their lands were taken from them and given to the MacIntosh Captain of Clan Chattan. The Macdonells did not, however, move from Lochaber, with the result that they and the MacIntoshes fought and squabbled for three centuries.

This clan provides yet another example of clan-power at work, for when John, their chief, surrendered to the Captain of Clan Chattan one of his clansmen who had committed some offence and placed himself under his chief's protection, the clan rose up, deposed him and elected his cousin in his place.

Ranald Macdonell of Keppoch and Cameron of Lochiel were arrested together by William MacIntosh, the Captain of Clan

Chattan, for rebellion, handed over to the Earl of Huntly and finally beheaded together at Elgin in 1547.

Like all the MacDonalds, the Keppochs took the side of Montrose and Dundee and later supported James II and the Jacobite cause.

The clan has the distinction of having taken part in 1688 in what was the last of the clan battles, at Mulroy. Inevitably it concerned the MacIntoshes and the rents for the Lochaber lands which the Keppoch clan had never quit and for which they did not see why they should pay rent. Clan Chattan were supported by a company of government soldiers, but they were soundly defeated and the Captain of the clan was taken prisoner by the Macdonells.

Coll, the Macdonell chief, escaped the worst consequences of this battle by joining Graham of Claverhouse's army, and Claverhouse nicknamed him 'Coll of the Cows', seemingly because he made off with most of the MacIntosh cattle.

Coll of the Cows was at Sheriffmuir in 1715 fighting for the Prince, and his son Alexander, or Alasdair, was killed at Culloden. The story of the death of Alasdair Macdonell of Keppoch is well known to most Highlanders. His clan hung back, along with the other MacDonalds, and Keppoch advanced alone against Cumberland's army, his sword in one hand and his pistol in the other, and was shot down. Donald Roy MacDonald of Clanranald's regiment went after him to try to draw him back, but the wounded chief refused to retreat, and shortly afterwards was killed by a second shot.

It was the Keppoch Macdonells who had the honour of striking the first blow for Prince Charles in 1745, when eleven of them intercepted and captured two companies of the Royal Scots and marched them prisoner to Glenfinnan, where the unfortunate Government soldiers had the mortification of witnessing the raising of the Jacobite standard!

There are many smaller branches of this great group of descendants of Gillebride, father of Somerled, ancestor of the Kings and Lords of the Isles, which was such a formidable Highland power.

22. MacDougall

The MacDougalls have a common origin with the MacDonalds. Somerled, the son of Gillebride, had three sons by his Norwegian wife the Princess Ragnhildis, daughter of King Olaf of Man—Dougal, Reginald and Angus. It is from Dougal, the eldest, that the Clan MacDougall springs. Reginald's son Donald was the MacDonald progenitor.

Dougal and his brothers Reginald and Angus were all styled Kings of the Isles.

The origin of the name Dougal is said to be '*Dugh-gall*' meaning 'the black stranger' or 'foreigner', which was one of the two names used to describe the Norse invaders—the other being '*Finn-gall*', 'white' or 'fair-haired stranger' (cf. MacFhionghuin, meaning 'son of the fair-headed', which is the MacKinnon patronymic).

The MacDougalls and MacDonalds are both, of course, of ancient Celtic origin, but early marriage with the Norse invaders meant that they, like so many Hebridean and west Highland clans, have a mixed ancestry with a strong Norse infusion.

King Dougal of the Isles received lands in Lorn, and his sons are said to have been recognized by the Norwegian King as 'Kings in the West Beyond the Sea', which is surely one of the most romantic and poetic of royal titles ever devised.

The third MacDougal chief, whose titles were 'King in the Hebrides and Lord of Lorn' (one has to admit that they had stirring titles) was the father of Alisdair, fourth Lord of Lorn, who married a sister of the Black Comyn (some authorities say it was his granddaughter not his sister, but the timing seems to favour the sister). As a consequence the MacDougalls supported the Comyns against Robert Bruce, the Comyns having a substantial claim of their own to the Scottish crown.

The best-remembered story of Robert the Bruce, more exciting by far than the story of the spider in the cave, is of his pursuit by three MacDougall brothers, followers of the Lord of Lorn. Following his defeat of Methven in 1306, Bruce had to take to the Highlands to escape his enemies. There the MacDougalls chased him, and the three brothers almost caught him. Bruce killed one; a second grasped his stirrup, but Bruce stood on his fingers, trapping his hand, and dragged him along the ground beside his horse, and the third came so close that he snatched at Bruce's cloak, hoping to pull him off the saddle. Instead the brooch holding the cloak gave way, and Bruce made his escape.

The 'brooch of Lorn', as it is called, is in the possession of the MacDougall clan chief to this day.

After Bruce had triumphed over his enemies, the MacDougalls were deprived of their lands and of Dunstaffnage and Dunolly Castles. They managed to get back some of their lands by marrying a granddaughter of Bruce, but they lost all their island possessions except the island of Kerrera, and they never recovered Dunstaffnage. It became a MacArthur possession and ended up in Campbell hands.

The Lorn lands passed in 1388 to the Stewart ancestors of the Stewarts of Appin, and the MacDougalls were left only with the lands of Dunolly and Oban and Kerrera. The full title of the MacDougall chiefs today is MacDougall of MacDougall and Dunolly, but their Highland patronymic is simply MacDhughaill.

There are considerable gaps in the MacDougall history between 1451 or 1457, when they were confirmed in their Dunolly and Oban possessions, and 1715, when the clan rose for the Old Pretender and fought for him at Sheriffmuir. Once again they lost their estates, but the Government, by luck or good judgement, restored them shortly before the rising of 1745, and the MacDougalls quite understandably remained neutral during the final Jacobite struggle. Their fighting strength was estimated as two hundred so it was a useful piece of Government diplomacy.

There were MacDougall branch clans of Ardencaple and Gallanach and Soraba, and the Galloway MacDowalls are said to be a Lowland branch of this undoubtedly Highland clan.

It is the custom in the Highlands of Scotland for the heiress to a chiefship or chieftainship to be called the 'Maid' of her inheritance—for instance the heiress to the chieftainship of MacLean of Ardgour is styled the 'Maid of Ardgour', and the Colquhoun heiress as the 'Fair Maid of Luss'. The MacDougall heiresses, however, are not called 'Maid of Dunolly' but by the old and splendid title 'Maid of Lorn'.

23.   MacFarlane

The MacFarlanes are descended from Gilchrist, the brother of Aluin the 3rd Earl of Lennox who lived *circa* 1200. They derive their name from Pharlain, their fourth chief, the grandson of Duncan who was Gilchrist's son. Pharlain's son Malcolm is described as MacPharlain or MacFarlane in an early charter confirming him in the lands of Arrochar.

Malcolm's son, Sir Duncan MacFarlane the 6th chief, obtained a charter from the Earl of Lennox confirming him in the clan lands of Arrochar. The early origins of this clan and the descent of the chiefs from the Earls of Lennox are extremely well documented at a period when historians normally rely on the bardic oral traditions for genealogical information.

The clan acquired yet further grants of land in 1395 after Sir Duncan MacFarlane married a sister of Lord Campbell, the chief of the Clan Campbell.

When Donald, the 6th Earl of Lennox, died in 1373, the MacFarlanes claimed the earldom, but it passed through Donald's daughter Margaret to her son Duncan, who became the 8th Earl. Duncan, however, also died without sons, in 1460, and once again the earldom became the subject of contest. In 1488 it was finally settled on the Darnley Stewarts, Duncan's daughter Isabella having married a son of the Regent Albany (cf. here the similarity between the position of the MacFarlanes and the MacPhersons who contested the Clan Chattan chiefship when it passed through an heiress).

The outcome of the dispute was a bitter enmity between the MacFarlanes and the Stewarts until finally Andrew MacFarlane of Arrochar, the chief, married into the new Stewart-held Earldom of Lennox, again uniting his clan to the earldom, and the quarrel seems to have ended there.

Andrew MacFarlane's son, Sir Iain, used the title 'Captain of Clan Pharlain' and was killed at Flodden in 1513 fighting along-side the Earls of Lennox and Argyll, both his kinsmen.

His grandson Duncan was a supporter of Lennox Stewarts and because of that fought with the Earl of Lennox at the Battle of Glasgow Muir in 1544, as a result of which Lennox had to flee to England. Duncan managed to save his life and his lands and was finally killed at Pinkie in 1547, fighting for the Scots against the English invaders.

His son, another Andrew MacFarlane, naturally enough sided with the Regent Moray and fought against Mary, Queen of Scots, at the Battle of Langside in 1568, where the Clan MacFarlane captured three standards and distinguished themselves in the fighting.

Time was running out for the MacFarlanes. By the Act of 1587 the chief was made responsible for his clan's behaviour. Five years later, when Colquhoun of Luss was having an affair with their chief's wife, the MacFarlanes besieged him at Bannachra Castle, and Colquhoun was slain. At this time the MacFarlanes were too friendly with the MacGregors, and there was no doubt that both were well-known raiders and thieves. In fact in Loch Lomond-side the full moon became known as 'MacFarlane's Lantern'. It was probably their association with the MacGregors, rather than the death of the Colquhoun chief, who had undoubtedly given great provocation, which was responsible for the MacFarlane chief being denounced in 1594 as a robber, thief and oppressor. After a series of rigorous prosecutions, the clan was finally broken up in 1624, their name was proscribed, as was that of MacGregor, and their lands were declared forfeit.

Nevertheless, the chiefs managed to retain some of their possessions, and the clan was able to give support to Montrose in 1644 and 1645, as a result of which Cromwell destroyed their castle at Inverglas.

Walter MacFarlane of that Ilk who died in 1767 was a noted historian.

There is a story that a seer had predicted that, when a black swan appeared among the MacFarlane swans in Loch Lomond, the chief would lose everything, and that the black swan actually did appear in 1785, before the 23rd chief sold Arrochar, which had been in his family's possession for six hundred years, and emigrated to North America.

24.   MacFie (MacPhee, MacDuffie)

This is one of the Siol Alpin family of seven clans whose origins are dealt with in Appendix I. Their clan land consisted of the island of Colonsay, and they were hereditary Keepers of the Records to the Lords of the Isles whom, like most Hebridean clans, the MacFies followed during the time of the Lordship.

The chiefs, following a normal Highland custom, styled themselves Captain of MacFie, as well as MacFie of Colonsay.

They are believed to descend from the MacKinnons, and one of their name was Lector of Iona in 1164, during the time of the hereditary abbacy of the 'sacred' clan MacKinnon, which suggests strongly that there was a family relationship since the MacKinnon abbots were not likely to bestow such offices outside their own number.

After the fall of the Lords of the Isles, the MacFies of Colonsay continued to follow the MacDonalds of Islay. In 1463 Donald MacDuffie witnessed a charter at Dingwall, and in 1531 Murdoch MacFie of Colonsay was accused of treason on account of his continued support of the MacDonald pretender to the forfeited Lordship.

The clan's adherence to the MacDonalds brought about their eventual downfall. They supported Sir James MacDonald of Islay, after his escape from Edinburgh Castle in 1615, and the Campbells had been promised Islay as a reward for getting rid of Sir James and his troublesome followers. Somehow the Campbells forced Coll MacGillespick MacDonald, who later won fame with Montrose under his nickname 'Colkitto', to take their side, and it was Colkitto, a MacDonald chief, who captured Malcolm MacFie of Colonsay and his followers and handed them over to the Campbells. In 1623 Colkitto finally slew the MacFie chief and annexed Colonsay for himself!

The clan became a broken clan, i.e. a clan without land (and therefore without shelter) and without a chief. The clansmen dispersed and the name is now to be found all over the Highlands.

The last official outlaw in Scotland is said to have been a MacFie—a sad ending for an ancient clan belonging to the family of the first kings of Scotland and descended from the early kings of Dalriada and their ancestors.

25. MacGillivray

While there were undoubtedly MacGillivrays in Morven and Lochaber at a very early time, and there is even a theory that the clan are connected with Gillebride, the father of Somerled who is the proud ancestor of the MacDonalds, the clan is regarded as one of the oldest and most important branches of the Clan Chattan confederation. One version of their Gaelic name is Mac Ghille-Breac, meaning 'sons of the freckle-faced one'.

Their distant origin seems to have been Dalriadic, and the clan were anciently to be found in Mull. One of the more amusing clan anecdotes concerns the Mull MacGillivrays. Around 1640 the Reverend Martin MacGillivray went out to collect his stipend from his patrons and coming across MacLaine of Lochbuie asked him for his share. Martin carried a sword, as did so many Highland clergymen in those days, and after some bantering, MacLaine dared him to take his money by the sword. This Martin promptly did, forcing the surprised MacLaine to yield to him—and the stipend was paid.

From a very early time, however, the main branch of the Clan MacGillivray was settled in eastern Inverness-shire under the protection of the MacIntosh Captains of Clan Chattan, and in 1330 they took part in a MacIntosh battle against the clan Cameron. The MacGillivray history is bound up so closely with that of the MacIntoshes that there are large gaps in it, which is the case with so many of the Clan Chattan clans.

The MacGillivrays acquired the lands of Dunmaghlas, from which their chief took his title, and they also possessed lands at Aberchallader, Daviot, Dalcrombie and Faillie.

It was Alexander MacGillivray of Dunmaghlas who was chosen by Lady Anne MacIntosh to lead the MacIntoshes in 1745 when her husband Aeneas, the chief of the clan, was serving in a Hanoverian regiment.

The Clan Chattan regiment under Alexander distinguished itself against the Hanoverian left wing, but Alexander was killed, as were many of the MacGillivray and MacIntosh clansmen with him, in what was undoubtedly the hottest fighting of the Battle of Culloden.

Of the only three officers of the Clan Chattan regiment who survived Culloden, one was William, brother of Alexander MacGillivray, who later served in the 89th Regiment, and another was Farquhar of Dalcrombie, whose grandson Neil MacGillivray of Dunmaghlas eventually became clan chief.

26. MacGregor

Clan MacGregor, the 'Children of the Mist', proclaim their Alpinian descent in their motto '*S Rioghal Mo Dhream*'—'Royal is my race'. They have never failed to assert their seniority in the Alpinian 'family', a meaningless seniority since the clans always acted independently and were bound only by a common origin. In fact, as the table in Appendix I shows, if anybody was senior it was The MacNab, who was a generation nearer the ancient throne than MacGregor, MacKinnon or MacQuarrie. But it is a pointless argument since the clans never fought together as an army under a high chief.

The MacGregor's earliest lands were in Glenorchy, as far back as the reign of Malcolm Canmore. John of Glenorchy, who was chief in 1292, was captured by the English in 1296, and his successor, Malcolm, fought for Bruce at Bannockburn and afterwards accompanied Edward Bruce to Ireland, where he was wounded at the Battle of Dundalk and known thereafter as 'the Lame Lord'.

Despite this support it was Bruce's son, King David II, who gave the Campbells a title to the MacGregors' Glenorchy lands. A situation arose similar to that of the Macdonells of Keppoch, whose lands were given to the MacIntosh chiefs. Neither the Macdonells nor the MacGregors were prepared to quit their land, but in the case of the MacGregors their enemies were the powerful Campbells who used legal processes to obtain their ends, and the MacGregors fared far worse than their northern neighbours the Macdonells.

The second son of Iain of Glenorchy, 'the One-Eyed', who died in 1390, was Iain Dubh, who founded the Glenstrae branch of the clan, which succeeded to the chiefship when the Campbells ousted the house of Glenorchy.

If the Campbells are to be accused of the deliberate and ruthless persecution of any clan, it is not the great Clan Donald, with whom they were engaged in a power-struggle for the supreme ascendancy in the western Highlands, but the infinitely smaller clan of MacGregors whose Balquhidder lands the Campbells coveted for themselves.

There is no doubt at all that the Campbells pursued a policy of provoking the MacGregors into acts of violence—acts which gave the Campbells a legitimate excuse for obtaining government authority to 'subdue' them. Nor is there any doubt that the MacGregors allowed themselves to be provoked. In 1488 James IV gave Sir Duncan Campbell of Glenorchy and Ewen Campbell of Strachur royal authority to enforce an Act to pacify unruly behaviour in the west, and this was promptly used to eject MacGregors from Campbell lands and lands wanted by the Campbells. In 1502 Campbell of Glenorchy succeeded in getting a charter for the MacGregor lands in Glenlyon. It was a game of cat and mouse, and one has to admire the Campbell skill in playing it, but it is not a pretty story.

In 1589 the MacGregors murdered John Drummond of Drummond Ernoch, forester of the Royal Forest of Glenartney—which was an offence against the King himself—and fresh letters of fire and sword were issued. It was declared to be an offence to shelter them or even to have any dealings with them. But worse was to follow.

When the MacGregors trapped and slaughtered the Colquhouns at Glen Fruin on 7 February 1603 (see also under Colquhoun), an Act was promptly passed by the Privy Council, on 3 April of the same year, proscribing the MacGregor name. 'Proscribe' sounds innocent, but what it actually meant was that anybody bearing the name MacGregor could be beaten up, robbed and killed by anybody who felt like it, with total impunity. Nobody with the name MacGregor could be baptized, married or buried by the Church, nor could they hear Mass or receive

Communion. All MacGregor charters (what few of them the MacGregors had troubled to obtain) were automatically voided. All debts due to MacGregors were cancelled.

It was at this time that the Lamonts in Cowal gave refuge to Alexander MacGregor of Glenstrae and his clansmen, for which they left themselves liable to the direst penalties, to say nothing of the anger of the Campbells who had been quietly ousting the Lamonts from their property too.

In October Glenstrae was taken prisoner; then he escaped and was finally recaptured in January 1604. The 7th Earl of Argyle is said to have promised to spare him and his followers by sending them out of Scotland. He kept his word—he sent them to Berwick but immediately brought them back again and sent them to Edinburgh, where all were hanged, Glenstrae his own height above his clansmen. It was this treachery, rather than their tug-of-war with the MacDonalds, which gave the name Campbell such a bad reputation among the other clans.

Despite continued persecutions, and from this time on the Government took a perverse delight in persecuting MacGregors, the clan managed to retain its identity, although of course they had been reduced by Act of Parliament to the status of outlaws.

King Charles I renewed the Acts against them, despite which they followed Montrose in 1644–5 when he fought for the King against the Covenant. As they could not have been inspired by love for the King, it is reasonable to assume that they welcomed the chance to hit back at the Campbells, and obviously, if they helped win the King's cause, there was always the chance that he would relax the penalties against them and restore their ancient lands.

All did not go well, of course, and it was not till 1661, after the restoration of Charles II, that finally the Acts were repealed, but for only thirty-two years, for in 1693 William III renewed them with full vigour.

Not surprisingly therefore, the clan supported the Stuart cause in 1715 and 1745, while they were still outlaws. It was not till 1775 that the Acts against the MacGregors were finally repealed for all time.

The most famous member of the clan is undoubtedly Rob Roy, whose father, Donald MacGregor of Glengyle, was a lieutenant-colonel in the service of James VII and II. His mother was a sister of Captain Robert Campbell of Glenlyon who commanded the Government troops who carried out the massacre of Glencoe! Rob Roy's exploits fill a book and were mainly directed against the Duke of Montrose, against whom he conducted a daring and swashbuckling one-man feud which reads like a Hollywood film-script but which is in fact well attested. He died in his bed some time after 1738, aged nearly eighty.

Robert, the chief of the clan, was imprisoned after Culloden and died in 1758. His brother Ewen, who succeeded, served with distinction as an officer in the 41st Regiment in Germany. Ewen's son John was a general in the service of the East India Company and was rewarded with a baronetcy in 1822. His only son was Major-General Sir Evan MacGregor of MacGregor GCH, KCB, Governor of the Windward Isles, whose son in turn, Sir John, the 3rd baronet, was Lieutenant-Governor of the Virgin Islands.

It is worth noting the bewildering transition from savage outlaw to prominent public service. It not merely underlines the extent to which the MacGregors had been manœuvred into outlawry by the Campbells, whose persecution of the Lamonts, MacArthurs and MacGregors is a far more substantial charge against them than their relationship with the powerful MacDonalds who could take care of themselves. It also underlines the stupid waste of valuable manpower which the Government either neglected or provoked over centuries. The brothers and sons of wild primitive savages outside the laws of civilization do not overnight make outstanding generals and administrators.

The MacGregor chief's seat at Lanrick Castle was sold in 1830, since when the chiefs have had their seat at Edinchip in Balquhidder in the very heart of MacGregor country.

27.   MacInnes

Almost nothing is recorded about the history of this clan except its extreme antiquity. Its Gaelic name is Clan Aonghas, and Angus is one of the oldest Gaelic names. Frank Adam asserts that the MacInneses and the MacGillivrays are descended from the original Dalriadic settlers in Scotland and that they are kin to the O'Duine—Clan Duibhne being the progenitors also of the Campbells. It therefore seems that in very early times the Campbells, MacArthurs, MacGillivrays and MacInneses all sprang from the same ancient Celto-Irish stock and were original settlers in Western Argyll from the establishment of the Dalriadic kingdom in 501, or even earlier.

Morven, now MacLean territory, is said to have been the earliest MacInnes territory, which they shared with the MacGillivrays. The MacInneses did not follow the Campbells, despite a common ancestry, but the MacDonald Lords of the Isles, and were Captains or Keepers of Kinlochaline Castle up to as recently as 1645.

But of the clan and the chiefs little is known, and it is possible that they may have suffered in the fall of the Lords of the Isles.

One family of MacInneses were hereditary bowmen to the Skye MacKinnons, and from them the name MacInnes became common in Skye.

The clan must be regarded as one of the ancient clans of the Highlands which did not survive the upheavals in the western Highlands where they had their home, so that only their name survived the medieval period in Highland history. That they were one of the original Highland clans is beyond dispute.

28. MacIntosh

The name of this great clan derives from *Mac-an-Toisach*, meaning 'son of the great chief', and it is an unnecessary interpolation to spell it with a K (as is the case also with MacKinnon, which should properly be spelled MacInnon). Since the MacIntoshes were Chiefs and Captains of Clan Chattan from 1291 till 1938, Clan Chattan has not been treated separately.

The MacIntoshes trace their origins to Shaw, son of Duncan the Earl of Fife in the twelfth century. Shaw was made Constable of Inverness Castle. The use of the name Toisach, which signifies a very considerable leader indeed, is believed to derive from the clan's descent from the MacDuff Thanes or Earls of Fife.

In 1291 Angus, the 6th MacIntosh chief, married Eva, the daughter and heiress of the 5th chief of Clan Chattan, and from her he inherited the Clan Chattan chiefship, becoming 7th chief of that clan in right of his heiress wife. Eva, however, had a brother, and the MacPhersons, who were the ancient chiefs of Clan Chattan, hotly contested the right of the incoming MacIntosh to the chiefship of their clan, which they asserted should have passed to them on the death of the 5th chief.

The debate continues to the present day, but at the Court of the Lord Lyon, where all genealogical matters in Scotland are settled, the rights of the MacIntoshes were upheld in a celebrated court case of 1672. The MacIntoshes have in any case *been* Captains of Clan Chattan for six and a half centuries, and when the chiefship of the MacIntosh clan was separated from that of the Clan Chattan in 1938, it was to another MacIntosh that the chiefship of Clan Chattan went. Today therefore there are two chiefs: the MacIntosh MacGilliechattan Mor, Chief of Clan Chattan, and the Mac-an-Toisach MacKintosh of MacKintosh.

There was never any question at any time of Salic Law in the Highlands, and a great many chiefs obtained both their lands and their clans by marriage to an heiress (cf. Fraser), and it was not on these grounds that the MacPhersons disputed the MacIntosh intrusion but on grounds of name.

Angus, who acquired the Clan Chattan chiefship by marriage,

supported Robert Bruce and was present at Bannockburn. After his death the MacIntosh-Cameron feud started over disputed lands at Loch Arkaig, which the MacIntoshes obtained by charters dated 1337 and 1357 but which the Camerons refused to part with. The celebrated clan battle on the North Inch of Perth is said to have arisen from this feud. Around 1380 at the Battle of Invernahaven, the MacPhersons stood aside because the Davidsons had been given the right wing, and they did not join in until the Davidsons had been slaughtered. Thereafter the MacPhersons turned the tide of the battle, and the Camerons were beaten—but the Davidsons became deadly enemies of the MacPhersons.

When Lachlan MacIntosh of MacIntosh died in 1407, he was succeeded by Farquhar, who was deposed by the clan for his lack of warlike leadership (yet another of the many instances of clan-power overthrowing the chiefs, which gives the direct lie to the current idea that the chiefs were comparable with early Norman barons and that the clansmen mere downtrodden serfs).

Farquhar was succeeded by Malcolm, who was one of their most warlike chiefs and who fought with Donald, Lord of the Isles, at Harlaw in 1411. In 1431 Malcolm received a grant of Lochaber lands which had belonged to the forfeit uncle of the Earl of Ross, and he became Bailiff of Lochaber *circa* 1445.

In 1493 James III confirmed Duncan MacIntosh, Captain of Clan Chattan, in the lands of Keppoch and the office of bailiff. Two years later his son Farquhar was thrown into prison by the King; he escaped but was recaptured and was not released until after the Battle of Flodden.

Farquhar's son Lachlan, 'a verrie honest and wyse gentleman', was murdered in 1526. He had married a sister of the Earl of Moray, and because of this his son William became embroiled with the Gordon Earls of Huntly. William was beheaded in 1550, and thereafter the MacIntoshes and the Gordons were at one another's throats. Because of this enmity with the Catholic Earls of Huntly, the MacIntoshes sided with the Argyll Campbells against them and fought against them at Glenlivet in 1595. Nevertheless, the MacIntoshes, MacPhersons, Farquharsons and other Clan Chattan clans supported Montrose and opposed Cromwell in 1650.

In 1665 the MacIntosh dispute with the Camerons was finally settled and the Camerons were left in possession of Loch Arkaig.

The clan did not rise in support of James VII. In 1688 they fought the last clan battle at Mulroy against the Macdonells of Keppoch and were defeated, the Clan Chattan chief actually being taken prisoner. Thanks to the timely arrival of some MacPhersons, he was released.

The MacIntoshes were out for the Old Pretender in 1715 under MacIntosh of Borlum, and again in 1745 when Lady Anne MacIntosh (a Farquharson of Invercauld) raised the clan, despite the fact that her husband Aeneas, the 22nd chief, was an officer in the Black Watch (some authorities say Loudoun Highlanders— both were Government regiments at the time).

The clan was commanded by Colonel Alexander MacGillivray of Dunmaghlas. The MacIntoshes won one of the most hilarious military victories in 1745 when a handful of them bluffed Loudoun's Highlanders into thinking that they were surrounded, forcing them to retreat in haste.

There was nothing hilarious about Culloden, however. It was the MacIntoshes on the right who led the charge on Cumberland's army, while on the left the MacDonalds hung back and looked on while one of their chiefs, Keppoch, died alone under enemy bullets.

The original MacIntosh castle is a ruin on an island in Loch Moy, and the present seat of the MacIntosh chief is Moy Hall, near Inverness.

29.　MacKay (Mac-Y)

MacKay is another of the names in which the letter K is intrusive (as is the case with MacKinnon and MacKintosh). The Gaelic rendering is MacAoidh, which in distant times was frequently spelled MacY, and the Christian name Aoidh (Hugh) is also rendered Y.

The Hugh from whom the MacKays take their name was the eighth of his House of which there is any definite record, the genealogy being:

Alexander, alive in 1214, who appears to have been the founder.

Walter, his son, who was chamberlain to the Bishop of Caithness and married the Bishop's daughter.

Martin, his son.

Magnus, his son, who fought for Bruce at Bannockburn, 1314.

Morgan, his son (from whom the clan is sometimes called Clan Morgan, and who counts as the first clan chief).

Donald, his son, married a MacNeil of Gigha.

Aoidh or Y, his son, counted as the 3rd chief, from whom the clan takes the name MacKay or Clann Aoidh.

Donald, son of Aoidh, the first MacY (*son* of Y) who was killed in 1395 at Dingwall.

The Clan MacKay is of much older origin than Alexander, however, for they are believed to be a branch of the old royal House of Moray, and in the twelfth century the MacKays were Earls of Ross for a short time until the earldom was bestowed elsewhere.

The MacKays therefore belong to one of the greatest Celto-Pictish families who dominated northern Scotland in early times, and it was not till the late twelfth century or the early thirteenth that the MacKays were physically removed from Morayshire to that extreme north-west corner of Scotland which they made famous as MacKay country. It was from the time of their removal north that their real rise to Highland prominence dates.

In 1411, when Donald, Lord of the Isles, swept across Scotland in an effort to establish his claim to the earldom of Ross, it was Black Angus MacKay of Farr who unsuccessfully attempted to stem the west Highland horde at Dingwall. Angus was taken prisoner, but some idea of his importance can be judged from the fact that the Lord of the Isles got him to marry his daughter Elizabeth, thus uniting the two Houses. Angus was known in his lifetime as Angus the Absolute!

The northern extremity of Scotland above the Moray Firth was inhabited by the Caithness Sinclairs, the MacKays of Strathnaver, the Sutherlands and, as a buffer state in the midst of them, Clan Gunn, and not unnaturally there was a good deal of fighting among them with constant switching of support to prevent either the Sinclairs or Sutherlands, who were the most numerous, from becoming too powerful.

In 1464 Angus MacKay, aided by the Clan Chattan Keiths who had obtained a foothold adjoining the Gunn territory, invaded Caithness, and in 1475 he was burned to death in the church at Tarbet. In 1487 his son John MacKay, helped by some of the Sutherland men, defeated the Rosses at Aldy-Charrish.

In 1517 yet another John MacKay, who had had some land taken from him by the new Gordon Earls of Sutherland, invaded Sutherland, and it took the Gordons five years to pacify him. The Sinclair Earl of Caithness of course helped the MacKays!

In 1587, however, the MacKays and the Sutherlands joined forces and made war on the Caithness Sinclairs.

Hugh MacKay, who died at Tongue in 1614, aged fifty-four, married firstly Lady Elizabeth Sinclair, daughter of the 4th Earl of Caithness, and secondly Lady Jane Gordon, daughter of the 11th Earl of Sutherland. By his second marriage he had two sons, and of whom, Sir Donald MacKay of Strathnaver and Farr, who was the clan chief, was created Lord Reay by Charles I in 1628, and thereafter Strathnaver became known as 'Lord Reay's Country'. This 1st Lord Reay gained much fame in the service of Gustavus Adolphus of Sweden. He spent a large part of his fortune helping Charles I and died in Denmark in 1649.

His son was also a Royalist and also spent much of his fortune in the Royalist cause, he was taken prisoner at Balveny in 1654. The third Lord Reay, however, supported the Government in 1715 and 1745.

The Scourie branch of the clan descends from a son of Y MacKay the 3rd clan chief, the one who gave the MacKays his name. Hugh MacKay of Scourie was the well-known general who fought the Royalist clans at Killiecrankie and who founded a military dynasty which served with distinction in Holland, where they raised the MacKay Dutch Regiment.

Unhappily the Reay country had to be sold to the Earl of Sutherland by the 7th Lord Reay.

30. MacKenzie

The MacKenzies appear to have belonged to the family of the original Earls of Ross, and their name, Mac Coinnich, means 'son of the bright one' and does not strictly equate with the name Kenneth, although the clan is known as Clan Kenneth, and Kenneth is one of its most widely used Christian names.

In the old pronunciation of the name, the letter Z is pronounced gy, giving MacKing-yie (cf. also Menzies, pronounced Ming-yies).

The earliest known MacKenzie ancestor is Kenneth, whose son Murdoch received a charter for the lands of Kintail in 1362. The clan rapidly grew to power, for by 1427 it was reputed to be able to muster two thousand fighting men, which was an extremely large number.

In 1463 the Earls of Ross gave considerable grants of land to the MacKenzies of Kintail, and the MacKenzies opposed all MacDonald attempts to gain the Ross earldom. They fought and defeated the MacDonalds at Blar na Pairc in 1477, and James III rewarded them with further grants of land.

Kenneth Og was chief in 1493 and was imprisoned in Edinburgh Castle by James IV. He escaped but was taken and slain by the Laird of Buchanan in 1497. He was succeeded by his brother John. Their mother, Agnes Fraser, was a daughter of Lord Lovat.

In 1508 the clan lands at Kintail were erected into a barony, for which the rent was a stag, and it is from this that the MacKenzies derive the stag's head on their coat of arms, and the chief's famous Gaelic designation '*Caberfeidh*' which means 'deer's antlers'. The ancient motto of the clan, '*Cuidiche an Righ*', refers to the 'payment' of the stag to the king for their barony.

John MacKenzie (Kenneth Og's brother) fought with the clan for James IV at Flodden in 1513. John was taken prisoner but released, and later he accompanied James V on his famous expedition to the Isles in 1540.

The clan fought at Pinkie in 1566 and for Queen Mary at the Battle of Langside in 1568, when Colin MacKenzie was the 11th chief of the clan.

It was not until 1609 that Kenneth MacKenzie of Kintail, the 12th chief, was finally raised to the peerage as Lord MacKenzie of Kintail, surprisingly late considering their great land-holdings and military power, and the political importance of the clan whose chiefs had been feudal barons (*not* to be confused with Lords of Parliament, who are peers and an entirely different thing) since 1508.

His son Colin was promoted in the peerage to become Earl of Seaforth in 1623, and the MacKenzies supported the Stuart kings, the 4th Earl being made a titular Marquis in the Jacobite peerage by James VII, a title which was not recognized by the new ruling House.

The 5th Earl took part in the rising of 1715 and was forced to go into exile. He was subsequently pardoned and died in Lewis in 1740. Officially the MacKenzies did not support the Stuarts in the rising of 1745, but in fact many of the clansmen were at Culloden fighting for Prince Charles Edward. Indeed, probably the most celebrated MacKenzie clansman was Roderick MacKenzie, who joined the Prince's army in Edinburgh in 1745 and was one of Charles's lifeguards. He bore a remarkable general resemblance to the Prince, close enough to deceive anybody who did not know Charles personally.

After Culloden Roderick took to the heather as the Prince did, and he was a refugee in the Highlands trying to avoid capture by the redcoats. About the middle of July 1746 he was discovered by a party of soldiers, and after making a stand he was shot fatally. As he lay dying, he called out to them, with remarkable presence of mind, 'you have killed your prince.'

The soldiers, delighted no doubt at the prospect of touching the £30,000 reward for Charles dead or alive, cut off his head and bore it in triumph to Fort Augustus. Even the Duke of Cumberland was deceived and posted off immediately to London carrying his grim trophy, and it was not till he arrived in London that the deception was discovered. The dying Roderick had bought time for his prince, for during a number of days or weeks the search for him was virtually dropped.

It was the grandson of the Jacobite 5th Earl who raised the Seaforth Highlanders (the old 78th Regiment) in 1778. The regiment saw service in India, and in 1793 a second regiment was raised, also as the 78th, the first one having been renumbered

72nd. The amalgamation of the two regiments into the first and second battalion of the Seaforth Highlanders took place in 1881.

The clan's estates stretched from the outer Hebrides in the west to the Black Isle in the east, right across the northern neck of Scotland. Their rallying-cry was 'Tulloch Ard' from the name of the place where they gathered in Kintail. Their most picturesque castle was Eileandonan on Loch Duich, which their devoted kinsmen and followers, the Mathiesons and the MacRaes, held for them, and the chief's residence was at Brahan Castle.

31. MacKinnon

The Clan MacKinnon is one of the Siol Alpin family (see Appendix I) and is among Scotland's most ancient clans. Its associations have always been Hebridean.

The clan counts King Alpin as its founder, and its slogan or war-cry is '*Cuimhnich bas Alpein*', meaning 'Remember the death of Alpin', who was beheaded in 841, in memory of which the MacKinnon chiefs have a second crest showing a severed head crowned with an antique crown.

It was Alpin's great-grandson Findanus, the 4th MacKinnon chief, who gave the chiefs their Gaelic patronymic of MacFhionghuin, sons of Fingon of Findanus, which is now the clan surname. It was Findanus too who brought Dunakin into the clan around the year 900 by marrying a Norse princess nicknamed 'Saucy Mary'. The castle, Dun Haakon, was an old broch or fortress commanding the narrow sound between Skye and the mainland, through which all ships had to pass or else attempt the longer, stormy passage of the Minch. Findanus and his bride ran a heavy chain across the sound and levied a toll on all shipping passing up and down!

The Princess lies buried on Beinn-Caillaich in Skye, her face reputedly turned towards Norway.

It was in the shadow of Dunakin that King Haakon IV's war galleys mustered in 1263 before the Battle of Largs, at which their power was finally broken in Scotland.

Findanus, however, had his lands in Mull, and there were MacKinnons in Arran too who gave shelter to Robert Bruce. The clan did not receive its great Skye estate until after Bannockburn, when Bruce rewarded them with it. It stretches from Kyleakin up to Broadford and then runs across Skye to Elgol and includes the islands of Pabay and Scalpay.

The chiefs, after Bannockburn, took their Lowland title from this estate of Strath Swordale or Strathardale and had their seat at Dunringill Castle, of which nothing now remains, and Dunakin was held by a collateral branch of the chiefly family.

Like all the Hebridean clans, the MacKinnons were vassals of the Lords of the Isles, and they were made hereditary custodians of the standards of weights and measures.

From the beginning the clan had very strong links with Iona, where for centuries a branch of the chiefly family were hereditary abbots, a position of such great prestige in the Highlands that it is certain that the MacKinnons belonged to the kin of Columba. Iona is the burial ground of MacKinnon chiefs as well as of Scottish kings. There was a Fingon abbot of Iona in 966, and the last abbot of the holy island was John MacKinnon, who was also Bishop of the Isles and who died in or around 1500.

During the time of the Lordship of the Isles the MacKinnons were frequently at feud with the MacLeans. One of the more pleasing clan stories describes an early incident, probably four-teenth century, when MacLean of Duart and MacLaine of Lochbuie seized the lands of the MacKinnon chief in Mull at a time when he was away in Skye. On his return The MacKinnon heard about it and obtained the help of forty warriors from the Earl of Antrim. On his way back to Skye to raise more of his clan, he stopped on Mull to find out how the land lay and heard that the MacLeans were lodged in Ledaig House without sentries and that their followers were sleeping off a heavy carousal.

The MacKinnon made every man in his party cut and trim a fir caber, which they planted in the ground before Ledaig House during the night. The chief himself planted an untrimmed one in front of the others and left his naked sword above the door. Next morning the MacLeans realized that they had been at the mercy of the MacKinnons and had been spared, and they are said to have withdrawn from the MacKinnon lands.

After the fall of the Lordship of the Isles, the MacKinnons and the MacLeans are generally to be found acting in concert and were frequently linked by marriage ties.

The MacKinnon crest is an unusual one. It is a boar's head, which is common enough in the Highlands, but with the shank-bone of a deer in its mouth. The story of this crest is that in the fourteenth century The MacKinnon was hunting on the shores of Loch Scavaig in Skye. He became separated from his hunting party and sheltered for the night in a cave, where he kindled a fire to broil some venison. A wild boar entered the cave and attacked him just as he was slicing some meat from a haunch. With presence of mind, he thrust the bone into the jaws of the beast, jamming them open, and killed it with the knife.

The MacKinnons were always a small clan but seem to have enjoyed a prestige greater than one would expect, perhaps from their Iona and Columban connection. Sir Iain Moncreiffe has described them as a 'sacred' clan.

They had supported Bruce, and in due course they supported Montrose too and took part in the attempt to restore the Stuart monarchy in 1650–1, being present at the Battles of Inver-keithing and Worcester. At Worcester Sir Lachlan Mor, the 28th chief, rendered some sort of special service to Charles II for he was created a knight banneret on the field of battle, the last or second-last such creation ever made.

The estate of Strath had been erected into a barony by Charles I on 15 January 1628 in favour of Sir Lachlan MacKinnon, the 26th chief, who died shortly afterwards.

The MacKinnon chief Iain Dubh was out in '15 and '45 and has been described in Part One of the book. His son was forced to part with the clan lands, and his grandson John died unmarried in 1808.

The chiefship now passed to the descendants of the second son of Sir Lachlan Mor, the 28th chief, who became a banneret at Worcester. This second son Donald had emigrated to Antigua *circa* 1680, as a result of a quarrel with his hot-tempered father. The present chiefly family was therefore in the West Indies all during the Jacobite risings and had nothing whatever to do with events in Britain. When the Antigua branch succeeded to the chiefship in 1808, there were no clan lands left, and they there-fore had also nothing to do with the shameful episode of the Skye clearances.

The only MacKinnon possession still in clan hands is Dunakin Castle, which belongs to the author, who is a direct male descendant of Findanus who obtained it by marriage early in the tenth century; he also belongs to the Antigua branch of the chiefly family.

32. MacLachlan

The MacLachlan lands were in Strathlachlan in Cowal on the eastern shore of Loch Fyne, and their seat was Castle Lachlan. No Highland title whatever can be more rousing than MacLachlan of MacLachlan of Castle Lachlan in Strathlachlan!

The origins of this clan are very ancient indeed, and their exact relationship with the Lamont proprietors of Cowal are not clear. One account says that the MacLachlans originally inhabited Lochaber and obtained Strathlachlan by marriage to a Lamont heiress. Another claim is that they were the original Celto-Irish settlers in Strathlachlan and were of the same original stock as the MacNeils, the MacEwens and the Lamonts.

It seems fairly certain that their descent is from the ancient Irish O'Neils, and it is probable that their presence in Cowal is as long standing as that of the Lamonts themselves, so possibly the Lochaber MacLachlans of Coire-uanan were an offshoot of the original stem, and the Lochaber lands came later.

Their ancestor from whom they derive their name was Lachlan Mor, who lived early in the thirteenth century. In 1230 Gilchrist MacLachlan witnessed a Lamont charter, and in 1292 Gilescop or Archibald MacLachlan received a charter confirming his possession of Strathlachlan from King John Balliol.

In 1296 the chief was Ewen, and his son Archibald supported Robert Bruce. His name appears on a letter to Philip IV of France in 1308, and in 1314 he granted 40 shillings yearly to the Preaching Friars of Glasgow. He is described as living at 'my castle called Castellachlan'.

Archibald died *circa* 1322 and was succeeded by his brother Patrick. Mention of the early MacLachlan chiefs is to be found in a number of charters dated 1410, 1430, 1456, 1485 and 1490, and the clan is really remarkably well documented between 1230 and the end of the sixteenth century. The chiefs were persons of importance in Cowal and were followers of the Campbells who had rapidly risen to power. The MacLachlans were directly involved with the Campbells in the massacre of over two hundred Lamonts at Dunoon in 1646.

Despite their Campbell association, by 1689 they were on the side of King James VII and fought with Dundee at the Battle of Killiecrankie—although as recently as 1679 their chief had been helping the Campbells against the MacLeans!

The 26th chief, Lachlan MacLachlan of MacLachlan, lord of Strathlachlan, was at Sheriffmuir in 1715 fighting for the Stuarts, and his son, also named Lachlan, followed Prince Charles in 1745, accompanying him on the march into England as far as Carlisle, when he was sent back to Scotland to raise reinforcements. He was at Culloden, where he commanded the MacLachlan regiment which included some MacLeans and probably some of the 'mixed clans' who were not numerous enough to form separate units. He was killed in the fighting.

The clan chief still owns land on the shores of Loch Fyne, and Castle Lachlan in Strathlachlan is still the chief's seat, having been rebuilt in 1790.

Not many people still live at the same address as their ancestor who fought with Bruce, and on the very same land which has probably been in their family for at least twelve hundred years!

33. MacLaren

The MacLarens are another extremely ancient clan. Their name suggests descent from Laurin or Lorn, the brother of Fergus Mor MacErc who founded the kingdom of Dalriada in 1501. Laurin settled in Argyll in 503, and the clan is said to have received its Balquhidder lands from King Kenneth MacAlpin himself. They are also believed to have fought at the Battle of the Standard in 1138, and their name certainly appears on the

Ragman Roll of 1296, so that once again we seem to be dealing with a clan of original settlers on the land.

At a very early date, when the Crown annexed the earldom of Strathearn in 1370, the MacLarens lost their lands, becoming tenants. This did not apparently affect their loyalty to the Crown, for they fought with Bruce at Bannockburn (1314), with James III at Sauchieburn (1488), with James IV at Flodden (1513) and for the infant Mary, Queen of Scots, at Pinkie in 1547.

The MacLarens were closely related by marriage to the Appin Stewarts, and in 1497, when the MacLarens and the Macdonells of Keppoch were embroiled in an affair which concerned a *creach* or 'lifting' of cattle, the Stewarts came to the support of the MacLarens, and Dugal of Appin was killed in the fighting.

In 1588 the MacGregors seized the lands of eighteen MacLaren families in Balquhidder and slaughtered all the occupants. Thereafter the MacLarens seem to have attached themselves to the Appin Stewarts more closely. They were 'out' for Prince Charles with their Stewart kinsmen in 1745, and, presumably, earlier in 1689 and 1715.

MacLaren of Invernentie was taken prisoner after Culloden, and his escape was spectacular. He was being marched to Carlisle to stand trial for his life. Near Moffat he jumped aside, rolled down a steep hillside and ran into a morass where he sank up to his chin, covering his head with a large piece of turf. His pursuers could not find him, and eventually he was able to make his way home disguised as a woman and lived undiscovered until the Act of Indemnity made it safe for him to show himself.

The MacLarens are yet another example of one of the most ancient of the Highland clans whose power went into a decline at a very early date. Some of these clans disappear altogether as clans, but the MacLarens managed to preserve their identity and their chiefly line through all their many misfortunes.

The story has a satisfactory ending, for there is still a MacLaren of MacLaren, and the family managed to re-acquire the clan's ancient rallying-place at Creag an Tuirc, 'the boar's rock', the place which gives the clan both its rallying-cry and its chiefly motto and which may very well have been given to them in the first place by King Kenneth MacAlpin in the first half of the ninth century.

34.   MacLean (MacLaine)

The origin of the name MacLean is somewhat tortuously given as Mac-Ghille-Eoin meaning 'son of the servant of John', but no explanation is provided as to the identity of John, which is extremely rare among the clans, who invariably know the name of the founder from whom they derive their patronymic. It is probable therefore that Gilleathain derives from *'Leathan'* meaning 'broad' or 'broad-shouldered' and that the Gillian who gave the clan its name was a burly man.

. This founder was known in Gaelic as Gilleathain na Tuaidh, Gillian of the Battle-Axe, and he was alive in 1263. His ancestry, however, is said to go back to Lorn, the brother of Fergus Mor MacErc, founder of the Dalriadic kingdom, and the MacLeans are said to have possessed lands in Glen Urquhart before settling in Argyll.

Gilleathain the founder fought at the Battle of Largs, and his son Gillemore is mentioned in the Ragman Roll of 1296. The clan supported Bruce at Bannockburn, and some time after Bannockburn the MacLeans settled in Mull and so came into conflict with the MacKinnons who were already settled there.

There are two accounts of what happened in Mull. One is that the MacLean chief, Iain Dubh, called MacGilliemore, killed the MacKinnon chief and seized the person of the Lord of the Isles and forced him to swear on sacred stones that he would not punish the MacLeans but would reward them with some of the MacKinnon lands. The other version is that Iain Dubh's son, Lachlan Lubanach, kidnapped the Lord of the Isles in order to marry his daughter Mary, in the course of which the MacKinnon chief was murdered, and that the Lord of the Isles approved of his daring and rewarded him for it. In any event, The MacLean did marry Mary, daughter of Iain the first Lord of the Isles, so the second version seems substantially correct, and the MacLeans grew steadily in favour with the MacDonald lords and dispossessed the MacKinnons of many of their Mull possessions.

Lachlan Lubanach was the founder of the family of Duart who became chiefs of the whole clan, and his brother Hector founded the branch clan of MacLaines of Lochbuie. The other principal branch clans of Ardgour and Coll are offshoots of the chiefly line of Duart.

Duart Castle, which is still the home of the chief of the clan, was already in existence when the MacLeans arrived in Mull and received it from the Lord of the Isles.

During the Lordship the MacLeans and MacKinnons were in constant conflict, possibly kept at one another's throats by the MacDonalds as a matter of simple policy. After the fall of the Lordship, however, the enmity seems to have ceased, helped no doubt by the fact that the MacKinnons possessed alternative clan lands in Skye and that they supported the rising MacLean power which turned Clan MacLean into a third party, holding the balance between the MacDonalds and Campbells for a long time.

By the time of the fall of the Lordship, the MacLeans possessed lands in Mull, Coll and Tiree, and in Morven and Ardgour on the mainland.

Lachlan Lubanach's son was Red Hector of the Battles, a celebrated MacLean warrior who fought at Harlaw on 24 July 1411, on the MacDonald side. It was during this battle that Sir Alexander Irvine of Drum and Red Hector MacLean sought out one another and engaged in a long personal combat in which both were killed. Thereafter the two families were in the habit of exchanging swords when the chiefs met.

Lachlan MacLean of Duart, who supported the MacDonald insurrection in 1503, was among the clan chiefs killed with James IV at Flodden in 1513. Ten years later the MacLeans and Campbells were involved in a bitter feud over Lady Elizabeth Campbell who was the wife of the chief Lachlan MacLean, and the daughter of the 2nd Earl of Argyle. The story is that she twice tried to kill her husband and that he in exasperation tied her to a rock at low tide and left her to drown (a similar punishment was meted out in different circumstances by MacDonald of Clanranald against a thief). Lady Elizabeth was saved by a passing boat and taken back to her family where she told a tale of woe, and her husband was murdered by her brother Sir John Campbell of Calder. In 1529 the MacLeans and the MacDonalds of Islay ravaged the Campbell lands, and the Campbells retaliated and much blood was shed.

Later a dispute arose between the MacLeans and the

MacDonalds of Islay over the possession of the Rhinns of Islay, during the chiefship of Lachlan Mor MacLean around 1578. In 1594 both chiefs were declared forfeit by Parliament for having failed to appear before the Privy Council to explain their fighting, but such declarations counted for more in Edinburgh than in the western isles, and in the same year the MacLeans redeemed themselves by their courage at the Battle of Glenlivet when they supported the Government against the Catholic Earls. In 1596 Lachlan Mor was restored to full favour, his forfeiture cancelled, and he was given the Rhinns of Islay.

In 1632 Lachlan Mor was created a baronet, and thereafter the clan was devotedly Royalist, following Montrose in his campaigns, fighting for Charles II at Inverkeithing and Worcester. The story has been told in Part One of how the seven foster-brothers of Hector MacLean died for him at Inverkeithing.

In 1689 the clan was out again on the side of James VII at Killiecrankie.

The MacLeans went into debt to support the Stuart cause, and as a result they lost their Mull lands and with them Duart Castle, their ancient stronghold, which were taken by force by the Marquis of Argyll in 1680.

The clan rose again in support of the Stuarts in 1715, and the chief, Sir Hector MacLean, became Lord MacLean in the Jacobite peerage in 1716. Sir Iain Moncreiffe mentions the interesting fact that this Sir Hector founded the Grand Lodge of Freemasons in Paris while he was still in exile in France, in 1736, and was its first Grand Master—a consequence of the Auld Alliance which the French could hardly have foreseen.

Sir Hector was arrested by the Government on the eve of the Jacobite rising of 1745 and held in custody till 1747, but the MacLeans were out under MacLean of Drimmin and took part in all the battles, including Culloden, where Drimmin was killed at their head.

Duart Castle was recovered in 1911 and restored and made habitable and is the home of the present chief of the clan, whose Gaelic title is Mac' illEathain. Breacadach Castle, the old seat of the Coll MacLeans (Clan Iain Abrach) is now a ruin. It was here that the son of MacLean of Coll entertained Boswell and Dr Johnson in 1773, but it was sold in 1848. The Lochbuie

MacLeans no longer possess their estates but the MacLeans of Ardgour have retained their home and their clan lands.

The hunting tartan of the MacLeans is the oldest tartan of which there is any documentary evidence and was described in both 1587 and 1630. The clan's war-cries are the famous '*Fear Eile air son Eachuinn*' ('Another for Hector') and '*Bas no Beatha*' ('Death or life').

35. MacLeod

The MacLeods are of Norwegian origin and are divided into two branches, the Siol Tormod, from whom descend the Skye MacLeods and the chiefs of the whole clan, and the Siol Torquil, who were the MacLeods of Lewis. Both branches descend from Leod, son of Olave the Black who brother was King of Man and the Isles.

Dunvegan Castle, the home of the chiefs, is said to have been acquired by Leod through marriage, as were the Glenelg lands. Although the MacLeods were early Norwegian 'incomers', they rapidly rose to become one of the most important of the island clans.

Tormod's son, also called Tormod, supported Bruce, and his son Malcolm received a charter from King David II confirming his Glenelg lands. Inevitably the MacLeods became involved with the powerful MacDonald faction and frequently opposed them, although they formed part of the Highland host which followed John, Lord of the Isles, at the Battle of Harlaw in 1411.

Despite the fact that the earlier chiefs were styled 'of Glenelg', it is with Skye that this clan is inevitably associated and where they had possessions from the dawn of their history as a clan. Inevitably they came into frequent conflict with the Skye MacDonalds, which was the other major power in Skye. Skye is a three-clan island, the third clan being the numerically inferior MacKinnons. The most probable explanation of why the MacKinnons were allowed to remain in more or less peaceful possession of their territory, which runs right across Skye, is its sacred connection with Iona, for either the MacLeods or the MacDonalds could have overrun them at will, and there must have been times when it would have been greatly to their advantage to do so.

One of the principal bones of contention between the Skye MacLeods and MacDonalds was the possession of Trotternish in the north of Skye. In this quarrel the Lewis MacLeods sided with the MacDonalds against their kinsmen, and in the end the MacDonalds occupied Trotternish.

Alexander the Humpback, the famous chief, who is described as 'of Dunvegan' and no longer 'of Glenelg', built the Fairy Tower at Dunvegan and unfurled the Fairy Flag twice, thus considerably shortening its life, for according to the clan legend the flag's magic powers will work only three times. Alexander used them twice when engaged in desperate struggles with the Clanranald MacDonalds. The Fairy Flag is real and is carefully preserved at Dunvegan to this day. It is described as probably being of tenth-century manufacture and of Eastern origin, and tradition says that the Norwegians brought it back from Istanbul and that it came into MacLeod possession via their Norwegian ancestors.

The flag is closely guarded in a metal chest and can be waved once more before it loses its powers. There is probably no MacLeod alive who does not believe, secretly if not openly, in its supernatural powers, and when there was a fire at Dunvegan in 1938, and the flag in its metal box was being carried to safety past the flames, the fire mysteriously extinguished itself as it passed.

When William MacLeod, Alexander the Humpback's son, died in 1554, he left only a daughter, but two brothers also survived him. Mary, the rightful chief, married a Campbell and came under the protection of the Earl of Argyle. Her elder uncle, Donald, inherited the MacLeod lands of Trotternish which had been given to the clan by James IV in 1498 but which the MacDonalds had continued to occupy in defiance of everybody. Donald seized his niece's estates but was murdered afterwards by an ambitious relative, Iain Og, who remained in possession of the chiefly estates and in command of the clan till 1559. Mary, who had been a maid of honour to Mary, Queen of Scots, surrendered her claims to her younger uncle, Tormod, who became chief in 1559 and who was a staunch adherent of the Queen.

Sir Rory Mor, the 16th chief of the clan, was knighted by James VI. He was another of the clan's more celebrated chiefs, and his horn is preserved at Dunvegan along with the sword of Alexander the Humpback.

The MacLeods supported the Stuarts and fought at Worcester under the 18th chief, Roderick, but the clan's losses were so heavy at this battle that it was decided they should not take the field again till they had had time to recover. Nevertheless, they rose again in 1715 for the Stuarts; but in 1745 the MacLeod and MacDonald chiefs on Skye both refused to support Prince Charles, who had arrived in Scotland empty-handed against all advice. Nevertheless, many MacLeods slipped away to join the Jacobite forces, and the MacLeods of Raasay were out under their chieftain.

What is most remarkable about this clan is not a historical fact at all but the very real bond of affection which existed and exists still between the chiefs and the clansmen. This is something which perhaps only a MacLeod can understand, and it reached its climax in the aftermath of the '45 when the MacLeod chiefs carefully protected their clansmen on their lands. Here there were no evictions but instead every effort to improve the condition of all the MacLeod clansmen on the island. It was in startling contrast to what was going on elsewhere (including on Skye itself).

The MacLeods are extremely proud of their race and of their chief's home at Dunvegan, which is in a real sense the spiritual home of them all.

Such a clan, of course, has a long history full of interesting anecdotes, but perhaps one of the most typically 'Highland' is that of the famous Alexander or Alasdair, the Humpback, who on a visit to the royal court was taunted by a Lowland courtier, who supposed that The MacLeod had never seen such finery or magnificence. Alexander retorted that he had a better table and better candlesticks at home than the court possessed, and he ended up by having a wager with James V over it. The following year, when James V visited the Isles, Alexander had a feast set out on the higher of MacLeod's Tables, two quite extraordinary flat-topped hills which face Dunvegan. For candlesticks he had his clansmen, fully armed, holding flaring torches. James conceded that he had lost the wager.

The Lewis MacLeods fared less well than their Skye kinsmen. Their line of chiefs became extinct following feuds with the

MacKenzies which culminated in 1597 when Torquil Dubh MacLeod was beheaded by the MacKenzie Lord of Kintail. Thereafter the MacKenzies claimed Lewis by right of marriage (some say the heiress was bogus), the MacLeod lands passed into MacKenzie hands, and the title Lord MacLeod became a secondary title of the MacKenzie Earl of Cromartie and still is—which confuses a great many people, as does Lord Cromartie's seat, which is Castle Leod.

The MacLeods of Assynt belonged to the Siol Torquil or Lewis MacLeods and not to the Skye clan.

36. MacMillan

There now seems to be no doubt that the MacMillans are *not* an offshoot of the Buchanan clan as the Buchanans have so often claimed. They were a distinct clan with their own chiefs and had no connection at all with Clan Buchanan.

The MacMillan origins are priestly, and the name is a translation of the Gaelic MacMhaoilean, 'son of the tonsured one' (i.e. of the priest), and they spring from a race of hereditary abbots in Perthshire.

By the middle of the fourteenth century the MacMillans were established as a major clan in Knapdale, and the title of the chiefs today is MacMillan of MacMillan and Knap. They appear to have received Knap first of all from the Lords of the Isles, and they were one of the clans who were with John, Lord of the Isles, at Harlaw in 1411, where Lachlan MacMillan, the clan chief, was killed in the fighting.

The clan was numerous in Argyll, and there is a beautiful stone Celtic cross in the churchyard of Kilmorie in Knap, showing a chief in hunting costume chasing deer and which commemorates Alexander MacMillan of MacMillan.

In the fifteenth century Alan MacMillan of Knap married the MacNeil heiress of Castle Sween, and one of the castle's towers is known as MacMillan's Tower.

The lands of Knap were lost after the downfall of the Lords of the Isles, and the MacMillans would seem to be one of the unfortunate lesser adherents of the Lordship whose lands were too close to the Campbells and who were swiftly dispossessed by them.

The family of the Knap chiefs died out in the mid-seventeenth century, but the clan had been in decline for a long time before that. The chiefship passed to the MacMillans of Dunmore.

The MacMillans have the interesting distinction of having the charter for their Knapdale lands engraved on a rock, which stood on the shore on the edge of their estates and which proclaimed that the MacMillans' right to Knap would endure for as long as the rock stood. In 1615 the Campbells deliberately tumbled it into the sea.

It was undoubtedly an unfortunate day for this clan when it left Perthshire to establish itself in a district where it was caught up in, and became a casualty of, the great Campbell-MacDonald struggle for power in the west. Many of the small mainland clans who supported the Lords of the Isles paid dearly for it later, and the lack of mention of the MacMillans after the fall of the Lordship indicated their fate.

Nevertheless, the line of chiefs continued and today the clan has its chief and its clan organization.

There was a fairly numerous offshoot of the clan in Lochaber which followed the Cameron chiefs and which acquired a reputation for bravery and daring among the Camerons.

37. Macnab

The name is correctly spelled with a small n as it is not MacNab ('son of Nab') but Mac-'n-Abba ('son of the abbot').

The *Clann an Aba*, 'children of the abbot', are, according to the traditional Alpinian descent, the senior of the four stem clans in the Siol Alpin family of seven (see Appendix I). Like the MacKinnons, they were one of the ancient 'sacred' clans and were hereditary Abbots of Glendochart and the heirs of St Fillan, who was one of the Dalriadic princes, as indeed were several of the early hereditary abbots. Like the other clans which were founded by the close descendants of King Alpin, they are equally descended from all Alpin's Scottish and Pictish ancestors back to the first Dalriadic king and the first Pictish king.

The clan's possessions from an early time were on the shores of Loch Tay, and the Macnabs were friendly with their neighbours the MacDougal lords of Lorn and supported them and the Comyns against Bruce, as a result of which many of their lands became forfeit after having been ravaged and burned.

The clan survived Bruce's revenge, however, and Gilbert Macnab of Bowain managed to obtain a charter for his barony of Bowain lands from Bruce's son, King David II, in 1336.

Gilbert's son Finlay, who died in the reign of James I (1406–37) was a celebrated bard and is said to have composed some of the Gaelic poems later attributed to Ossian (and which, curiously, were favourite reading of Napoleon!).

From now on, the name Finlay proliferates bewilderingly. Finlay the bard's grandson, Finlay the 4th chief, was successful in expanding the clan's possessions and received charters from James III and James IV.

Finlay Macnab the 5th (*dominus de eodem*, 'lord of the same' or 'lord of that ilk') witnessed a charter in 1511, and Finlay the 6th unwisely mortgaged some of his lands to an ancestor of the Campbell Earls of Breadalbane in 1552. This inevitably led to trouble with the Campbells, who tried to use the mortgage to turn the Macnabs into a Campbell sept.

Finlay the 7th was the Finlay who signed a bond of manrent with Lachlan MacKinnon of Strathardale in 1606, setting out their common ancestry among other things. He is also the subject of a grimly amusing clan story. The Macnabs were deadly enemies of the Neishes who had been numerous in Strathearn. The few surviving Neishes now inhabited an island in Loch Earn called Neish Island, where they existed by plunder. One Christmas they waylaid a servant of Finlay the 7th, who was bringing home Christmas provisions from Crieff. The servant turned up empty-handed with his tale of theft.

Finlay had a dozen sons, of whom the elder was 'Smooth John', noted for his athletic prowess. The chief and his sons brooded on the robbery until Finlay said meaningly in Gaelic, 'The night is the night if the lads were but the lads.' Smooth John took the hint, and he and his brothers set off in the dark with a heavy boat which they carried overland from Loch Tay to Loch Earn. There they launched it and rowed to Neish Island, dirked the luckless Neishes and returned with the stolen Christmas fare plus a boat-load of severed Neish heads. On arrival back home, Smooth John told his father drily, 'The night *was* the night and the lads *were* the lads.'

This Iain Mion or Smooth John succeeded as chief and supported Charles I and Montrose and fought for Charles II at Worcester in 1651. He was killed in 1653 attacking Cromwellian troops in Breadalbane. He had earlier had a lucky escape from execution following the Battle of Kilsyth in 1645.

During Cromwell's Commonwealth the Campbells finally managed to gain possession of the Macnab estates. Some of the lands were recovered in 1661 after the restoration of Charles II, and Robert Macnab of Macnab poured oil on troubled waters by marrying Anne Campbell, Breadalbane's sister, thus intelligently playing the Campbells at their own game.

The eldest son of Robert was an officer in the Black Watch, which put him on the Hanoverian side during the Jacobite uprisings, and he was taken prisoner by the Jacobites at the Battle of Prestonpans in 1745. The clan, however, did not share his politics and fought for the Stuarts under Macnab of Inshewan.

The most spectacular of the Macnab chiefs was almost certainly Francis, the 16th Macnab, who died on 15 May 1816. His portrait by Raeburn shares with that of Alasdair Macdonell of Glengarry the distinction of being one of the two best-known portraits of Highland chiefs in all their glory. But whereas Glengarry looks out distantly and disdainfully from the canvas (he was by nature both), Francis scowls menacingly, lower lip out-thrust, as if suspecting that there might be excisemen in the vicinity. He had a positive hatred for excisemen, whom he termed 'vermin'—perhaps because he had his own distillery, said to make the best whisky in the Highlands and which almost certainly made a lot of whisky on which no duty was ever paid.

He was the complete Highland chief of fiction, tall and immensely strong, full of self-esteem, as befitted the descendant of ancient kings, a man certainly born out of his time (he only just missed being alive when Queen Victoria was born!). He is said to have wooed one lady with the boast that he had the most beautiful burial ground in the world—the island of Innis Buie in the River Dochart which was the burial place of Macnab chiefs.

Two stories illustrate his character. On one occasion, when he was marching at the head of the Breadalbane Fencibles of which regiment he was colonel, the baggage carts contained much whisky on which no duty had been paid. Some excisemen fell on the rear of the column and attempted to search the baggage carts. Macnab hurried to the scene. When they said they were on the king's business, he pointed out that so was he, and promptly demanded to see their commissions as excisemen. They were not carrying them, and Macnab gleefully denounced them as highwaymen and footpads and gave orders to his soldiers to take aim and fire. The excisemen beat a hasty retreat, and the chief resumed the march, telling his men, 'Proceed, the whisky is safe.'

The other story concerns a sheriff's officer who arrived at Kinnell House to serve a summons on him (one suspects that many summonses were taken out but that not many were served). Macnab got the man roaring drunk and put him to bed, the summons unserved. He then hung a fully clothed dummy from a tree facing the bedroom windows. When the sheriff's officer woke next morning, bleary-eyed and hung-over, he demanded in alarm from the housekeeper who was hanging from the tree. 'Oh,' she said cheerfully, 'just a wee misguided baillie who came here trying to serve the laird a summons.' The officer left hurriedly with the summons and without breakfast.

Francis let others pay for his fun, leaving on his death numerous illegitimate children and debts amounting to £35,000. The estates were finally sold to the Earl of Breadalbane, but after World War II Archibald Corrie Macnab of Macnab recovered them, and The Macnab still lives today at Kinnell House which has been the family home since 1654, when Eilean Ran Castle was burned down by the English Roundheads.

38. MacNaughten

Also spelled MacNaughtan and MacNaughton, but the present chiefs have made MacNaughten the official spelling. The name derives from the Gaelic meaning 'son of Nechtan', which is an ancient Pictish name and which supports the theory that the clan's founder, Nechtan Mor, who lived in the tenth century belonged to the family of the early Thanes of Loch Tay. The clan also claims descent from Fearchar Fada, one of the Dalriadic kings, which is perfectly possible.

Originally the MacNaughtens possessed lands between Loch Awe and Loch Fyne, and their seat was at Dunderave on Loch Fyne. As early as 1246 Malcolm MacNachtan's son Gilchrist gave a church to Inchaffray Abbey, and in 1267 or 1287 he himself was made hereditary keeper of the royal castle of Fraoch Eilean on Loch Awe.

Gilchrist's grandson Donald was related to the MacDougal lords of Lorn and so fought against Bruce for a time, but he eventually changed sides, inspired, it is said, by Bruce's personal prowess in a skirmish. Although some authorities said that the estates became forfeit to Bruce, Donald's son Duncan was in favour with Bruce's son King David II, and his son Alexander was even given lands in the island of Lewis where there was a MacNachtan Castle. Indeed, this clan possessed quite a number of castles at one time or another.

A younger son of the chiefly family was Bishop of Dunkeld in 1436.

Sir Alasdair MacNaughtan of that Ilk was with James IV at Flodden and was killed there. A later chief, Sir Alexander, was a loyal Stuart supporter, and in 1627 he was given a commission by Charles I to raise a levee of two hundred bowmen to serve in France, among them being the MacKinnon chief and some of his men (and, one assumes, the family of MacInneses who were hereditary bowmen to the MacKinnons). Sir Alexander was a favourite of Charles II, who kept him at court and gave him a pension for life, a form of generosity to which the Merry Monarch was not greatly addicted. Alexander was known as Colonel

MacNaughtan, and he was buried in the Chapel Royal in London at the King's expense.

Alexander's successor fought for Dundee at Killiecrankie and lost his lands, partly by forfeiture and partly on account of accumulated debts. The chiefly line failed before the Jacobite risings of 1715 and 1745, and the clan does not figure on the list of clans of Lord President Forbes, but quite probably MacNaughten clansmen fought for the Stuarts with the mixed clans.

One unfortunate clansman died in the Jacobite cause without ever having supported it. John MacNaughtan, who was born in Glenlyon, was a servant of James Menzies of Culdares. Menzies had been taken prisoner by the Government in 1715 and decided to stay at home peacefully during the '45. But he could not suppress his Jacobite sympathies entirely, and he decided to send a white charger to Prince Charles, who was on the march into England. He sent John MacNaughtan to deliver the horse, which he duly did, but he was taken prisoner by the English and sent to Carlisle. His judges knew very well that he was an innocent messenger, and they offered him a pardon if he would say on whose behalf he had delivered the horse. MacNaughtan refused to betray his master despite the enticements offered to him, and in the end he was executed.

The Clan MacNaughten chiefship has now passed to a family of baronets who are descended from a younger son of the Dunderave family who settled in Antrim around the year 1580.

39. MacNeil

The MacNeils claim descent from the Irish King Niall of the Nine Hostages, who lived around the year 400, and Gillieonan MacNeil, who received a charter from the Lord of the Isles for Barra, in 1427, is said to have been the 10th laird of Barra and 30th in line of descent from Niall.

Certainly the MacNeils are a very ancient clan indeed, belonging to the same group of families as the Lamonts and the MacLachlans and possessing lands in Cowal and Knapdale. The first clan chief to figure in a charter is Neil Og, who lived during the time of Robert Bruce and was Constable of Castle Sween. He received a charter for Barra from Bruce.

Neil Og's great-grandson Gilleonan received a new charter for Barra from the Lord of the Isles in 1427. Charters were frequently granted to early chiefs who were already in possession of their lands, so that the claim that the MacNeils were in Barra as early as 1049 is quite feasible.

The MacNeils of Gigha, to whose family also belonged the MacNeils of Colonsay, were the early chiefs of the clan and are so described by the Privy Council as late as 1530. But the Gigha power declined and the Barra power grew, and the Barra chiefs became established as chiefs of the whole name.

Certainly the MacNeils of Barra acknowledged no master and were a remarkably high-handed and proud line. It would appear that the chief of Barra's trumpeter used to stand on the ramparts of Kisimul Castle, after his master had dined, blow a fanfare and then solemnly announce to wind and waves that, The MacNeil of Barra having dined, 'The princes of the earth may dine.'

The Barra MacNeils were picturesque pirates, and Kisimul Castle was well known as a corsair lair from which the MacNeil galleys set out on swift, successful raids. They were almost impregnable on Barra, and certainly safe from all attack at Kisimul, which rises sheer from the sea on a small island and which could not in those days be assaulted by land.

During the Lordship of the Isles, the MacNeils generally supported the MacDonalds. Roderick Og MacNeil of Barra was celebrated for his bravery. He was one of the chiefs who accompanied the Earl of Argyle on his expedition against the Catholic Earls, which ended disastrously for Argyle. Roderick Og fell at the Battle of Glenlivet in 1594.

His son was a splendid character called Roderick 'the Turbulent', one of the greatest sea-rovers of a clan which had the sea in its blood. Queen Elizabeth of England complained of his piracy, and he was peremptorily summoned to appear before the Privy Council in Edinburgh. Naturally he ignored the summons, and eventually he was captured by a trick, being invited aboard the ship of a friendly MacKenzie, where he and his henchmen were got drunk and then secured while the boat made off with them. When he arrived in Edinburgh, he took a high tone. He explained that he had made war on English ships because he was honour bound to avenge the murder of the King's mother (Mary, Queen of Scots) by Elizabeth, and he had assumed that the King would be pleased by what he had done. One feels that he deserves the pardon which he then received.

Black Rory MacNeil of Barra received a charter from James VII raising Barra into a barony, and he fought with Dundee at Killiecrankie in 1689 and took his clan out in 1715 in the Stuart cause.

In 1745 the MacNeils, a Catholic clan, were out again. Their chief, known as Roderick 'the Dove of the West', was imprisoned for his part in the rising.

Barra had to be sold in 1838, but a century later, in 1938, it was repurchased, including that most romantic stronghold Kisimul Castle, which has been restored and modernized inside and which is once again the home of The MacNeil of Barra.

The Gigha MacNeils sold Gigha to James MacDonald of Islay in 1544. It was repurchased in 1590 but later sold again and finally became the property of the MacNeils of Colonsay who, however, had to part with their lands in 1704.

40.   Macpherson

The name Macpherson derives from the fact that this clan were originally hereditary lay clergy in Kingussie, and means simply 'son of the parson'. The clan tradition is that the progenitor from whom they derive their earliest name was Mhuirich, a parson and son of a parson, and the clan's ancient Gaelic name was Clan Vurich (Clann Mhuirich). The Macphersons therefore have two Gaelic patronymics which in English mean 'sons of the parson' and 'sons of Vurich'. Macpherson is usually spelled with a small p, since 'parson' is not a Christian name, and MacVurich is spelled with a capital V because Vurich is.

The Macphersons belong to the Clan Chattan, and indeed they have never renounced their claims to be the rightful chiefs and captains of Clan Chattan, contesting the MacIntosh 'usurp-ation' of the chiefship by marriage into the clan. There is a good deal of doubt about who *ought* to be the chiefs of Clan Chattan, but the whole matter was legally settled (although not to Macpherson satisfaction) in the celebrated court case of 1672, when the Lord Lyon King of Arms, Scotland's genealogist, settled the chiefship in favour of the then chief of Clan MacIntosh. (see Appendix III.) Whatever the rights or wrongs, the MacIntoshes have in fact *been* chiefs of Clan Chattan since 1291.

The Clan Chattan is of very ancient origin, and Mhuirich, the Macpherson name-father, was chief of Clan Chattan in 1153 and was the great-great-grandson of Gillichattan Mor, who was the name-father of Clan Chattan. Mhuirich's grandson was Dugal Dall, who left a daughter, Eva, as heretrix of the clan. He also had brothers, and when Eva married the MacIntosh chief, her uncle claimed the chiefship of Clan Chattan by right of name, since Eva's husband retained his own clan name. In Scotland it is not necessary to be a son to become chief. Eva could inherit and transmit the chiefship, but she had also to transmit the *name*, since chiefship and name are inseparable (the principle involved is that the clan name *must* live on).

Kenneth was the Macpherson chief at the Battle of Inver-nahaven which led to the Davidson-Macpherson feud which has been mentioned at length under Clan Davidson and which gave birth to the celebrated clan battle on the North Inch of Perth.

But in fact, despite their claim to the chiefship of Clan Chattan and their undoubted independence as a considerable clan in their own right, the Macphersons were remarkably tolerant of, even loyal to, the MacIntoshes. The inevitable bitter blood-feud which once would reasonably look for between two clans who disputed something as important as the Clan Chattan chiefship never developed. This is greatly to the credit of the Macphersons, who, although they did not always support the MacIntoshes, never made war on them.

The clan received its Badenoch lands for having supported Bruce against Comyn, their earlier clan lands being in Lochaber. Later they received lands in Strathearn and Strathnairn. The older branches of the clan, Pitmean and Invershie, contested the ascendance of the Cluny branch, but it was Macpherson of Cluny (usually known as Cluny-Macpherson, in the same way as Robertson of Struan is known as Struan-Robertson), whose lands were in Badenoch, who became acknowledged as chief of the whole name of Macpherson.

Andrew Macpherson of Cluny supported the Catholic Earls against the Government in the reign of Mary, Queen of Scots, and fought at Glenlivet in 1594, helping to defeat Argyle and his west Highland army. Donald of Cluny was a supporter of Charles I, and his grandson Duncan who died in 1722 rose for the Stuarts in 1715.

The famous Cluny Macpherson of the '45 was Ewen, who married a daughter of Simon Fraser, Lord Lovat. Although his father, Lachlan, did not die till 1746, it was Ewen who raised the clan, which provided about six hundred Macphersons for the army of Prince Charles. Ewen, an officer in the army, had thrown up his commission in the Government service to join the Prince when the standard was raised at Glenfinan, and for this reason the Government put a price on his head after Culloden.

The clan was not present at Culloden when Jacobite hopes tumbled; in fact, Lord George Murray had advised the Prince not to give battle till the Macphersons had come up with the rest of the army, but it was one of several pieces of good advice which the Prince ignored on that fateful day.

After the defeat, Cluny helped the Prince to escape and also took charge of his military chest, which included a lot of money, which he eventually took to the Continent with him and delivered when he made his own escape from Scotland.

The Government had put £1,000 on his head, an enormous sum for the time, but he lived on his estates for nine years, in 'Cluny's Cage', a secret hiding-place on Ben Alder, without being caught. His son, who succeeded to the chiefship, was nicknamed 'Duncan of the Kiln' because he was born in a corn-kiln in 1748 while his father was in hiding from the redcoats.

Ewen died in exile at Dunkirk in 1776, the year following his eventual escape to France.

Although the clan lands eventually had to be sold, several acres of the old lands have been purchased back by the Clan Macpherson Association as a perpetual 'rallying-ground' for Macphersons all over the world, and this clan has its own interesting clan museum at Newtonmore. The ancient Cluny Castle, near Kingussie, was rebuilt early in the nineteenth century but had to be sold.

The Macpherson war-cry of 'Creag Dhu' is the name of a rock near Cluny Castle where the clan rallied in time of emergencies.

41. MacQuarrie

The MacQuarries are one of the four stem-clans of the Siol Alpin family of seven, and their descent is given in Appendix I. The name, 'son of Guaire', means 'son of the proud one', and their progenitor was the brother of Findanus or Fingon who gave the MacKinnons their name. Like their kinsmen the MacKinnons, the MacQuarries are said to have been kindred of St Columba. Like all the Siol Alpin clans, they are descended through the line of Dalriadic kings from that great ancestor of kings, Niall of the Nine Hostages, who reigned at Tara in 400 while the Romans were still in Britain.

The early MacQuarrie lands were on Ulva, an island near Iona, and in Mull, which they shared with the MacKinnons in early times. The two clans are closely linked from the very earliest times by place of residence as well as descent.

In 1249 Cormac Mor, the chief of Ulva (ancestor of the 'Lord of Ulva's Isle' made famous by Sir Walter Scott), supported King Alexander II against the Norwegian invaders and was killed by Haco of Norway.

Hector MacQuarrie of Ulva supported Bruce and fought at Bannockburn with his clan. John MacQuarrie of Ulva, who died in 1473, was a follower of the MacDonald Lords of the Isles and was one of the Council of the Isles, and his name appears on a MacDonald charter of 1463. Under his son Dunslaff, the clan became independent following the forfeiture of the Lordship. Thereafter the clan supported the MacLeans (as also did the MacKinnons, which again suggests a very close relationship between the chiefs of these two clans).

In 1504 the MacQuarrie chief was accused of treason by the

Scottish Parliament and was repeatedly summoned to appear before the Privy Council, but, as was the habit with the island chiefs, he contemptuously ignored such summonses. Eventually, in 1517, he and Lachlan MacLean of Duart were pardoned for their offences.

Allan MacQuarrie, 13th lord of Ulva, was killed at Inverkeithing on 20 July 1651, fighting alongside the MacLeans for Charles II against the forces of Cromwell and the English. The link with the MacLeans remained very strong, for Allan's brother Hector married a daughter of MacLean of Torloisk, from whom he obtained the lands of Ormaig, and his family frequently intermarried with the MacLeans of Duart and the MacLaines of Lochbuie.

The clan had been so badly weakened at Inverkeithing that afterwards it was in no state to support the Jacobite cause actively, and it did not take part, as a clan, in the risings of 1715 and 1745.

Lauchlan MacQuarrie of Ulva entertained Johnson and Boswell during their celebrated tour of the Hebrides in 1773, but five years later he was forced to sell Ulva. He then joined the army, at the age of sixty-three, and served as an officer in the American War. He had been born in 1715 and did not die till 1818 (at Glenforsa, Mull), having lived 103 years—the last of a proud line of Lords of Ulva's Isle, and a descendant of Irish, Scottish and Pictish kings.

His kinsman General Lachlan MacQuarrie succeeded Captain Bligh of the *Bounty* as Governor of New South Wales, and in honour of him MacQuarrie River, Port MacQuarrie and MacQuarrie County are all named. He too was buried in Mull, in 1824.

The MacQuarrie war-cry was '*An t'arm breac dearg*', 'The red-tartaned army'.

42. MacRae

The MacRaes are always associated with the MacKenzie Lords of Kintail, but in fact they have an interesting history prior to their joining the ranks of MacKenzie followers.

The name MacRae means 'son of good luck', from which one can assume that the early MacRae chiefs were successful in their various exploits. The founder from whom they take their name is not known at all, which supports the theory of the great antiquity of the clan.

In the twelfth century Mary, the daughter of the last Lord Bisset of Lovat, was fostered with MacRae of Clunes. As the Bissets were great magnates in the north, prior to being broken up by William the Lion (1165–1214), the MacRaes must have been of considerable standing to be chosen to foster a Bisset daughter. Mary Bisset married a Fraser and there was a tradition in the Fraser clan that no MacRae would ever lack shelter while a Fraser lived at Lovat Castle. This promise is said to have been carved on a stone over the door of the castle.

The MacRaes are of Celto-Irish extraction. They were present at the Battle of Largs in 1263, fighting against the Norse invaders, and at an early date they settled in Kintail, and their chiefs became known as 'of Kintail'.

It is not clear exactly when they allied themselves with the MacKenzies, but there is a story that during the Lordship of the Isles the MacKenzies were forced to seek MacRae assistance in helping to protect Wester Ross from MacDonald invasions. During one of the ensuing battles the MacRae warrior killed a number of MacDonalds, including one of their chieftains, on whose dead body he sat down to watch the fight. When MacKenzie of Kintail demanded to know why he was not fighting, he pointed out that, if everybody killed as many MacDonalds as he had, the MacKenzies would soon win the battle. The MacKenzie urged him to rejoin the fight with words along the lines made famous by Scott, 'He who does not reckon with me, I will not reckon with him.'

What is interesting about this is that Walter Scott may have borrowed this story to include in his novel *The Fair Maid of Perth*, in which a Perth blacksmith, Henry Gow, sat back after he had killed his man in the Battle of the North Inch of Perth and was egged on with the same words.

From the fourteenth or early fifteenth century the MacRaes became known as 'MacKenzie's Shirt of Mail' from their fame as bodyguards to the MacKenzie chiefs. They were unwaveringly loyal to the MacKenzies despite the fact that seemingly the MacKenzies had reduced them from the status of proprietors in Kintail to that of MacKenzie tenants.

The MacRaes were Chamberlains of Kintail, and around 1520 they became hereditary constables of the beautifully picturesque castle of Eilean-Donan. They were usually referred to as 'the wild MacRaes' on account of their warlike spirit, but they were also noted in the Highlands for their love of poetry and music.

The clan lost many men at the Battle of Auldearn in 1645, fighting in support of Montrose, and at this time the chiefs of the clan were styled 'of Inverinate'.

The Reverend John MacRae of Dingwall, who died in 1673, founded the Conchra branch of the clan, a distinguished family who, however opposed the Inverinate chiefship on the most unusual grounds that the MacRaes did not have a chief.

The clan fought at Sheriffmuir in 1715 in support of the Stuarts, and the oldest piece of authentic clan tartan in existence is a piece of MacRae tartan worn at this battle. The sword of Duncan MacRae who was killed at Sheriffmuir used to be on display in the Tower of London.

There is at present no MacRae chief, but Eilean-Donan Castle, a very beautiful and much-photographed castle in the western Highlands, of which the MacRaes were hereditary constables for centuries, is now in the possession of a MacRae.

43. Mathieson

The Mathiesons were at one time one of the most powerful clans in the north, capable of bringing two thousand warriors into the field, it was said. The name MacMhathain derives from '*Mathaineach*', 'the heroes'. The clan held lands in Lochalsh as early as the time of Kenneth MacAlpin.

Like the MacRaes, the Mathiesons have long been associated with the MacKenzies, both the MacKenzie and Mathieson chiefs holding lands under the Earls of Ross; but whether the Mathiesons are a branch of the MacKenzie clan or whether in fact the MacKenzies are an off-shoot of the Mathiesons is not clear.

In 1264 Cormac, the 2nd Mathieson chief, is mentioned as supporting the Earl of Ross against Norse invaders. He was also constable of Eilean-Donan Castle and later, when Eilean-Donan became a MacKenzie possession, the Mathiesons seem for a time to have shared the constableship with the MacRaes.

The clan was involved in the rising of Donald, Lord of the Isles, in 1411 and fought for the MacDonalds at Harlaw that year.

In 1427, when James I held a Parliament at Inverness, he promptly seized the Highland chiefs who were becoming either too powerful or too troublesome, and the Mathieson chief was among those arrested, which indicates that at that time the clan was of political importance. The Mathieson estates were seized by the Crown.

It is probably from this time that the Mathiesons became MacKenzie followers. The clan feuded with their Glengarry neighbours, and in 1539 the Mathieson chief, Donald Dhu, held Eilean-Donan against the Sleat MacDonalds. Another Mathieson chief, Murdoch Buidhe, was constable of Eilean-Donan in 1570. A branch of the clan settled in Sutherland, but the Lochalsh Mathiesons were the stem clan and provided the clan chiefs.

Their disappearance from the Highland scene seems to be connected with the MacKenzies, whom, like the MacRaes, they served faithfully. Both of these ancient clans, who were considerable powers in their own right, seem to have lost their lands to the MacKenzies and contented themselves thereafter by supporting the MacKenzie chiefs, who were extremely well served by them.

It is not clear how this was achieved without bloodshed. Perhaps the MacRaes and Mathiesons were absorbed peacefully by marriage. In any event it makes a pleasant change from the less peaceful fate of some of the ancient clans in Argyll who got in the way of the MacDonalds and Campbells and became geographical casualties of that particular power struggle.

In 1851 Sir Alexander Mathieson was able to purchase the clan estates in Lochalsh which had been forfeit since 1427. A descendant of Murdoch Buidhe, who was constable of Eilean-Donan in 1570, was recognized as chief of the clan in 1963. As has happened in a surprising number of cases, the wheel has come full circle, and the clan has been 'restored'.

44. Menzies

This clan is believed to be of Anglo-Norman origin, and the name was spelled Meyneris in the early thirteenth century. The English surname of Manners is said to be of the same early Norman origin, which has been identified as the place-name of Mesnières in France.

Sir Robert de Mayneris was appointed Lord High Chamberlain of Scotland on the accession of Alexander III in 1249. His son Alexander possessed lands at Weem and Aberfeldy, in Atholl, as well as the family seat at Durisdeer in Nithsdale. To these possessions Alexander's brother Thomas added the lands of Fortingall, which eventually passed to the Stewarts when a Menzies heiress married James Stewart, son of the famous Wolf of Badenoch.

The Menzies chiefs of Weem followed Bruce. Their seat at

this time was Comrie Castle on the River Lyon, and Bruce granted them several land charters after Bannockburn, where they fought for him.

In 1423 David Menzies de Wimo was appointed Governor of Orkney and Shetland under King Erik and Queen Philippa of Denmark, 'Swedland' and Norway, which indicates that the chiefs were using the style 'of Weem' *before* the destruction of Comrie Castle in 1487. After 1487 Weem became their seat, but the mansion of Weem was burned in 1502, and Menzies Castle was built to replace it. It was in 1487 that the Weem estates were turned into the barony of Menzies. In 1665 Sir Alexander Menzies of Castle Menzies was created a baronet.

The clan is mentioned in the Parliamentary Rolls of 1587. In 1644 the Menzies were opposed to Montrose. They shot (whether deliberately or by accident is not certain) a herald sent by Montrose, as a result of which their lands were burned and plundered by the Royalist forces.

Understandably in 1688 the chief favoured the new monarchy rather than the cause of the exile James VII. The clan fought against the Government, however, in 1715, and it was at Dunblane that Menzies of Culdares was taken prisoner and later pardoned. It was he who decided to send the gift of a valuable horse to Prince Charles in 1745, as has been related in detail under Clan MacNaughten.

The Menzies chief was not active in 1745, but his clan was out in strength under Menzies of Shian.

This clan has also recovered its ancient seat, which had been sold by Sir Neil Menzies of Menzies, Bt, in 1910; and a descendant of Menzies of Culdares was officially recognized as chief of the clan in 1958 (see Appendix III).

The clan's war-cry, '*Geal 'us dearg a suas*', means 'The red and white for ever' and alludes to the chief's coat of arms, which is a shield, the top third of which is red and the bottom two-thirds white, without any figures or ornaments on it, a sure sign of a very ancient coat indeed.

45. Munro

The Munroes were early followers of the old Earls of Ross, and their home has always been in Ross-shire on the north shore of the Cromarty, Firth. The name is said to derive from an unidentified place-name, but the chiefs have been known as 'of Foulis' for many centuries, the earliest known mention being of Hugh Munro of Foulis who died in 1126.

Robert Munro of Foulis supported David I and Malcolm IV in their wars in the twelfth century, and George, the 5th chief, obtained charters from Alexander II early in the thirteenth. Sir Robert Munro of Foulis, the 6th chief, fought for Bruce at Bannockburn, where his son was among those killed; and his grandson George died at Halidon Hill in 1333. Robert, the 8th chief of Foulis, married a niece of Euphemia, the Queen of Robert II, and was killed during a skirmish in 1369.

The Munroes held their lands from the Scottish kings in return for a ball of snow to be delivered on Midsummer Day on request—this they could do because there were gullies in the mountains on Munro land where snow lay all year round. Nowadays a castle and estate for a snowball would be considered a very fair rent indeed.

Robert the 14th laird died fighting against the English at Pinkie in 1547, and his son, Robert the 15th laird, was a devoted follower of Mary, Queen of Scots, and later of her son James VI. Robert must have been a favourite name for the 16th and 18th chiefs are also Roberts, the latter being called 'the Black Baron'.

The Black Baron joined the army of Gustavus Adolphus of Sweden, along with a regiment of his clan, all of whom wore gold chains round their necks so that they could ransom themselves if taken prisoner. It is said that under Robert, the Black Baron, there were three Munro generals, eight Munro colonels, five Munro lieutenant-colonels, eleven Munro majors and over thirty Munro captains all serving the King of Sweden at the same time. Robert died of wounds at Ulm in 1633. He was succeeded by his brother, whom Charles I created a baronet in 1634.

Robert the 21st chief and 3rd baronet succeeded in 1651 and was created Commander in Chief of the army in Scotland by

Charles II, following his restoration. He died in 1688. The 4th Baronet took the part of the new monarchy against James VII in 1688. He was a big, strong man and a very staunch Presbyterian and was nicknamed 'the Presbyterian Mortarpiece'.

Sir Robert Munro of Foulis the 6th Baronet was killed at Falkirk in 1746 along with his brother George, fighting against the Jacobites. He had been appointed Lieutenant-Colonel of the Black Watch when it was formed as a regiment in 1740, and commanded it at the Battle of Fontenoy. The third brother, Captain John Munro, was tragically waylaid and shot beside Loch Arkaig by Dugal Roy Cameron, who mistook him for a Government officer named Grant who had shot his son.

The clan's war-cry of '*Caisteal Foulis na Theine*', 'Castle Foulis in flames', does not refer to an actual burning of the chief's home but was meant to rouse the clansmen into a fury at the mere prospect. Oddly enough, the old castle was accidentally burned in 1750, and the present castle was built by Sir Harry Munro, the 7th Baronet.

Foulis Castle remains the seat of the chiefs who were never dispossessed at any time and who have lived at Foulis for nine centuries at least.

46. Murray

The ancestor of the Murrays is described as Freskin, a Fleming who settled in Scotland *circa* 1120 and who acquired both Highland and Lowland lands from King David I. His grandson was known as William de Moravia and seems to have been regarded as the representer of the old Pictish mormaers of Moray, which indicates that one of the family had married a Moray heiress.

The younger son of William de Moravia was Malcolm, and it is from his son William that the Tullibardine family of clan chiefs descend, William having married the heiress to the Tullibardine estates. His name appears in charters of 1282 and 1284 as the lord of Tullibardine.

The Murrays who fought with Wallace and Bruce during the

Wars of Independence represented the senior and Lowland branch of the family, but it was the Tullibardine or Atholl branch which eventually came to be recognized as chiefs of the whole name of Murray.

It is slightly misleading to think of the Murrays as a clan in the ordinary sense, since there were numerous prominent Lowland branches, and the Tullibardine branch itself was one of those powerful 'frontier' clans which were half-Highland half-Lowland. Nevertheless, Tullibardine could bring three thousand Highlanders into the field, so it is as a Highland clan that they are considered here.

Sir William Murray of Tullibardine, the 7th laird, was sheriff of Perthshire in 1446 and married Margaret, daughter of Sir John Colquhoun of Luss, the Great Chamberlain of Scotland.

The 12th lord* of Tullibardine, John, was Master of the Household to James VI in 1592 and was created Earl of Tullibardine in 1606. His son William, the 2nd Earl, married Dorothea Stewart, the heiress of the Stewart Earls of Atholl, through whom the Atholl earldom passed into the Murray family in 1629 by letters patent granted by Charles I.

John the 1st Murray Earl of Atholl was a staunch Royalist and supported Montrose, and his son the 2nd Murray Earl, who succeeded in 1642, was also a Stuart supporter. After the Restoration he became Sheriff of Fife and later Lord Justice General of Scotland. He was created Marquis of Atholl in 1676. His son John was Earl of Tullibardine during his father's lifetime and was one of the commissioners who inquired into the Massacre of Glencoe. He became Lord Privy Seal, and after his father's death in 1703 he was created Duke of Atholl by Queen Anne and made a Knight of the Thistle.

He was not 'out' for the Stuarts in 1715, but his son William, who was Marquis of Tullibardine, was and as a result was excluded from the succession to the dukedom, which passed to a

---

* The terms 'lord' and 'lordship' in the Highlands have nothing to do with peerage titles and are much older and equate with the French '*seigneur*'. The Lowland version of 'laird' is often used nowadays to prevent confusion. The 'lord of Tullibardine' does *not* mean Lord Tullibardine, which is a modern peerage form connected with the comparatively modern institution of Parliament.

younger brother, James. A third brother was Lord George Murray who was the famous Jacobite general of the '45 and whose son succeeded eventually as 3rd Duke of Atholl!

During the '45, therefore, there were three brothers, two professed and notorious Jacobites (the Marquis of Tullibardine and Lord George Murray) and the youngest, James, Duke of Atholl, head of the whole name of Murray and nominally loyal to the Government. His clan were, of course, mostly Royalist and followed his two brothers.

Tullibardine died in the Tower of London in 1746, and Lord George Murray had to go into exile.

James, the 2nd Duke of Atholl, who had succeeded 'over the heads' of his two elder brothers because of their politics, was sovereign of the Isle of Man. He died in 1764 and was succeeded by his daughter, who had married John Murray, son of Lord George Murray. John Murray had not been attainted along with his father, and so he was allowed to succeed as 3rd Duke of Atholl. He surrendered his sovereignty of the Isle of Man to the British Crown in 1765 for a paltry £70,000 (which is scarcely more than twice the sum put on the head of Bonnie Prince Charlie!). It would be interesting to know what price the Isle of Man would fetch today, if it were in private hands and could be sold.

The Tullibardine and Atholl Murrays were extremely closely linked to their neighbours, the Highland family of Moncreiffe of Moncreiffe, and there was much marriage between the families. Today the Moncreiffes wear Murray of Atholl tartan.

The seat of the chiefs of Clan Murray, the Dukes of Atholl, is at Blair Castle in Perthshire. The Duke of Atholl has the extraordinary privilege of being the only person in the United Kingdom who has his own private army, the Atholl Highlanders. Originally raised as a bodyguard, they became a clan regiment and Queen Victoria presented them with a pair of colours in 1845 which in effect officially recognizes the Atholl Highlanders as a regiment, and they possess many rare regimental privileges even although they are not a part of the British Army. Nowadays they are used only on ceremonial occasions.

47. Ogilvie

The Ogilvies were an active 'frontier' clan, part Highland and part Lowland in their tradition. Their surname is a place-name in the parish of Glamis in Forfarshire, and their ancestor Gilchrist received the barony of Ogilvie from William the Lion in 1163. He was a son of the Earl of Angus, one of the seven earls of Scotland who ruled as princes.

The Ogilvies supported Robert Bruce, who rewarded them with grants of land, and they became heritable sheriffs of Angus. Keeping the peace was no sinecure, however, and Sir Walter Ogilvie and his son George were killed at Glenbrereth fighting against some marauding Robertsons in 1394.

The Ogilvies supported the King's army under the Earl of Mar at Harlaw in 1411, when the Lord of the Isles and his west Highland host were marching to sack Aberdeen.

In 1429 Sir Patrick Ogilvie commanded the Scottish contingent that fought in France in support of Joan of Arc. It was his descendant who was created Lord Ogilvie by James IV in 1491.*

Airlie came into the Ogilvie possession early in the fifteenth century and was confirmed to Sir John Ogilvie in a charter of 1458. The Ogilvie Earls of Findlater are descended from Sir John's brother Walter, and the Ogilvie Earls of Seafield descend from the Findlater earls.

In 1591 the Campbells attacked the Ogilvies and ravaged their lands, burning 'the bonnie House of Airlie', an act for which they paid dearly in 1645, when the Ogilvies and MacLeans destroyed Castle Gloom, the Campbell castle near Dollar, and devastated the Campbell lands.

---

* The lowest Scottish peerage title is *lord*, not baron as in England. A baron in Scotland is still to this day a medieval title and refers to the possessor of a medieval barony which has nothing to do with Parliamentary peerage titles. In various parts of the text, reference is made to lands being made into baronies— this does not mean that the chiefs were Lords of Parliament. The medieval barony is a much older creation and existed before Parliament.

James the 8th Lord Ogilvie of Airlie became the first Earl of Airlie in 1639 and was recognized as chief of the whole clan of Ogilvie. The Gaelic name for this clan incidentally is Siol Gilchrist, after their progenitor Gilchrist the son of the Earl of Angus. The Ogilvie surname therefore derives not from their progenitor's name or nickname but from the lands he acquired, which is a Lowland rather than a Highland practice.

The Ogilvies supported Charles I and the later Stuarts with great devotion and were known for their chivalry and gallantry. The 2nd Earl was taken prisoner at Philiphaugh in 1645 and condemned to death by the Covenanters. He was imprisoned at St Andrews and escaped on the eve of his execution when his sister was permitted to visit him. She wore a voluminous cloak with a hood, and once in his cell brother and sister changed clothes, and the Earl walked out dressed as a woman.

The clan was active in the Jacobite cause in 1715 and 1745, and Lord Ogilvie, the son of the 4th Earl, had to go into exile in France after Culloden. He was later pardoned and died in Scotland in 1813.

There is an Ogilvie tradition that the ghost of a drummer-boy haunts Airlie Castle and can be heard beating his drum when an Earl of Airlie is about to die. This actually occurred in 1900, when the Earl of Airlie was killed during the Boer War, and Lady Ogilvie in Scotland heard the sinister drumming on the day of his death.

It was during the invasion of Scotland by Cromwell in 1652 that the regalia of Scotland was saved by the courage of two women, who buried the crown, sceptre and sword of justice under the pulpit of Kinneff Church, just before Dunnottar Castle fell into English hands. Cromwell's men never found the regalia. The two women were Mrs Granger, the wife of the minister of Kinneff, and Mrs Ogilvie, the wife of George Ogilvie, the Governor of Dunnottar Castle, into whose keeping the regalia had been given to save it from Cromwell. After the Restoration the regalia was recovered from its hiding-place.

48.   Robertson (Duncan)

The Robertsons are known in Gaelic as *clan Donnachaidh* after Duncan, who led the clan at Bannockburn in 1314. The clan continued to be known as Duncan until around 1450, when they adopted the name of Robert, one of their chiefs who captured two of the murderers of King James I and handed them over to justice.

The clan's early history is obscure, several accounts being given—one that they are descended from the MacDonalds, another that they descend from the old Earls of Atholl, and yet another that they belong to the Kindred of Columba and would thus descend from very early Irish kings.

Duncan who led the clan at Bannockburn seems to be the earliest chief on record, and it is from his son Robert that the Robertsons of Struan descend. Their chiefly title of Struan-Robertson is derived from their Struan lands which were erected into a free barony in 1451. The question of style was a matter of chiefly choice, and the Robertson chief could just as easily have elected to be called The MacDuncan or The MacRobert of MacRobert.

William of Struan was killed by the Earl of Atholl in 1530, and the Earl seized nearly half of the clan lands. The 11th laird died in 1636 leaving an infant to succeed him, and the child's uncle Donald became captain of the clan during his infancy. He was a supporter of Charles I and followed Montrose in all his campaigns. He is said to have accounted personally for nineteen enemy dead at the Battle of Inverlochy.

Alexander Robertson of Struan who was born in 1669 was one of the most remarkable Jacobites of all. He succeeded to the chiefship in 1688 and as a youngster of nineteen took his clan out in support of Viscount Dundee, James VII's general in Scotland. He was attainted for treason and had to go into exile, but Queen Anne pardoned him in 1703 and he came back to Scotland. In 1715 he joined the Earl of Mar when he raised the Jacobite standard. He was captured at Sheriffmuir but escaped, and was recaptured shortly afterwards and again escaped. Once again he went into exile in France.

Yet again he was pardoned, in 1731, and came home again, aged sixty-two—no doubt regarded as harmless by the Government in London.

When the Jacobite standard was raised again at Glenfinnan in 1745, old Struan was seventy-six. He was too old to lead the clan in the field, but he sent them out nevertheless. After the collapse of Jacobite hopes in 1746, the Government sensibly decided to turn a blind eye to his pro-Jacobite dealings, and he was permitted to live out his life in peace, dying in 1749 aged eighty.

There were not many Highland chiefs who could boast in 1745 that they had been serving the Stuarts ever since they fought with Bonnie Dundee in 1688! Struan probably merits a special prize for long service to the Stuart cause, and the clan battle-cry of '*Garg'n uair dhuis gear*', meaning 'Fierce when roused', fitted him perfectly.

The clan's principal possessions were on Loch Tay and Loch Rannoch, and the chief's early seat was Dun Alister at one end of Loch Rannoch. There were branches of the clan further north in Inverness-shire. The clan Skene is believed to be descended from one of the early Struan-Robertson chiefs.

49. Rose

The Roses are a small 'frontier' clan whose lands in Nairn are in the Lowland belt but adjoin those of the MacIntoshes and Frasers and other Highland clans with whom the Roses have been linked throughout their history.

The Roses of Kilravock acquired lands in Nairn in the early twelfth century, and in the early thirteenth Hugh Rose of Geddes witnessed a charter for the founding of the Priory of Beaulieu. His son, also Hugh, inherited the barony of Kilravock by marriage to an heiress of the Bisset Lord of Lovat, and this was confirmed by King John Balliol in a charter of 1293.

His grandson, yet another Hugh Rose, was styled 'Hugo Rose, nobleman, lord of Kilravock'. There is a bewildering proliferation of Hughs over the centuries, this being a favourite Christian name among the clan chiefs and their immediate family, and as a result in the clan itself.

In 1431 John Rose of Kilravock obtained a fresh charter for all the clan lands, and his son, Hugh, built Kilravock Castle in 1460, since when it has continuously been the residence of the chiefs of the clan who live there to this day.

In 1467 Rose of Kilravock, Lord Forbes of Culloden and the MacIntosh of MacIntosh entered into the bond of friendship, pledging themselves to support each other, and in 1474 Kilravock was erected into a barony following the forfeiture of the Earls of Ross, since when the chiefs of the clan have always been known as the Barons of Kilravock (see footnote on page 226).

Hugh Rose of Kilravock, who was made prisoner at the Battle of Pinkie in 1547, had a distinguished career. Among other offices he held, he was Constable of Inverness Castle and Sheriff of Inverness-shire. He died at the age of ninety in 1597.

The Roses were loyal to the actual Government throughout their history and so did not support the Stuart cause in 1688, 1715 or 1745. In 1715 they, along with the Forbeses, were mainly responsible for recapturing Inverness from the Jacobites, and during the '15 they successfully defended Kilravock Castle from repeated attacks. The chief at this time was father-in-law of Duncan Forbes of Culloden, who became Lord President and who was an outstanding figure during the rising of '45.

Shortly before the Battle of Culloden, Prince Charles visited Kilravock and stayed to dinner, which must have been rather an awkward meal considering Hugh Rose's loyalty to the established Government in London. The Duke of Cumberland, who would dearly have liked to lay hands on his cousin the Prince, found out and arrived at Kilravock the next morning, but Charles had gone, and the loyalty of the Roses was never questioned, even by Cumberland.

It was a close brush, however, and one wonders what difference it would have made to events if Cumberland had found out in time to come and arrest Charles while he was dining at Kilravock with the Roses.

50. Ross

The Rosses are descended from Malcolm, the first known Earl of Ross, who died about 1150 and whose daughter married into the family of O'Beolain, the hereditary abbots of Applecross. From the O'Beolains, the Rosses are linked to the ancient Irish royal House of Tara. They are often referred to as the Clan Anrias from Anrias who was one of their O'Beolain ancestors.

The earliest chief of the Clan Ross was Fearchar Mac an t'sagairt, which means 'son of the priest' and obviously refers to his O'Beolain forefathers. Fearchar assisted Alexander II in 1214 against the son of Donald Bane, who was a claimant to Alexander's throne. For this loyalty Fearchar was knighted and eventually recognized formally in 1234 as Earl of Ross, by virtue of his descent from Malcolm whose daughter had married an O'Beolain. Fearchar is therefore the second known Earl of Ross.

William the 3rd Earl entered into a treaty with Llewellyn, Prince of Wales, in 1258, and William the 4th Earl supported Bruce, fought at Bannockburn and was a signatory to the Arbroath Declaration of Independence in 1320.

Hugh the 5th Earl had a daughter, Isabel, who in 1317 married Robert Bruce's brother Edward Bruce, King of Ireland. The 6th Earl died fighting in the Battle of Halidon Hill in 1333, and William, 7th Earl of Ross and Lord of Skye, died without male heirs in 1372. He was the 6th chief of Clan Ross, and the chiefship now passed to his half-brother Hugh, the first of the Ross chiefs of Balnagowan and the 7th chief of the clan. Hugh obtained a charter for his lands of Balnagowan in 1374.

The earldom of Ross passed out of the family through Euphemia, the daughter of William the 7th Earl, eventually came into the family of the MacDonald Lords of the Isles and was reverted to the Crown in 1476.

The surname of the Earls of Ross was, of course, not Ross at all, but O'Beolain, and it is conjectured that Hugh of Balnagowan when he became chief of the clan adopted the surname of Ross to show his family's connection with the earldom. Ross is a place-name therefore which became adopted as a surname quite late in the clan's history.

The Rosses of Balnagowan do not figure largely in the political history of Scotland. When David Ross the 13th of Balnagowan died in 1711, the chiefship passed to a collateral branch, the Rosses of Pitcalvie. The Balnagowan estates became the property of outsiders, and it was this which led to the savage and ruthless Ross evictions during the Highland Clearances (see Chapter 9)—evictions which had nothing whatever to do with the old line of clan chiefs.

The Pitcalvie Rosses were chiefs up to the time of the rising of 1745, for in 1740 Simon Fraser, Lord Lovat, refers to Ross of Pitcalvie as 'a brother chief'. But the Rosses were not Jacobite sympathizers and seem to have remained peacefully on their lands during the Jacobite era.

David Ross of Balnagowan, who died in 1711, had left his estate to the family of Ross of Hawkhead, who were of English descent and had no connection whatever with the Clan Ross but who assumed the chiefship nevertheless. But when the Hawkhead incomers died out, Miss Ross of Pitcalvie was recognized in 1903 as representer of the ancient chiefly line and became the 34th chief of the clan with the surname of Ross of Ross, so that the chiefship has been restored.

51. Shaw

The Clan Shaw is one of the important member clans of the great Clan Chattan con-federation and held lands in Rothiemurchus from the Bishops of Moray in the early part of the thirteenth century; later they held the same lands from the MacIntosh chiefs of Clan Chattan.

The clan's progenitor is Shaw Mor, a son of a MacDuff Earl of Fife, who helped to put down a rebellion in Moray around 1153. From Shaw also descend the MacIntoshes, and indeed the MacIntoshes may be a branch of the original Shaw clan, as are the Farquharsons, these three forming the most prominent of the Clan Chattan clans, apart from the Macphersons who were the original Clan Chattan chiefs before the MacIntoshes obtained that chiefship.

The Gaelic name for the Clan Shaw is '*Na si'aich*' which does not translate as 'Clan Shaw' but means 'Shaw-ites' or 'Shaw-people'. The chiefs of the clan never used the title, for instance, of MacShaw although Shaw was their famous founder. It is highly probable that the MacIntoshes, Farquharsons and Shaws were all Shaw-people originally. After 1396, however, the Gaelic term '*Na si'iach*' refers specifically to the Shaws of Rothiemurchus, chiefs of Clan Shaw.

It is not clear how the Shaws came to hold Rothiemurchus from the MacIntoshes. It is probable that the MacIntosh acquisition of the Captaincy of Clan Chattan gave them status above all the other Shaw-people.

James Shaw was killed at Harlaw in 1411 fighting for the Lord of the Isles. His son Alisdair Ciar obtained a charter dated 24 September 1464 for Rothiemurchus, from the 11th MacIntosh chief. It is curious that apparently in the charter he is described as Alasdair Ciar *MacIntosh*, which suggests that the Shaws and MacIntoshes at this late date still considered themselves one people, even if the Shaws had their own chiefs who were subordinate to the high chiefs of Clan Chattan.

The history of the Shaws is obscured by the MacIntosh history, as is often the case with Clan Chattan member clans, but they supported Montrose and fought for the Stuarts in 1715, although by that time they had been broken up as a clan and absorbed by the MacIntoshes and Macphersons. They appear to have had no separate chiefs after about 1600.

In 1970, however, the Lord Lyon officially recognized a descendant of the old Shaw chiefs as chief of the clan.

There remains at present a great deal of mystery about the early Shaw-MacIntosh relationship, and it is at least possible that if a MacIntosh had not been lucky enough to marry Eva, the heretrix of the great Clan Chattan, and so become high chief of the whole confederation, the Shaws might have been able to maintain their separate existence as a senior branch of the same original blood-line as the MacIntoshes. That the Farquharsons escaped the same fate as the Shaws, and were not broken-up as a clan, was probably due as much to their geographical location in Aberdeenshire as anything else.

52.   Sinclair

The Sinclairs or St Clairs are of Norman origin and are also descended in the female line from the famous French family of noblemen the Sires de Coucy, whose prestige rivalled that of kings.

The first Sinclair to arrive in Scotland appears to have been Henry, who received a grant of lands in Haddington in 1162. Sir William Sinclair, who was granted the barony of Rosslyn in 1280, was the son of Robert St Clair in Normandy and presumably of the same family as the Haddington Sinclairs who had arrived in Scotland earlier.

Both these families supported Bruce, and Sir William of Rosslyn was killed in southern Spain along with Good Sir James Douglas, carrying Robert Bruce's heart into battle against the Moors.

Sir William's son Sir Henry became Earl of Orkney. It was William the 3rd Sinclair Earl of Orkney who became the 1st Sinclair Earl of Caithness in 1455. In 1470 he was forced to surrender the earldom of Orkney to the Crown in return for the castle of Ravenscraig in Fife.

There had, of course, been Earls of Caithness for a long time before the arrival of the Sinclairs, and it would seem that when the family acquired the earldom they acquired a ready-made clan with it. The Sinclair clansmen, the original inhabitants of Caithness, are of much earlier origin than their Sinclair chiefs from whom they eventually took their surname. As has happened in similar cases, however, the incoming chief soon became as Highland as his clan and quickly settled down to a life of feuding with the Sutherlands, MacKays and Gunns. The far north of Scotland was not a peaceful place to live in!

The 1st Earl of Caithness disinherited his eldest son, Lord Sinclair, who is reputed to have been feeble-minded. He left Rosslyn to his second son, whose descendants are the Earls of

Rosslyn; and he was succeeded as 2nd Earl of Caithness by his third son William, who fell at Flodden in 1513 fighting with James IV.

John the 3rd Earl was killed fighting in Orkney, and the 4th Earl, George Sinclair, was something of a monster, imprisoning his own heir in a dungeon for seven years until he died in the end of hunger and thirst.

Around 1612 the Earl of Caithness discovered Adam Smith, a forger who lived in Banff. He had been arrested in 1599 but managed to escape execution by designing a curious lock for the King, who as a result pardoned him. Adam Smith was promptly installed in Girnigoe Castle (Sinclair Castle) under the patronage of the Earl. Within a short time the district was flooded with counterfeit coin.

Eventually one of the family of the Earls of Sutherland, who were avowed enemies of the Earls of Caithness, obtained permission to arrest Smith and bring him to trial. By this time Smith was living in a house in Thurso, and he was arrested, but the Sinclairs found out and tried to free him. There was a good deal of blood shed, during which Adam Smith, private forger by appointment to the Earl of Caithness, was allegedly killed 'to prevent him escaping'.

The 6th Earl, who died in 1676, was forced to leave all his property to his principal creditor, Sir John Campbell of Glenorchy, who promptly tried to assume the title of Earl of Caithness. The Sinclair heir seized the estates from the Campbells, and eventually there was a violent clan battle near Wick in 1680. The following year the Privy Council quite rightly recognized George Sinclair as 7th Earl of Caithness, and the Campbells of Glenorchy were created Earls of Breadalbane.

Although the Sinclairs were Jacobite sympathizers, they did not rise for the Stuarts in 1745. Their Castle of Mey now belongs to Queen Elizabeth the Queen Mother, but the present Earl of Caithness, who is chief of the clan, still owns Girnigoe Castle, facing Sinclair's Bay north of Wick, the ancient stronghold of his ancestors, now unfortunately in ruins.

53.   Skene

The Skenes are traditionally descended from a younger son of an early Robertson chief, and their Gaelic name is Siol Sgeine no Clann Donnachaidh Mhar which in effect says that the Skenes are the Robertsons of Mar.

There are differing accounts of how they came to break away from the stem clan and settle in the lowlands of Aberdeenshire. The popular one is that a young Robertson saved the life of one of the Scottish kings by killing a wolf with his *sgian* (hunting-knife, pronounced 'skene'). His lands were presumably therefore named to commemorate this feat. On the other hand it is claimed that the Aberdeenshire lands of the clan were called Skene before the clan ever appeared on them, and that the Skenes take their names from the land where they settled.

If the John Skene who signed the Ragman Roll of 1296 was styled 'de Skene', meaning 'of Skene', then the second explanation would seem likely. But one early account says that he was styled 'le Skene', which means something quite different, John 'the *Sgian*' (like Mack the Knife), which would support the popular theory.

As the three wolves' heads in the Skene arms are shown as being impaled on the points of three *sgians*, the clan tradition obviously prefers the more popular account of how they acquired their name.

Robert Skene fought with Bruce, and as a reward his lands of Skene were erected into a barony in 1318. The dirk (*sgian*, skene) with which he was invested is still in existence. Adam Skene, the chief of the clan, was killed at Harlaw in 1411 defending Aberdeen against the Lord of the Isles and his west Highland host.

Alexander Skene of Skene died at Flodden in 1513, and his grandson was killed at Pinkie in 1547, so that the clan has a proud record of fighting in the national interest. They were followers of Mary, Queen of Scots, and the chief lost a younger son fighting for her in 1562. They remained loyal to James VI and Charles I, but after James VII was forced into exile, they seem to have abandoned the Stuart cause.

The chiefly family failed in the male line in 1827, and the estates went to the Earl of Fife. There are, however, several branch families of the name of Skene, including the Moncrief-Skenes of Pitlour.

The coat of arms of Skene of Skene is of special interest to Highlanders, because in the original matriculation of arms in 1672 the right-hand 'supporter' of the shield is a Highlander wearing a kilt without a plaid—i.e. the little kilt of today, as opposed to the great belted plaid which was its forerunner. This makes nonsense of the claims that the little kilt was the invention of an Englishman more than fifty years later, since the Lyon painter could not very well have depicted something that did not exist.

The ancient seat of the chiefs of the clan was Skene Castle in Mar.

54. Stewart

It is one of the strange quirks of history that a name so closely identified with both Scotland and the Highlands, to say nothing of the ruling Houses of Scotland and of the United Kingdom, is not Scottish at all but of Anglo-Norman origin. The Stewart ancestors were the hereditary Stewards of Dol, near St Malo in Brittany, and are descended from Alan, Steward of Dol in 1045.

It was an Alan of this Breton family who became Baron of Oswestry in Shropshire under King Henry I of England, and his son Walter FitzAlan was created hereditary Steward of Scotland by King David I around 1140. Walter is celebrated as the founder in 1163 of Paisley Abbey and died in 1177. His brother was the ancestor of the present Dukes of Norfolk.

The 'royal' Stewarts are not strictly speaking Highland at all. They were members of a royal household which had its seat outside the Highlands, and eventually, as a result of Walter the 6th hereditary High Steward marrying Bruce's daughter, Princess Marjory, they became Scottish kings. They do not rightly concern us in this book, but their dynasty failed with Mary

Queen of Scots, who had married Henry Stuart, Lord Darnley, who was the father of James VI of Scotland and of England, and therefore the male ancestor of the ill-fated Stuart House (who spelled their name differently from the earlier Stewarts).* The House of Stuart finally failed in the male line when Henry, Cardinal Duke of York, brother of Bonnie Prince Charlie, died in Rome in 1807. Their line is perpetuated in the present royal family of Britain who are the Protestant descendants of James VI and I.

There are many Lowland and Border Stewart families in Scotland, but the principal Highland clan were the Stewarts of Appin. This clan traces its origins from Sir John Stewart of Bonkyl, younger son of Alexander the 4th Great Steward of Scotland. Sir John was killed in 1297 fighting for William Wallace. One of his descendants was John Stewart of Innermeath who married a daughter of John, or Ewen, the last MacDougal Lord of Lorn, and so became first Stewart Lord of Lorn. When John Stewart, Lord of Lorn, was killed by MacDougalls in 1463, his son Dougal, assisted by the MacLarens, tried to recover his lost possessions but was successful only in acquiring Appin, and he became the founder of the Appin Stewarts, one of the proudest of all the west Highland clans.

The Appin Stewarts were particularly friendly with their near neighbours the MacDonalds of Glencoe. They feuded bitterly with the Campbells and fought for Montrose, for Dundee and for the Stuart kings throughout the Jacobite period. There was never any doubt as to where their sympathies lay.

There were many branches of the Appin Stewarts, including Invernahyle, Ardshiel, Auchnacrone and Ballachuilish.

The Stewarts of Invernahyle had a long-standing quarrel with the Campbells of Dunstaffnage, and in the early sixteenth century all the family were killed by Green Colin of Dunstaffnage except for one small boy.

The child was taken to safety in Ardnamurchan and raised as a blacksmith's son. He became extremely strong, and from his ability to wield two heavy hammers at once, one in each hand, he

---

* Henry Stuart's father was Matthew Stuart, 4th Earl of Lennox, who became a French citizen in 1537 and adopted the French spelling of the name. A branch of the Darnley Stuarts had been Counts of Aubigny in France since 1423 and founded a notable Franco-Scottish family.

was nicknamed '*Domhnull nan Ord*', 'Donald of the Hammers'. When he reached manhood, his foster-father presented him with a sword and revealed his true identity. Donald and a dozen followers went to Dunstaffnage, where they killed Green Colin and his retainers and took possession again of Invernahyle.

He became Tutor of Appin during the minority of the clan chief and in 1547 led the clan at the Battle of Pinkie. It was following this battle that Donald Stewart of Invernahyle, Donald of the Hammers, stole poultry from a wedding feast being given by the Graham Earl of Menteith, subsequently killing the Earl and his followers, as a result of which the Grahams of Menteith became known throughout the Highlands as 'the Grahams of the Hens'.

The Appin Stewarts were out under Robert their chief in 1715. In 1745 Stewart of Ardshiel commanded the clan in the field.

Apart from the Appin Stewarts and their branches mentioned above, other famous Highland Stewart families included the Atholl Stewarts, descendants of that picturesque but ruthlessly ferocious character Sir Alexander Stewart, Earl of Buchan, fourth son of King Robert II and best known as 'the Wolf of Badenoch'. He had his lair at Lochindorb Castle, was excommunicated and burned down Elgin Cathedral (he had already been excommunicated when he did this). From him descend the Stewarts of Garth, one of whom, General David Stewart of Garth, wrote *Sketches of the Highlanders*, which is an invaluable source-book for information on the Highlands prior to 1746.

Sir John Stewart of Balveny was the son of Sir James Stewart, the Black Knight of Lorn, who had married the widow of King James I. He was created Earl of Atholl in 1547, but the title was lost to the family when the 5th Stewart Earl of Atholl died without a male heir and the earldom passed to the Murrays.

Grandtully Castle in Atholl was the lair of the Steuarts of Grandtully, another devoted Jacobite clan. The Bute Stuarts, who are illegitimately descended from King Robert II, are also a Highland branch of this great and widespread clan—more than a clan, for it has notable Lowland and Border Houses, including the Earls of Galloway who at present are the senior representatives of the old High Stewards of Scotland.

The Stewarts of Ardvorlich still hold their ancient Highland lands, but the Appin estates passed out of the clan's possession.

The chief of the Highland clan today is Stewart of Appin and Ardshiel.

55. Sutherland

The Sutherlands take their name from the district they inhabited and are of mixed Norse and Pictish origin with a later infusion of Gaelic-speaking Celto-Irish stock. The people of this area therefore represent all the principal fusions which went into the making of the Highlanders.

The Earls of Sutherland, who are the clan chiefs, descend from Freskin the Fleming, who has already been mentioned as the ancestor of the Clan Murray. Freskin's grandson Hugh acquired the lordship of Sutherland some time after 1197, and Hugh's son William became Earl of Sutherland around 1222 and died in 1248.

There were, of course, earlier magnates in the north, and there were Earls of Caithness who apparently ruled over Caithness and Sutherland, who were declared forfeit because of rebellion in 1197 and who predate both the Sinclairs and the Sutherlands.

The Sutherland Earls quickly became one of the most important families in Scotland. The 2nd Earl who succeeded in 1248 as a baby lived to fight at Bannockburn in 1314 and to sign the Arbroath Declaration of Independence in 1320, dying in 1325 after having been earl for seventy-seven years.

His son Kenneth, the 3rd Earl, died at Halidon Hill in 1333 fighting the English. The 4th Earl, William, married Princess Margaret, eldest daughter of Robert Bruce by his second wife, and his son John claimed the crown of Scotland and was even chosen by David II to be his heir in preference to Robert, son of the High Steward. But John died at Lincoln in 1361, and the succession went to Robert II, founder of the royal House of Stewart. Had John Sutherland lived, it might have been the Royal House of Sutherland!

Dunrobin Castle, the chiefly seat, is named after Robert the 6th Earl, who married in 1389 a daughter of Alexander Stewart, Wolf of Badenoch and a son of King Robert II.

When the 9th Earl died without a male heir in 1514, the succession passed through his daughter Elizabeth, Countess of Sutherland in her own right, to her husband, Adam Gordon of Aboyne, younger son of the second Earl of Huntly.

The Sutherlands, Sinclairs and MacKays were engaged in a long three-cornered feud with frequent shifting of alliances. The Gunns were usually involved also when they were not protecting themselves against the Keiths. The MacKays in particular had a grudge against Adam, the first Gordon Earl, and this led to the Battle of Torran Dubh near Rogart in Strathfleet in 1517, but it was the Sutherlands who won and the MacKays eventually had to submit to them.

The 11th Earl, John Sutherland, called 'the Good Earl', accompanied the Queen Regent to France in 1550 along with the Earl of Huntly. Shortly after Mary, Queen of Scots, returned to rule Scotland in 1560, Sutherland and Huntly were charged with rebellion, and the Good Earl had to seek refuge in Flanders. He came back to Scotland in 1565, and in 1567 he and his pregnant wife were both poisoned at Helmsdale Castle by Isobel Sinclair, a cousin of the Earl of Caithness. They died five days later at Dunrobin.

Alexander the 12th Earl succeeded as a minor. The Earl of Atholl, who was made his guardian, sold his wardship to the Earl of Caithness, hereditary enemy of the Sutherlands. Alexander was carried off to Caithness and forced to marry Lady Barbara Sinclair. When he came of age, he divorced her and married Lady Jean Gordon.

The 14th Earl opposed Charles I's new prayer book and did not support Montrose. The Sutherlands were loyal to the new rulers, William and Mary, in 1688, and to their successors. They fought for George II in 1745.

In 1746, when Dunrobin Castle was occupied by Jacobites, the Sutherlands attacked it and recaptured it. It is the last castle in Britain to have been captured in time of war, happily by its rightful owners.

The part played by the English husband of Elizabeth, Countess of Sutherland, during the clearances, has already been described in Chapter 9.

Dunrobin Castle is still the seat of the chief of Clan Sutherland, '*Ban mhorair Chataibh*', 24th Countess of Sutherland in her own right. It is constructed in the style of a French château and along with Inveraray must be one of the most beautiful and impressive homes in Scotland. The chief also has a home at Uppat House near Brora.

56. Urquhart

The Clan Urquhart derive their name from the district called Urquhart on the Black Isle, facing Dingwall. There do not seem to be any grounds at all for the earlier theory that they were a branch of Clan Forbes, who held Urquhart Castle on Loch Ness. The Urquharts were a clan in their own right from the earliest times.

In 1306 William Urquhart was Sheriff of Cromarty. He married a daughter of Hugh, Earl of Ross, and his son Adam succeeded in enlarging the clan's possessions.

Thomas Urquhart of Cromarty is said to have lost seven sons at the Battle of Pinkie in 1547. He was married to a daughter of Lord Abernethy. Legend has it that he was the father of twenty-five sons and eleven daughters but is discreetly silent on the question of their mothers.

The most famous chief of this clan was Sir Thomas Urquhart Knight of Cromartie, chief of the clan in the reign of Charles I. He made a scholarly translation of Rabelais and traced his ancestry back to Adam and Eve, and Charles I knighted him at Whitehall. He was loyal to the Stuarts and fought for Charles II at the Battle of Worcester. Afterwards his estates were declared forfeit by Cromwell. The date and place of his death are unknown, but tradition has it that he died laughing delightedly when he heard of the restoration of Charles II, which would place his death in 1660, at which time he was probably about sixty or sixty-five years of age at least, and possibly much older (his tutor was born in 1547, it is said).

The male line of chiefs ended in 1741, when Colonel James Urquhart died. In 1958, however, the Court of the Lord Lyon recognized an heir to the chiefship, in the United States, and the new chief recovered Castlecraig, the ancient and ruined fortress of the clan near Cromarty.

This clan also has therefore recovered an important part of its ancient heritage and a vital link with its past.

Appendix I

MacAlpin, the Clan That Wasn't

The Siol Alpin is one of the least-discussed and more mysterious clan alliances in Highland history. It is not a confederation of clans but rather a *family* of seven clans all of common descent from King Alpin I, the last of the Dalriadic kings.

There has never been a Clan MacAlpin living on its own clan lands and with its own hereditary chiefs and chieftains. The present-day MacAlpin (with or without the unnecessary e on the end) almost certainly belongs to one of the seven clans.

When the earnest Lowlanders, bent on giving surnames to Highlanders who had no surnames and spoke little English, realized the difficulty of their task, they must soon have discovered that the way to find out the 'name' of a Highlander was to question him about his chief. The clansmen had listened to the bardic recitals of clan genealogy from their earliest childhood, back to the first man to settle on the land *and beyond*. Thus a MacKinnon might say that his chief was the son of Fingon (or Findanus) or he might easily say that he was the son of Alpin ('son' meaning 'House of')—for the early MacKinnon chiefs were all known as So-and-so MacFingon MacAlpin, so-and-so of the House of Findanus (who gave the clan his name) who was of the House of Alpin (who gave the clan their lands).

The descent is as follows:

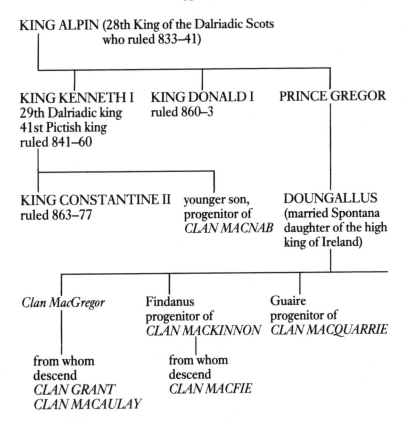

KING ALPIN (28th King of the Dalriadic Scots who ruled 833–41)

KING KENNETH I
29th Dalriadic king
41st Pictish king
ruled 841–60

KING DONALD I
ruled 860–3

PRINCE GREGOR

KING CONSTANTINE II
ruled 863–77

younger son,
progenitor of
CLAN MACNAB

DOUNGALLUS
(married Spontana
daughter of the high
king of Ireland)

Clan MacGregor

Findanus
progenitor of
CLAN MACKINNON

Guaire
progenitor of
CLAN MACQUARRIE

from whom
descend
CLAN GRANT
CLAN MACAULAY

from whom
descend
CLAN MACFIE

The Clan MacAulay in question here is that of Ardincaple and not that of Lewis, which has no connection at all.

It can be seen from this that the 'senior' branch of the Siol Alpin was the Clan Macnab, being descended from a younger son of King Kenneth MacAlpin. The MacGregors have always claimed seniority, but in fact the whole question is completely academic because these seven clans (Macnab, MacGregor, MacKinnon, MacQuarrie, Grant, MacAulay and MacFie) never acted in concert.

It has been the habit of early Highland historians to dismiss the Siol Alpin as a fanciful, if not fictitious, piece of Highland nonsense. The reason for this is perfectly obvious—they searched clan histories for mention of the Siol Alpin *doing* anything and

failed to find it. They compared it with the Clan Chattan confederation and could find no similarity, and so they dismissed the
Siol Alpin altogether.

The royal House of Alpin, Scotland's first kings, did not need
to be taught the ABC of their kingly craft, for they had been kings
for centuries. When they gave grants of land to the younger sons
of the family, they kept them well separated. They did not want
the younger sons and their descendants combining to put one of
their number in place of the current ruler. It was the old and
effective policy of divide and rule, and only a fool allowed younger
sons and cousins to congregate together. Thus of these seven
clans three are Hebridean and lived on islands, three are west
Highland, and the Grants settled right across Scotland in the
north-east. But then the Grants probably received their Strathspey lands by marriage, as did so many Highland clan chiefs.

The original MacKinnon lands were in Mull, from which they
spread to Arran and later to Skye, although they had an early Skye
stronghold at Dunakin sometimes called MacKinnon Castle.
The Grant lands were in Strathspey and Glenmoriston. The
Macnab lands were in Perthshire on the western shore of Loch
Tay, and from an early time they were Abbots of Glendochart.
The MacAulays had their seat at Ardincaple in Dumbartonshire.
The MacFies possessed Colonsay. The MacQuarries had lands
in Mull near the MacKinnons, but they also owned the island of
Ulva, to the west of Mull. The MacGregors had numerous
possessions, their early principal seat being Glenorchy, but they
had estates at Glenstrae, Glenlyon, Glengyle, Glenlochy and
Balquhidder, most of which passed into Campbell ownership in
the same way as a good deal of MacDonald territory did.

The clans share a common plant badge—the pine. The
MacKinnons and MacFies both had the same Alpin war-cry of
'*Cuimhnich bas Alpein*', meaning 'Remember the death of King
Alpin' (which the MacKinnons now have as a second motto); the
MacGregors were more explicit, adopting as their motto ''*S
Rioghal mo dhream*' which means 'My race is royal', which indeed
it is, but they are not alone in that, nor are the Siol Alpin clans.
Many clan chiefs married into the various royal families, perhaps
the best known being the 9th Duke of Argyll who married
Princess Louise, the daughter of Queen Victoria. He was not the
first Campbell to marry a princess, of course.

The evidence for the common descent of these particular clans is traditional, as is the greater part of Highland history, but bardic traditions are far more accurate than the garbled history of the early monkish chroniclers.

Although the clans never acted together as a confederation, there are interesting historical links. For instance, when the MacKinnon lands in Skye were forfeit after the Jacobite rising of 1715, it was the Laird of Grant who bought them (he had not taken part in the rising, although some of his clan had!). He then sold them back to a MacKinnon clansman who settled them on the heirs of the attainted Jacobite MacKinnon chief, so that in effect the lands were not lost. There can be no reasonable explanation of this act other than that of a feeling of common ancestry, of belonging to the same 'family', as indeed they did.

In 1591 a bond of friendship and mutual support (they were called 'bonds of manrent') was signed between MacGregor of Glenstrae and MacAulay of Ardincaple, and in a later bond of 1694 the MacAulays declared themselves to be a branch of Clan Gregor.

In 1671 James MacGregor of MacGregor and Lachlan MacKinnon of MacKinnon also entered into a bond of manrent the wording of which is, 'For the special love and amitie between these persons, and *condescending that they are descended lawfully fra twa breethern of auld descent*, quhairfore and for certain onerous causes moving, we witt ye to be bound and obleisit, likeas be the tenor hereof we faithfully bind and obleise us and our successors, our kin, friends and followers faithfully to serve one anither in all causes with our men and servants, against all who live or die.'

An earlier bond of manrent concerned Lachlan MacKinnon of Strathardill and Finlay Macnab of Bowain and was signed at Uir or 12 July 1606. It reads that, 'Happening to foregadder togedder, with certain of the said Finlay's friends, in their rooms in the Laird of Glenurchay's country, and the said Lauchlan and Finlay this long time bygane oversaw their awn duties till udderis in respect of the long distance betwixt their dwelling places, quhairfore baith the saids now and in all time coming are content to be bound and obleisit, *with the consent of their kyn and friends*, to do all sted, pleasure, assistance and service that lies in them ilk ane to uthers; the said Finlay acknoledging the said Lauchlan *as ane kind chieff and of ane house*; and likewise the said Lauchlan to acknoledge the said Finlay Macnab, his friend, *as his special kynsman and friend.'*

There really seems to be little doubt that these clans shared the same common origin, and the fact that it was royal is nothing out of the ordinary, for most of the west Highland Celtic clans were connected with both Irish and Dalriadic royalty. The MacGregor-MacKinnon bond is particularly interesting in that it spells out that the clans are descended anciently from brothers, as they were, the three sons of Doungallus founding the clans MacGregor, MacKinnon and MacQuarrie.

What is of real interest is that the MacGregors and MacNabs, who lived a long way from Skye, should have entered into bonds with the MacKinnon chiefs, and that the chief of Clan Grant who could hardly have been further removed from Skye, should have saved the MacKinnon clan lands in time of trouble, all these things happening centuries after the origins of the clans in question.

There is an amusing story that in the first quarter of the eighteenth century the Siol Alpin chiefs met in an attempt to band themselves together, but that the meeting broke up in disorder because they could not agree on seniority—an outcome which could easily have been anticipated, especially if the MacGregors expected the Macnabs to acknowledge their claims, which are based on bad genealogy.

There is a version which claims that Macnab, MacKinnon, MacGregor and MacQuarrie are all commonly descended from Fearchar Fada, the 15th King of Dalriada. Since those four are the stem clans descended from Alpin, they are of course descended from all Alpin's ancestors including Fearchar Fada— but they did not exist as clans before the death of Alpin in 841.

One final item of interest to MacAlpin is that the fusion of the Picts and the Scots in 843 under King Kenneth of Dalriada was not the first one but the second. The genealogical evidence for this given in *The Foundations of Scotland* by the late Dr Agnes Mure MacKenzie, in which she shows that the Dalriadic King Eocha-Annuine IV was King of the Picts in 836.

The table is:

DALRIADIC SCOTS	PICTS
25th king. **SELVACH II** (son of Eogan) 772–96	37th king. **BREST** (son of Constantine) 833–6
26th king. *EOCHA-ANNUINE IV* (Eoganan, Ewen) son of Aodh-Fin 796–839	38th king. *EOCAH-ANNUINE IV* (Eoganan, Ewen) son of Aodh-Fin 836–9
27th king. **DUNGAL** (son of Selvach II) 839	39th king. **WRAD** 839–42
28th king. **KING ALPIN** (son of Eoganan) 833 (or 839) –841	40th king. **BRED** 842–3
29th king.	41st king.

KENNETH I (MACALPIN)
SON OF ALPIN I
841–60 King of the Scots
843–60 King of the Picts and the Scots

Appendix II

The State of the Clans in 1745

The list of the Highland clans, both Hanoverian and Jacobite, which was provided by Lord President Forbes of Culloden to the Government in London in 1745 is given below.

Those who actually rose for the Prince are marked '(OUT)', and it will be noted that while Forbes's list contains twenty-one clans who came out for the Prince, there were at least twenty-six at Culloden. Furthermore, it is known that in the centre of the Jacobite army there were companies of mixed clans, not mentioned by name in the Jacobite battle-order and probably fighting under the MacLachlan chief or else with Colonel John Roy Stewart's Edinburgh Regiment. The total number of clans represented at Culloden is much more probably thirty-five or even forty.

Forbes's list illustrates the difficulty facing anybody who tries to find out just how many Highland clans there really were prior to 1746, for although some clans would be included among the followers of the greater chiefs, he does not mention clans such as MacNeil, which was out in 1715 and whose chief was imprisoned for his part in the rising of '45, nor the Macnabs, who were also out in 1715 and who came in strength under one of their chieftains in 1745. Nor does he mention his own clan or the MacFarlanes or the Grahams—to say nothing of the MacGillivrays and MacLarens, both of whom were at Culloden.

There is a considerable difference between the various clan lists compiled up to 1745, and the modern lists of clans in books—even allowing for the fact that modern clan books usually include Border clans and Lowland houses, plus a number of Highland 'Names' which were not clans at all in the real sense of the word but rather families attached to clans—such as the MacCulloughs, for instance.

The reader's attention is again drawn to the fact that the Camerons were out without their chief, who was in exile, and the MacLeans without their chief, who was in custody. The Grants, Gordons and Macnabs were all part of the Jacobite army *despite* their chiefs, and the Clanranald men came out under their chief's son, old Clanranald having flatly refused to rise. The MacKenzies and Campbells are generally regarded as Hanoverian, but they provided men for the Jacobites nevertheless, which makes absolute nonsense of the grim picture which some historians have tried to paint of savage medieval chiefs forcing beardless boys into the cannon's mouth at sword point.

Another point of interest is that the Highland fighting strength was estimated at around 22,000 of which 12,000 were supposedly Jacobite, but at no time did the Jacobite army contain anything even remotely like this number of Highlanders. Indeed, when the Prince's army crossed into England on the daring raid south to Derby, its total strength has been estimated at 5,000, a great part of which was non-Highland! Of course, it is true that there would never have been a rising of '45 unless the clans had mustered in some strength at Glenfinnan, but the Prince never received anything like maximum support from the Jacobite clans.

The question remains open—how many actual distinct Highland clans *were* there in the eighteenth century, and *who* were they? One can only make a reasoned calculation. There is no definitive answer. But a figure of around sixty seems to be generous considering that most lists give fewer than forty. There were certainly never the eighty or ninety who today claim to have been Highland clans.

Here then is Forbes's list, which contains a total of thirty-one clans, which includes listing MacDonald as five clans, not one, so that the basic list is of twenty-seven clans.

Cameron	(OUT)	Chief in exile.
Campbell		Some fought at Culloden where fifty were taken prisoner
Chisholm	(OUT)	
Drummond	(OUT)	
Farquharson	(OUT)	

Fraser	(OUT)	
Gordon	(OUT)	Chief not out
Grant	(OUT)	Chief not out
MacDonald of Sleat		
MacDonald of Clanranald	(OUT)	Chief not out
Macdonell of Glengarry	(OUT)	
MacDonald of Glencoe	(OUT)	
Macdonell of Keppoch	(OUT)	
MacDougall		
MacGregor	(OUT)	
MacIntosh	(OUT)	Chief with the Hanoverian army
MacKay		
MacLachlan	(OUT)	
MacLean	(OUT)	Chief a Government prisoner
MacLeod		The Raasay MacLeods were out
MacKinnon	(OUT)	
MacKenzie		There were MacKenzies with the Jacobite army
Macpherson	(OUT)	
Menzies	(OUT)	
Munro		
Murray	(OUT)	
Robertson	(OUT)	
Ross		
Sinclair		
Stewart	(OUT)	
Sutherland		

Appendix III

Succession to Chiefship

In this book there are several references to clans 'still' being without a chief or having 'acquired' chiefs, which may confuse those who do not know that the clan system is a living system and was *not* (as is popularly but wrongly stated) killed at Culloden. What was lost at Culloden was not the system but the leadership of the chief around whom clan life and the clan economy revolved. The clans became fatherless.

The question of chiefship of a Scottish clan is decided by the Lord Lyon King of Arms in Edinburgh, who is not only the head of the Scottish heraldic establishment (and a judge, sitting daily in his own court of law, Lyon Court) but also the official genealogist for Scotland.

The chiefship of a clan is absolutely linked to the possession of the undifferenced arms of the chief, and it is the Lord Lyon who investigates all claims to succession; in bestowing the arms (and the supporters, which are the hallmark of the chief of a whole name) he adjudicates both heraldically and genealogically. The Lord Lyon's 'recognition' of a chief is what in fact makes a chief. Such recognition of chiefs, chieftains and heads of territorial Houses in Scotland is notified to the Lord Chamberlain in London as it arises, and is published from time to time in lists in the *Government Gazette* (in the case of Scotland it is the *Edinburgh* not the *London Gazette*).

It is thus perfectly normal for a chiefship which has been long vacant to be applied for, and when that happens, the Lord Lyon will recognize the legal representer of an ancient chief, so that a chiefless clan can once more have its chief if the person with a legal claim to represent the old chiefs can be found.

In the case of the MacPherson-MacIntosh dispute, the Lord Lyon was the correct person to adjudicate, which he did in the light of information available at that time.

Today many clans are re-acquiring *some* part of their ancient lands, chiefs are being identified and gazetted by the Crown, and clansmen all over the world have a very real and living link with their ancient past.

GENEALOGY 1

THE VACANT THRONE

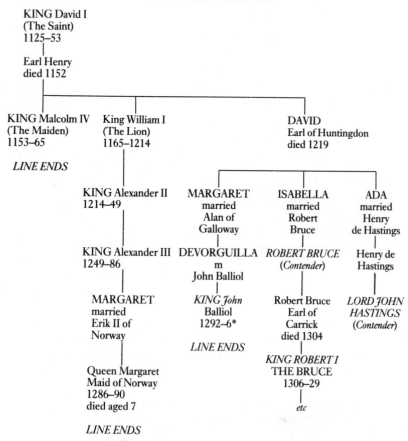

---

* King John was deposed by Edward I of England, *not* by the Scots. He did not abdicate, either, and he did not die till 1313, seven years after Bruce had had himself crowned.

GENEALOGY 2

THE HANOVERIAN SUCCESSION

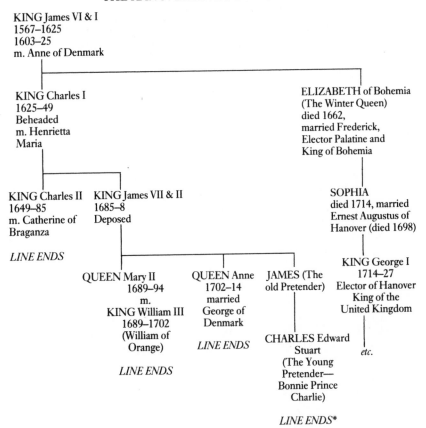

KING James VI & I
1567–1625
1603–25
m. Anne of Denmark

KING Charles I
1625–49
Beheaded
m. Henrietta
Maria

ELIZABETH of Bohemia
(The Winter Queen)
died 1662,
married Frederick,
Elector Palatine and
King of Bohemia

KING Charles II
1649–85
m. Catherine of
Braganza

LINE ENDS

KING James VII & II
1685–8
Deposed

SOPHIA
died 1714, married
Ernest Augustus of
Hanover (died 1698)

QUEEN Mary II
1689–94
m.
KING William III
1689–1702
(William of
Orange)

LINE ENDS

QUEEN Anne
1702–14
married
George of
Denmark

LINE ENDS

JAMES (The
old Pretender)

CHARLES Edward
Stuart
(The Young
Pretender—
Bonnie Prince
Charlie)

KING George I
1714–27
Elector of Hanover
King of the
United Kingdom

etc.

LINE ENDS*

* Strictly speaking, the line ended not with Prince Charles Edward but with his younger brother, Cardinal Henry, who outlived him. As a Catholic Cardinal, Henry was unmarried.

NOTES

These notes are not intended to be in any way exhaustive but are merely an amplification of the main index. The mention of battles can be very bewildering, and the mention of events happening in a particular reign can be equally bewildering unless there is an accompanying list of kings and queens with dates.

BATTLES MENTIONED IN THE TEXT

1138 THE BATTLE OF THE STANDARD: King David I was defeated at Northallerton while attempting to push the Scottish border southwards into northern England. Despite losing the battle, he did succeed in annexing Northumberland, Cumberland and Durham.

Clans/or clan chiefs known to have been present: MUNRO.

1263 THE BATTLE OF LARGS (2 October): King Alexander III, helped by a sudden fierce storm, defeated King Haakon of Norway in the latter's last attempt to restore Norwegian power in Scotland.

Clans/chiefs present: MACLEAN, MACRAE.

1314 THE BATTLE OF BANNOCKBURN (23/24 June): King Robert I (The Bruce) decisively defeated Edward II of England a few miles south of Stirling. The battle did not end the war between England and Scotland, but it turned the tide in Scotland's favour and finally led to the peace treaty at Northampton in 1328.

Clans who supported Bruce: BUCHANAN, CAMPBELL, COLQUHOUN, DRUMMOND, FORBES, FRASER, GRAHAM, MACALISTER, MACARTHUR, MACBEAN (MACBETH), MACDONALD MACDONELL, MACGREGOR, MACINTOSH, MACKAY, MACKINNON, MACLACHLAN, MACLAREN, MACLEAN, MACLEOD, MACNEIL, MACPHERSON, MACQUARRIE, MENZIES, MUNRO, MURRAY, OGILVIE, ROBERTSON, ROSS, SINCLAIR, SKENE, STEWART, SUTHERLAND (33 clans).

Clans who opposed Bruce: COMYN, MACNAB, MACDOUGAL.

N.B. Gordon and MacNaughten both started out by opposing Bruce and are said to have finished supporting him. Not all these clans were present at Bannockburn. The list of clans who supported Bruce is almost suspiciously long, but in fact all these clans appear to have been rewarded by him. Bruce was an unequivocal man who rewarded his supporters and harried his enemies, so the chiefs of these clans probably did support him. What is curious is that he had more clans supporting him than did Bonnie Prince Charlie in 1745!

1332 BATTLE OF DUPLIN MOOR (August): In the reign of King David II (the son of Robert Bruce) an army led by Edward Balliol (son of the late King John Balliol) defeated a Scottish army under the Earl of Mar (who was killed).

Clans who supported David II: FORBES.

1333 BATTLE OF HALIDON HILL (July): Also in the reign of King David II. Edward Balliol defeated a Scots army, under Archibald Douglas, which was attempting to relieve Berwick.

Clans who supported David II: FRASER, GORDON, MUNRO, ROSS, SUTHERLAND.

N.B. King David II may well have been supported by *more* clans than these, in the struggle to defeat the claims of Edward Balliol.

1411 THE BATTLE OF HARLAW (24 July): Reign of King James I. Donald the 2nd Lord of the Isles invaded the north-eastern plain of Scotland in an attempt to secure the earldom of Ross. He was halted at Harlaw by the Earl of Mar, and a particularly savage battle saved Aberdeen. Donald and his west Highlandmen and islesmen retired back into the Highlands.

Clans who fought for the Earl of Mar: MACKAY, OGILVIE, SKENE.

Clans who fought for Donald of the Isles: MACDONALD, MACDONELL, CAMERON, MACBEAN, MACINTOSH, MACLEAN, MACLEOD, MATHIESON, SHAW, probably also MACPHERSON and FARQUHARSON.

1488 BATTLE OF SAUCHIEBURN (11 June): King James III led an army against rebel barons and was defeated at Sauchieburn near Stirling. He was thrown from his horse and was stabbed to death at Beaton's Mill by an unknown priest for whom he had sent in order to be shriven.

Clans who fought for the King: FORBES, MACLAREN.

1513 BATTLE OF FLODDEN (9 September): King James IV was obliged to invade England in order to honour the Auld Alliance with France, because France had been attacked by Henry VIII of England (in league with the Pope!). James was brought to battle by the Earl of Surrey, Earl Marshal of England, and totally routed. King James, nine earls, thirteen barons and thousands of others were killed in Scotland's most disastrous battle. James had never wanted war against Henry VIII and had done everything in his power to prevent it. The Auld Alliance, which was extremely useful to France on occasion, was a disastrous union from the Scottish point of view.

Clans who fought at Flodden for the King: BUCHANAN, CAMPBELL, FRASER, GORDON, MACFARLANE, MACKENZIE, MACLAREN, MACNAUGHTEN, SINCLAIR, SKENE, MACLEAN.

1547   BATTLE OF PINKIE (September):   In the reign of Mary, Queen of Scots, and during the regency of her mother, Mary of Guise. This battle followed the 'rough wooing' of Henry VIII of England who wished his son to marry the infant Scots Queen. Henry died in January 1547, but the rivalry of French (Catholic) and English (Protestant) interests in Scotland led the Lord Protector Somerset to invade Scotland. He defeated the Scots army at Pinkie near Musselburgh. One result of this battle was that the infant Queen was betrothed to the Dauphin and sent to France for safety.

Clans who fought for Scotland: BUCHANAN, FARQUHARSON, MACFARLANE, MACKENZIE, MACLAREN, MUNRO, ROSE, SKENE, URQUHART.

1568   BATTLE OF LANGSIDE (13 May):   Mary, Queen of Scots, had been compelled to abdicate on 24 July 1567, while imprisoned at Loch Leven. Her son James was crowned at Stirling on 29 July 1567. Mary escaped from Loch Leven on 2 May 1568 and rallied her supporters. She was defeated at Langside (Glasgow) while trying to join forces with her northern supporters. After the battle she fled to England, which was the worst possible thing she could have done and which in the end cost her her life.

For the Queen: CAMPBELL, GRANT, BUCHANAN, MACKENZIE, probably SKENE.

Against the Queen: MACFARLANE.

1594   BATTLE OF GLENLIVET (October):   King James VI learned of an alleged plot by the Catholic Earls of Huntly and Errol to assist Spain, and sent an army against them led by the Earl of Argyle. Huntly defeated the royal army at Glenlivet.

For the King: CAMPBELL, MACINTOSH, MACNEIL, FORBES,   GRANT,   MACLEAN,   MACGREGOR, MACNEIL.

For the Catholic Earls: GORDON, MACPHERSON.

1644–5 MONTROSE'S CAMPAIGN: During the war between King Charles I and the Scottish Covenanters, Montrose won decisive victories at Tippermuir (1 September 1644), Inverlochy (2 February 1645), Auldearn (May 1645) Alford (July 1645) and Kilsyth (14 August, 1645). He was surprised and routed at Philiphaugh on 12 September 1645 while most of his army was dispersed.

Clans who fought against Montrose: CAMPBELL, FRASER, MACKENZIE, MENZIES.

Clans who fought for Montrose: CAMERON, FARQUHARSON, GORDON, GRAHAM, GRANT, LAMONT, MACALISTER, MACDONALD, MACDONELL, MACDOUGAL, MACFARLANE, MACGREGOR, MACINTOSH, MACPHERSON, MACKAY, MACKINNON, MACLEAN, MACRAE, MURRAY, OGILVIE, ROBERTSON, STEWART.

1651 BATTLE OF INVERKEITHING: Cromwell defeated a part of the Scottish army of King Charles II, in a short, sharp action.

Clans who fought for the King: BUCHANAN, FARQUHARSON, MACKINNON, MACBEAN, MACQUARRIE, MACLEAN.

1651 BATTLE OF WORCESTER (3 September): The Scottish army under Charles II, who had already been crowned King of the Scots at Scone, was decisively defeated by Cromwell, and Charles had to go back into exile until 1660.

Clans who supported Charles II: FARQUHARSON, FRASER, MACKINNON, MACLEAN, MACLEOD, STEWART, URQUHART.

1689 BATTLE OF KILLIECRANKIE (27 July): James Graham of Claverhouse, Viscount Dundee, routed the army of William and Mary under General MacKay. Any hope of a successful rising in favour of James VII and II perished at this battle because Dundee who was the driving force in Scotland, was killed at the moment of victory.

Clans who supported the Government: MUNRO, CAMPBELL.

Clans who fought with Dundee: CAMERON, FARQUHARSON, GRAHAM, GRANT, MACALISTER,

MACDONALD MACDONELL, MACKINNON, MAC-
LACHLAN, probably MACLAREN, MACLEAN, MAC-
NAUGHTEN, MACNEIL, ROBERTSON, STEWART.

1715 BATTLE OF SHERIFFMUIR (13 November): The 11th
Earl of Mar and the Jacobites defeated the Marquis of Argyll and
Government troops near Dunblane, Stirlingshire, in the Jacobite
rising of '15. The victory was not exploited and the Jacobite cause
dissipated. The Prince of Wales (i.e. The Old Pretender, son of
the exiled James VII and II) did not arrive in Scotland till 22
December, and he and Mar quietly left Scotland on 4 February
1716.

Government clans: CAMPBELL, FRASER, MACKAY,
MUNRO, ROSE, FORBES.

Jacobite clans: CAMERON, CHISHOLM, FARQU-
HARSON, GRANT OF GLENMORISTON, MAC-
DONALD, MACDONELL, MACGILLIVRAY, MAC-
GREGOR, MACINTOSH, MACKENZIE, MACKINNON,
MACLACHLAN, probably MACLAREN, MACLEAN,
MACLEOD, MACNEIL, MACPHERSON, MACRAE,
MENZIES, MURRAY, OGILVIE, ROBERTSON,
STEWART.

1745–6: THE SECOND JACOBITE RISING (the '45): This
was the final Jacobite attempt, led by Prince Charles Edward
Stuart. The standard was raised at Glenfinnan on 19 August
1745. General Cope was heavily defeated by the Jacobites on 21
September at Prestonpans, and the Jacobites pushed south to
reach Derby on 4 December. They were forced to return to
Scotland where they defeated General Hawley at Falkirk on 17
January, 1746. The Jacobite army was finally routed at Culloden
on 16 April 1746, the last pitched battle fought on British soil.

Government clans: CAMPBELL, FORBES, MACKAY,
MUNRO, SUTHERLAND.

Jacobite clans: CAMERON, CAMPBELL OF GLEN-
LYON, CHISHOLM, DRUMMOND, FARQUHARSON,
FORBES OF PITSLIGO, FRASER, GORDON, GRANT OF
GLENMORISTON, MACBEAN, MACDONALD, MAC-
GILLIVRAY, MACGREGOR, MACINTOSH, MACKEN-
ZIE, MACKINNON, MACLACHLAN, MACLAREN,
MACLEAN, MACLEOD OF RAASAY, MACNAB,

MACNEIL, MACPHERSON, MENZIES, MURRAY, OGILVIE, ROBERTSON, STUART.

SOME CLAN BATTLES MENTIONED IN THE TEXT

1330   MacGillivray and MacIntosh against Camerons.
(*c.*) 1380   Invernahaven. Clan Chattan against Camerons.
1394   Glenbrereth. Ogilvies against Robertsons.
1396   North Inch of Perth (23 October). Clan battle between Davidsons and Macphersons.
1438   Wick. Keiths against Gunns.
1464   Dirlot Keiths against Gunns.
1477   Blar na Pairc. MacKenzies against MacDonalds.
1517   Torran Dubh (near Rogart, Strathfleet) MacKays and Gunns against Sutherlands.
1544   Blar na Leine (Loch Lochie, 3 July). Frasers against MacDonalds of Clanranald.
1546   Kinlochlochy. Camerons and Macdonells of Keppoch against Frasers.
1572   Catt (Aberdeenshire). Forbes against Gordon.
1603   Glen Fruin (7 February) MacGregor against Colquhoun.
1688   MULROY. THE LAST CLAN BATTLE. Macdonells against MacIntoshes.

LIST OF SCOTTISH KINGS AND QUEENS

It is important to remember that in the beginning there was no rule of primogeniture (i.e. descent to the eldest son). This did not become established until after the reign of Malcolm III (Canmore). The first sixteen kings mentioned in the list which follows represent only *seven* generations, as the succession passed from brother to brother and then back and forth among the sons of the brothers and so on. Even after primogeniture became established, descent might pass to a brother or to a grandson if there was no son to inherit the crown.

Genealogy is the last bastion of male chauvinism, and the *dynasty* changes each time the succession passes through a daughter since the daughter's son belongs to his father's 'House' not his mother's (the Picts did it the other way round, and descent was usually through the mother's rights and not the father's).

In no ruling House in Europe (and very possibly the world) can or could descent be traced back from father to son (or grandson) in a broken *male* line of descent leading to the first king.

HOUSE OF ALPIN:

*KING ALPIN died 834

834–60	King Kenneth I
860–63	King Donald I
863–77	King Constantine II
877–8	Aedh
878–9	Eocha
889–900	Donald II
900–942	Constanine III
942–54	Malcolm I
954–62	Indulf
962–7	Duff
967–71	Colin
971–95	Kenneth II
995–7	Constantine IV
997–1005	Kenneth III
1005–34	Malcolm II

HOUSE OF ATHOLL:

1034–40	Duncan I
1040–57	MacBeth
1057–8	Lulach (who was MacBeth's STEPson!)
1058–93	Malcolm III (Canmore). Neither Malcolm nor the kings who follow have any blood ties with Lulach, who is an 'intruder' king.
1093–4	Donald Ban
1094	Duncan II
1094–7	Donald Ban Joint rulers. Donald ruled north of the Edmund Forth-Clyde line and Edmund south of it.

* King Alpin belonged to the original royal House of Dalriada, the House of Fergus Mor MacErc. The change of 'House' here denotes *not* a female descent but the merging of Picts and Scots under Alpin's son King Kenneth I. Strictly speaking the 'House' did not change at all with Alpin or Kenneth; but it is normal historical practice to refer to the first kings of a combined Scotland as being of House of Alpin rather than, for example, the House of Fergus.

1097–1107	Edgar
1107–24	Alexander I (The Fierce)
1124–53	David I (The Saint)
1153–65	Malcolm IV (The Maiden)
1165–1214	William I (The Lion)
1214–49	Alexander II
1249–86	Alexander III (The Great)
1286–90	Margaret
1290–92	THE CONTEST FOR THE CROWN
1292–6	John
1296–1306	THE INTERREGNUM UNDER EDWARD I OF ENGLAND DURING WHICH JOHN REMAINED THE RIGHTFUL KING OF SCOTLAND (which, it can be argued, he remained till his death in 1313)

THE HOUSE OF BRUCE:

1306–29	Robert I (Robert Bruce)
1329–71	David II

HOUSE OF STEWART:

1371–90	Robert II
1390–1406	Robert III
1406–37	James I
1437–60	James II
1460–88	James III
1488–1513	James IV
1513–42	James V
1542–67	Mary, Queen of Scots

HOUSE OF STUART:

1567–1625	James VI (who was James I of England from 1603 to 1625)
1624–49	Charles I
1649–85	Charles II. (Charles did not occupy the throne till 1660 when the monarchy was restored after Cromwell's death.)
1685–9	James VII and II
1689–94	Mary II
1694–1702	William III
1702–14	Anne

HOUSE OF HANOVER:

1714–27   George I (second cousin of Queen Anne and great-grandson of James VI and I). Here follows the present reigning dynasty of the United Kingdom. George II was king during the second Jacobite rising of 1745–6.

Index

Compiled by I. D. Crane